# AUTISM AND
# THE FAMILY

# AUTISM AND THE FAMILY

## UNDERSTANDING AND SUPPORTING PARENTS AND SIBLINGS

Ready-to-implement resources
and approaches for professionals
in school and clinical settings

## KATE E. FISKE

### FOREWORD BY TRISTRAM SMITH

W. W. NORTON & COMPANY
*Independent Publishers Since 1923*
New York · London

**Note to Readers:** Standards of clinical practice and protocol change over time, and no technique or recommendation is guaranteed to be safe or effective in all circumstances. This volume is intended as a general information resource for professionals practicing in the field of psychotherapy and mental health; it is not a substitute for appropriate training, peer review, and/or clinical supervision. Neither the publisher nor the author(s) can guarantee the complete accuracy, efficacy, or appropriateness of any particular recommendation in every respect.

To my children,
who taught me to understand
the strength of a parent's love.

# CONTENTS

# FOREWORD
## by Tristram Smith

Kate Fiske takes on a big problem in services for children with autism spectrum disorder (ASD): Providers and families need to work together in order to provide the best possible support for a child with ASD, but they are largely on their own in figuring out how to do so. Although researchers have identified many intervention strategies that can help children with ASD learn new skills, they have provided little guidance on how providers and families can collaborate to select and implement these strategies. Moreover, although many of the strategies are rated highly by families whose children receive them in research studies, providers may get a less enthusiastic reaction because the families that they encounter in practice are likely to differ from families in research. For example, families seen in practice could have different beliefs about acceptable strategies for their children, less time and fewer resources to use the strategies themselves, greater caution about accepting recommendations from providers, or children who are less well-suited to the strategies.

Along with a research gap, there is a training gap. All professions that serve children with ASD emphasize the importance of engaging families in intervention, but few training programs delve into the complexities of this process. As Dr. Fiske documents, numerous factors influence how families interact with providers and make decisions about intervention, including their previous experiences with providers, their child's history of progress in intervention, stress lev-

els in the family, parents' goals and preferences for their child, relationship status of the parents (living together or apart, in agreement
about the needs of the child or not), siblings and extended family,
financial situation and employment status, cultural background, and
many others.

Miscommunication or outright conflict between providers and
families of children with ASD is all too common. Dr. Fiske recounts
many poignant and instructive examples. These examples dovetail
with findings from surveys of families of children with ASD, which
report that these families are much more likely than other families to
express dissatisfaction with their primary care pediatrician (Kogan
et al., 2008). Many also report receiving too little guidance at the
time their child received the diagnosis of ASD (Hennel et al., 2016).
In addition, they report less coordination of care and shared decision making with providers than do families of children with other
disabilities (Hubner, Feldman, & Huffma, 2016; Vohra, Madhaven,
Sambamoorthi, & St. Peter, 2014). Families of children with ASD are
more likely than families of children with other disabilities to report
having difficulty using school and community services (Montes,
Halterman, & Magyar, 2009). They are also more likely than other
parents to initiate mediation or due process hearings with their children's schools (Mueller & Carranza, 2011). In about one-third of due
process hearings, the primary complaint is lack of parental participation in the special education process (White, 2014).

Families often make valiant efforts to compensate for shortcom-
ings in their relationships with providers. As an illustration, one
mother disclosed to Dr. Fiske, "I remember sitting in contentious
meetings where providers told me I lacked the qualifications to make
recommendations about interventions for my son. As you can imagine, that was quite a motivating factor." While raising her son and
working full-time, she spent seven years taking online courses and
doing fieldwork in order to earn her master's degree and become a
board certified behavior analyst. This mother went to extraordinary
lengths to place herself on equal footing with providers and make
sure her son got appropriate services. Even so, it would have been
much better if she had been able to join forces with her son's provid-

ers from the outset. Other families show resilience in different ways, such as finding new social supports or mobilizing previously overlooked resources (Bayat, 2007). This resilience is laudable and valuable, but it is not a substitute for effective services from providers.

Clearly, then, children with ASD and their families have much to gain from better collaborations with providers. So what can providers do to make this happen? One well-established approach is to systematically teach families to deliver intervention to their children. Doing so empowers families to make informed decisions about the intervention and use it to help their children learn skills that are important to the family. Some parent education programs arrange for parents to work as apprentices with experienced providers during intervention sessions (Smith, 2010). In the sessions, the parent and provider take turns implementing the intervention and give each other feedback on their work. After a few months, many parents become proficient enough to conduct sessions on their own. Other parent education programs involve scheduling sessions for the purpose of teaching the parents about the intervention (Bearss et al., 2013; Oono, Honey, & McConachie, 2013). These sessions begin with the provider giving didactic instruction about an intervention strategy. Next, the provider models the strategy or shows a video that does so, then roleplays it with the parent, and finally guides the parent to practice the strategy with the child. The session ends with the provider and parent jointly developing a homework assignment that will allow the parent to try out the strategy with the child during the daily routine until the following session.

As useful as parent education can be, it is only a partial solution. Families and providers still interact frequently about health care and educational services implemented by professionals for the child with ASD. These interactions usually extend over many years. Also, family members may themselves seek professional services because, as Dr. Fiske describes, having a child with ASD can be highly stressful.

For all of these situations, understanding and incorporating family perspectives are vital. This is where Dr. Fiske's book becomes absolutely invaluable. It provides insights on family experiences across the lifespan of their children with ASD, the spectrum of needs that these children may have, the range of priorities that families set, the variations in family structure, and the diverse personal and cultural backgrounds that family members have. It then describes practical ways that providers can gain an understanding of the perspectives of individual families, foster rapport, and offer child and family-centered services. In short, it gives providers the tools they need to improve relationships with families and lay the foundation for improving the outcomes of children with ASD.

## REFERENCES

Bayat, M. (2007). Evidence of resilience in families of children with autism. *Journal of Intellectual and Disabilies Research, 51*(Pt 9), 702-14.

Bearss, K., Lecavalier, L., Minshawi, N., Johnson, C., Smith, T., Handen, B., . . . Scahill, L. (2013). Toward an exportable parent training program for disruptive behaviors in autism spectrum disorders. *Neuropsychiatry, 3*(2), 169-180.

Hennel, S., Coates, C., Symeonides, C., Gulenc, A., Smith, L., Price, A. M. H., & Hiscock, H. (2016). Diagnosing autism: Contemporaneous surveys of parent needs and paediatric practice. *Journal of Paediatrics and Child Health, 52(5)*, 506-511.

Hubner, L. M., Feldman, H. M., & Huffman, L. C. (2016). Parent-Reported Shared Decision Making: Autism Spectrum Disorder and Other Neurodevelopmental Disorders. *Journal of Developmental and Behavioral Pediatrics, 37(1)*, 20-32.

Kogan, M. D., Strickland, B. B., Blumberg, S. J., Singh, G. K., Perrin, J. M., & van Dyck, P. C. (2008). A national profile of the health care experiences and family impact of autism spectrum disorder among children in the United States, 2005–2006. *Pediatrics, 122(6)*, e1149-e1158.

Montes, G., Halterman, J. S., & Magyar, C. I. (2009). Access to and satisfaction with school and community health services for US children with ASD. *Pediatrics, 124(Supplement 4)*, S407-413.

Mueller, T. G., & Carranza, F. (2011). An examination of special education due process hearings. *Journal of Disability Policy Studies, 22*(3), 133-141.

Oono, I. P., Honey, E. J., & McConachie, H. (2013). Parent-mediated early intervention for young children with autism spectrum disorders (ASD). *Cochrane Database Syst Rev*(4), CD009774.

Smith T. Early and intensive behavioral intervention in autism. In J. R. Weisz & A. E. Kazdin (Eds.), *Evidence-Based Psychotherapies for Children and Adolescents* (2nd ed., pp. 312-326) New York: Guilford.

White, S. E. (2014). Special Education Complaints Filed by Parents of Students With Autism Spectrum Disorders in the Midwestern United States. *Focus on Autism and Other Developmental Disabilities, 29*(2), 80-87.

Vohra, R., Madhavan, S., Sambamoorthi, U., & St Peter, C. (2014). Access to services, quality of care, and family impact for children with autism, other developmental disabilities, and other mental health conditions. *Autism, 18(7)*, 815-826.

# ACKNOWLEDGMENTS

I would like to express my gratitude to the many people who contributed to the development of this book. First, I thank Andrea Costella Dawson for approaching me with this opportunity, and Benjamin Yarling at Norton for his thoughtful feedback and seeing the project across the finish line. Special thanks to Sean Massey, Suzannah Iadarola, Sandra Harris, and Naomi Warren for reading and offering input on early versions of this book; to Erica Dashow for helping compile the resources included within; to Erica, Ethan Eisdorfer, and Katelyn Selver for conducting interviews; and to Courtney Butler and Daniela Silva for their assistance in coordinating interviews and transcriptions.

Many thanks to my colleagues at the Douglass Developmental Disabilities Center of the Graduate School of Applied and Professional Psychology at Rutgers, The State University of New Jersey, and to my loving family for their support in the development of this book.

Finally, I would like to thank all of the individuals and families with whom I have had the opportunity to work over the years, who taught me the many lessons that I have included in this book. To the parents and siblings who so openly and honestly shared their experiences with me: I hope that your words are as influential on the careers of other practitioners as they have been on mine. I am truly grateful for all that you have contributed, through your help with this book, to the care and support provided to other families like yours.

# INTRODUCTION

The medical, behavioral, social, and communication needs of individuals with autism spectrum disorder (ASD) are complex and many. When one considers the different types of professionals who provide services directly to individuals with ASD to address all of these needs, the number can be astonishing. One student alone might receive treatment from a teacher, teacher's aide, pediatrician, neuropsychologist, psychologist, behavior analyst, speech therapist, occupational therapist, physical therapist, and any number of other medical professionals who may address additional medical concerns. Each of these professionals will strive to fully understand the symptoms of the individual with ASD and how they manifest uniquely in this specific individual. Each professional will use his or her own specialized training to implement the best treatment possible for the individual, be it medical treatment, therapy, or educational lessons. Some of these professionals may log as many as 30 hours a week with the individual with ASD, and after a time start to feel that nobody could possibly know the child better than they do.

However, sometimes professionals focus so exclusively on the individual with ASD that they fail to take into account perhaps the most influential factor in the individual's life, and the people who will always know the child best: his or her family. No individual with ASD exists outside of a network of caregivers, which may include parents, siblings, and extended family. Disregarding these family members in treatment is a critical omission for practitioners, because with the knowledge and support of family any possible treatment can be strengthened and carried out in the home setting. A solid, working relationship with parents and other family members should be a primary goal of any practitioner.

In 1977 George Engel introduced the biopsychosocial model to the medical field. This model urges practitioners to take into account the whole individual: not only body and mind but also the system in which the individual lives, including the family, social group, institutions that provide care, and culture and community. Engel's primary concern was that the health condition of the individual would have an effect at each level within the larger system, and each level within the system would have an effect on the individual. Accordingly, the individual could not, and should not, be treated without consideration of the full context, because knowledge of the system would best inform the practitioner's understanding of the individual as well as the recommended treatment (Engel, 1977).

Yet, so often within my work with individuals with ASD I find practitioners who focus intensively on the individual with ASD without an understanding of or appreciation for the individual's family or cultural context. These practitioners will make recommendations to parents that are not always easily implemented and then express frustration that parents are not taking advantage of the services that are offered. They demonstrate little understanding of the experiences of family members raising an individual with ASD and often see these members as barriers to the work that needs to be done rather than collaborators in treatment. Most troubling, practitioners do not always appreciate the incredible source of support they themselves can be for families of individuals with ASD, even while still maintaining focus on the individual.

Each year I teach a class of prospective behavior analysts how to apply the principles of applied behavior analysis (ABA) to their work with children, adolescents, and adults with ASD. As part of the course, I focus on the importance of working effectively with families. I spend some time lecturing about the parent training models that can be effective when working with parents and siblings, and I review the literature base on the unique experiences of siblings and parents of individuals with ASD. However, despite the broad reach of the overall course curriculum, I feel the most influential component of this course content is a panel of parents and siblings that I invite to the class to share, in their own words, their day-to-day experiences with their family member with ASD. Each summer these parents and siblings openly share the joys and heartache of caring for an individual with ASD with my class of students, recalling their memories of effective relationships that they have had with professionals and the steps professionals can take to best support them and their child.

The responses I receive from students each year about this panel of parents and siblings are overwhelmingly positive. My students, some of whom have worked with children with ASD for years, often share that they had never considered the perspective of family members when working with individuals with ASD. They talk of having a newfound appreciation for how the experiences of family members should be taken into account when providing treatment, and a better understanding of the challenges that parents face that can impact not only their child but also their work with the practitioner. In the feedback I receive from students at the end of the semester, the parent panel is resoundingly the best-received aspect of the course.

What my students learn from the panel is that, for families of children with ASD, the impact the diagnosis has on their daily lives is far-reaching, unsettling, and in some ways as difficult as the diagnosis itself. The aim of this book is to share these same lessons with a broader range and number of professionals by describing the challenges parents and siblings face and offering practical ideas for how professionals can best provide support. No matter how well trained the practitioner, he or she may struggle with how best to work with and support parents and siblings who are affected by having a family member with ASD. This book does not offer recommendations for the diagnosis or treatment of a child with ASD. Instead, this book provides practitioners with an understanding of the impact of ASD on family dynamics, to increase empathy and understanding in their work with the family. Additionally, this book provides specific recommendations practitioners can use to help parents and siblings overcome the many challenges they face in their daily lives. In a sea of books that teach practitioners how to help the individual with ASD, this book will teach practitioners how to help the *family* of the individual with ASD.

In my work as a practitioner, I have seen firsthand the impact ASD has on the family. I have seen parents in shock from the news of diagnosis, and as their child grows I have seen them express every emotion from desperation to elation. I have watched parents tirelessly push their child to grow and succeed while simultaneously trying to accept their child's limitations. I have seen parents grapple with how to balance their career and their family life, manage the financial impact of ASD treatment, struggle with the strain ASD puts on their relationship, and grieve the loss of their life prior to their child's diagnosis. I have watched siblings work hard to understand their brother's or sister's disability, show pride in their sibling's accomplishments, vie for their parents' attention, and navigate their role in the family. These family experiences form the basis of this book, and my recommendations for practitioners are based on my own clinical work as well as that of others. Additionally, while my description of family experiences and recommendations for support draw on snippets of research, the book relies heavily on the personal stories shared with me by parents and siblings in individual and group interviews. Conducted over the course of 2 years, these interviews have an honesty that informs this book in a way that no other source could. In a sense, I have worked to take the contents of the parent and sibling panels that are so informative for my students and put them into written form so that the messages from parents can reach a wide range of practitioners.

One of the most important aspects of the biopsychosocial model proposed by Engel is that it can be adapted for application by any practitioner. Medical doctors, psychologists, teachers, and other professionals can easily learn to take into account the family system, as well as the greater impact of culture and community, when working with individuals with ASD. To that end, though many examples that I use in this book are drawn from my own experiences as a teacher, behavior analyst, and clinical psychologist working in the field of

ASD treatment, I have written this book to apply to all professionals working with individuals with ASD. Additionally, psychologists
and family therapists working directly with family members of individuals with ASD will gain insight into the experiences of the family
in reading this book. Finally, in some cases providing this book as
a resource for parents and other family members could be helpful,
because the words offered by other parents and family members in
interviews can be a source of support and solace for others raising a
child with ASD.

I have written this book so that it first addresses the experiences
of family members of individuals with ASD and then offers recommendations for practitioners to use in the treatment of the individual with ASD to build effective working relationships with family
members. Chapter 1 explores one of the most important events in a
parent's life, the time of the child's diagnosis. The chapter provides
professionals with insight into the events that lead up to the child's
diagnosis, as well as the emotions the parents may experience following their child's diagnosis. Chapter 2 conveys to professionals the
range of experiences that parents may have related to raising a child
with ASD through the life-span and the impact that this unique
parental role has on parent well-being. In Chapter 3, differences in
how parents respond to and cope with their child's diagnosis of ASD
are discussed, as well as the impact that the diagnosis has on the
relationship of parental couples and their social networks.

The experiences of siblings who grow up with an individual with
ASD are shared in Chapter 4, providing professionals with ideas for
how best to integrate these important family members into treatment. Similarly, Chapter 5 explores relationships among individuals with ASD, their parents and extended family members such as
grandparents, aunts, and uncles. Chapter 6 examines how culture
can impact a family's view of ASD and the treatment that the professional provides, as well as how the professional should take into
account culture and family context when working with the individual with ASD.

The final set of chapters offer professionals recommendations for
how to work most effectively with family members. Chapter 7 sum-

marizes coping strategies commonly used by parents of individuals with ASD and offers ideas for how to encourage the use of these
strategies by family members. Chapter 8 lays out suggestions for how
all professionals can build effective rapport and a successful working relationship with parents of individuals with ASD. In Chapter 9 I
offer recommendations for how to effectively teach parents skills in
ASD treatment, regardless of treatment approach, and how to help
parents evaluate the myriad treatment options that are available for
their child. A Resources section follows the Conclusion to provide a
wide range of information helpful for both families and practitioners.

My hope is that these comprehensive chapters and the resources
that follow provide practitioners with the knowledge they need not
only to provide effective treatment to individuals with ASD but also
to reach and support the greater family system in which the individual grows and develops. With this biopsychosocial approach, all
practitioners can best effect therapeutic change across the full family system.

# AUTISM AND
# THE FAMILY

# CHAPTER 1

# Understanding the Experience of Diagnosis

When many of us think about diagnosis, we often think about a finite, discrete period in time: that moment in the doctor's office when the doctor delivers the diagnosis, whatever it may be, to the individual or family. We imagine the immediate reactions the family may have to the diagnosis while still in the office: the shock, disbelief, sadness, or in some cases relief. Occasionally, we also consider the processing that the family must do over the few days that follow that diagnosis. However, rarely do we consider the period of time before that or beyond that. We are talking about the period of diagnosis, after all: what more could there be to consider beyond the moment of diagnosis itself?

However, when we talk about a family of an individual with ASD, diagnosis can be a lengthy period of time that parents will continue to process and reference for much of their lives. Thus, any professional working with a family of an individual with ASD will have to consider the impact of this time on the family. For instance, professionals such as psychologists, behavior therapists, speech therapists, physical therapists, pediatricians, and others may be working with the family to address the child's needs before a diagnosis has been given. These professionals may have concerns about the child and should be able to provide parents with resources they can use to seek out an appropriate diagnosis. They should also be able to recognize the barriers that parents will face in attaining a diagnosis—from the process itself to the reactions they will receive from loved ones—and help parents determine how to respond. They should understand the emotions the family experiences and be prepared to support them as they struggle to manage these emotions.

At the time of diagnosis, diagnosticians will be added to the team of care providers already working with the child with ASD. Diagnosticians may include pediatricians, psychologists, school personnel, and other professionals who provide assessment and diagnosis. These professionals should be highly attuned to the experiences of parents to ensure that they are as empathic and supportive as possible during one of the most vulnerable and challenging periods of parents' lives. Stories of diagnosticians, school staff, and other service providers who are highly insensitive are unfortunately all too common. Diagnosticians will need to recognize the impact that their diagnosis will have on the family, immediately and in the long term, and deliver their news with the utmost care. Immediately after diagnosis many more professionals will begin to work with the family as ASD-specific treatments are identified and initiated with the child, and all of these practitioners must understand the toll that the recent news can have on the family.

Many professionals in the field of ASD treatment come to know a child and the family years after diagnosis. Perhaps the professional is a teacher providing education in a classroom for children with ASD, or a speech therapist working with a child after school. The professional could be a service provider supporting an adult in vocational work in the community, or a psychiatrist providing medication. Regardless of the context in which professionals meet the family, the diagnosis may seem to be well behind parents, and professionals may not expect the parents' experience with the time of diagnosis to be relevant to the treatment plan moving forward. However, for many parents the struggle that they faced when thinking about, seeking, and receiving their child's ASD diagnosis will be one of the most profound and memorable periods of their life. Few parents I speak with can remember back on the time their child was diagnosed without tears coming to their eyes.

Even if a professional is not working with the family at the time of diagnosis, understanding the family's experiences during that period can help build a foundation of understanding for where the family has been and how far they have come. Asking about and realizing the stressors of this early time, as well as the range of emotions that parents experienced during the process, will help set the stage for a greater sense of empathy with parents going forward. At any stage of treatment, asking parents how they learned about their child's diagnosis, how they felt about that diagnosis then, and how they feel about it now will demonstrate the practitioner's interest in not only the child but also in the parents' experiences and will begin to build a sense that the practitioner is interested in including all members of the family in treatment, not just the individual with ASD. This chapter introduces the practitioner to the different stages of diagnosis and the experiences of families during each stage. Highlighting the challenges that families face at these specific times, recommendations are offered to maximize the sensitivity and support practitioners in the field provide to families.

## SUPPORTING THE FAMILY BEFORE THE DIAGNOSIS

The diagnostic experience for parents of children with ASD is more confusing and uncertain than for parents of children with other special needs. For example, sometimes babies have complications at birth or in early development that immediately raise concern for parents. These parents monitor their child's development closely, as all parents do, but with a genuine rationale for their concern. This awareness that their child may not develop as other children do is present from the moment the child is born. Compare this with the experience of parents of a child with ASD, who likely have no indications at the time of the child's birth—and sometimes for a year or two after—that their child is developing in any way other than typically. These parents, like all parents, will think about their child's future within the cultural norms of society; they will talk about traditional goals they have for their child: graduating from high school, marrying, getting a job, having children of their own, and being healthy and happy.

The smallest things a child does will make their parents imagine what that will mean for that youngster as an adult. I remember when my son was a toddler he had an affinity for all things tools—tape measures, toy hammers, and any kitchen utensil that looked like it would be handy on a construction site—and my husband imagined him growing up to be a woodworker just like his grandfather. When my daughter's facial expressions would send us into fits of laughter, we would imagine her debut on a Broadway stage. Though it may seem silly to base these dreams on the tendencies of infants and toddlers, the point is that parents whose children are born without apparent complication view their child's future from the vantage point of parents raising a neurotypical child. Though they may not be wedded to the dreams they have for their child, they think about their child's future without fear of that future becoming clouded or less certain over time.

However, at some point, the parents of a child with ASD become aware that their child's development differs from that of other children. Maybe they begin to realize it themselves as they compare their child with other children at the playground or with older siblings. Maybe somebody else tells them about their concerns. An ability to recognize these signs and to not ignore them may be affected by parents' belief that their child is developing as all children do. The process of identifying these signs of ASD and understanding what they may mean is a difficult course for parents and one that should be appreciated by practitioners. Professionals working with families during this time should be familiar with the signs of ASD to best provide direction to families concerned about their child's development. Individuals with ASD will manifest symptoms in two significant areas: deficits in social communication and interaction, and restricted and repetitive patterns of behavior, interests, and activities. Examples of these symptoms are provided in Table 1.

| Table 1. **Examples of Symptoms of ASD** | |
|---|---|
| Deficits in Social Communication and Interaction | Restricted or Repetitive Pattern of Behavior, Interests, or Activities |
| • Slow or nonexistent development of language | • Repetitive motor movements or vocalizations |
| • Poor or undeveloped back-and-forth conversational skills | • Lining up toys or other items |
| • Infrequent social initiation or response to adults or peers | • Repeating the words of others, movie scripts, or passages from books |
| • Reduced sharing of interests, emotions, and affect | • Insistence on routines and resistance to change |
| • Poor integration of eye contact, body language, and gestures in social interaction | • Intense focus on unusual objects or highly specific topics of interest |
| • Limited use or understanding of facial expressions | • Unusual reactivity to sensory input, including sounds, tastes, smells, sights, or textures |
| • Difficulty understanding, developing, and maintaining friendships with others | |
| • Absence of imaginative play | |

For a diagnosis of ASD to be given, these symptoms must be present beginning in early development, cause significant impairment, and not be accounted for by intellectual disability or global developmental delay. The severity of the diagnosis (Level 1, 2, or 3) is assigned based on the level of support required by the individual, with Level 1 requiring support and Level 3 requiring very substantial support (American Psychiatric Association, 2013). Any professional working with young children should be cognizant of these criteria and, if concerned that the child may meet criteria for the diagnosis, be prepared to refer the family to a reputable diagnostician.

As an aside, practitioners should also be aware of the differences in the diagnostic criteria between the fourth (*DSM-IV*) and fifth editions (*DSM-5*) of the *Diagnostic and Statistical Manual of Mental Disorders* (American Psychiatric Association, 2000, 2013), because the differences in diagnostic criteria between the two editions are significant. In brief, the *DSM-5* did away with the use of categorical diagnoses on the autism spectrum, such as Asperger's disorder; pervasive developmental disorder, not otherwise specified; and autistic disorder. Instead, it subsumed all three diagnoses under the diagnosis of ASD. The challenges of differentially diagnosing individuals using the *DSM-IV* were significant, because practitioners found considerable gray area between, for instance, an individual with "high-functioning" autistic disorder and Asperger's disorder. While the new diagnostic criteria limit these diagnostic challenges, parents may be confused by the change, especially if referencing older resources that have not been updated, or if their child was initially diagnosed using the *DSM-IV* and the diagnosis is changed using the *DSM-5*. Practitioners should be prepared to address their questions.

Professionals should also be mindful that parents' awareness of the signs of ASD, and how they present in their child, will differ based on the child's development. The difference between parents who report a regression in their child's development and those who notice differences in their child's development from that of other children early on is meaningful and will impact parents' willingness to respond to a practitioner's recommendation for an evaluation.

Understanding parent concerns about regression. Some parents speak of their child's diagnosis as a regression in skills following a period of what appeared to be typical development. These parents describe a child who smiled at his caregivers as a baby, kicked his legs wildly in joy when a caregiver entered the room, and reached for caregivers to be picked up and cuddled. "He was the ideal baby," one father remembered of his son. "He didn't cry, he didn't make a fuss. He was happy with whatever you did with him. He was happy if you didn't do anything with him." By all accounts, these babies appeared as other babies did, and parents had no concerns about their development.

However, these same parents talk about the change in their baby that occurred later, often at the age of 2 or 3 years. In many cases the change that parents recount was gradual. One mother remembers her son's change in development at the age of 15 months:

> He was very happy and loving, interactive, smiley; he was the kid that when you walked into the room he was flailing his arms and grinning, and so engaging. Just a little bit, it seemed like almost a little bit every day, he started withdrawing. He was less and less and interactive, and less engaged, and he stopped babbling, stopped making sounds, started doing these really repetitive things like open and close the cabinet doors, open and close the cabinet doors—he could do that for hours. Or he would run in circles, not spin but in a little loop, and he would just run around a coffee table, around and around and around and around, and it would be really, really hard to get him to stop and be engaged with anything else. At that point, with the combination of things, I knew that something wasn't right.

For other parents who talk of regression, it occurs not slowly but very suddenly. One parent described her son's loss of language following what seemed like typical language development. "He was talking a lot; he seemed so bright and everything, and he had stopped talking. . . . It almost seemed like he had an accident. It almost seemed like he had a stroke."

The prevalence of regressive ASD, or the development of ASD that robs a child of predeveloped social and communication skills, is unknown, but research estimates it occurs in between 15 percent and 50 percent of population samples (Fombonne & Chakrabarti, 2001; Kurita, 1985; Lingam et al., 2003; Lord, 1995; Tuchman & Rapin, 1997). In these cases we do not always know whether the child was truly typically developing or whether the parents and pediatricians missed subtle early signs of ASD that may have indicated an earlier onset of the disorder.

As a clinician, I have seen videos of children I have worked with as babies, often snippets of birthday parties or family trips. Sometimes the change between the toddler in the video and the child I am working with in the moment is shocking. I see videos of toddlers engaged in their exciting event, smiling and making eye contact with the adult behind the camera, referencing their surroundings and then checking with mom or dad using eye contact to seemingly ask, "All of this is okay, right?" or "This is so exciting!" The children point at splashing water or a burst piñata. These children are so tangibly different, sometimes, from the grown child with whom I am working, who struggles to make eye contact, connect socially with his family members, and share in his surroundings. Watching these videos, I can certainly understand how these parents would say that they had no concerns about their child's early development but that he regressed completely once ASD took hold.

Regardless of whether the child had been developing typically and then began to regress, or early signs of ASD had been missed, the point is that the parents *thought* that their child would continue typical development. They did not expect their child's development to take a turn and that they would be faced with the prospect of a developmental disability. Therefore, the period of regression for parents is emotionally exhausting and scary. "I was losing him," a mother recounted:

> It was beyond heartbreaking and devastating. Every day there was a little bit less. It got harder and harder and harder to make contact with him. . . . I would go into his crib when he was sleeping and stand there looking at him . . . and I just wished he would wake up and be like my old [son]. As stupid as it sounds, every morning I would hope that maybe he would wake up and he would be back.

The memories parents have of their engaged, smiling child begins to slip away, and these parents are faced with the very real fear that they may never get that child back.

For professionals working with a family whose child appeared to regress, they must be aware that parents not only are managing the daily challenges of their child's diagnosis but also may be struggling with the loss of the child they once had. This could especially be the case if the child had language and social skills at a young age that slowly disappeared over time. Some of these parents may continually seek treatment that will recover their child's lost skills. Some of these parents may be apt to try several different treatments, one after another or at the same time, in the hopes that one will help their child regain skills. They may also be discouraged and frustrated with treatments—even if their child is making gains—because their child is not making the progress they originally envisioned and recapturing early skills. Professionals may feel unappreciated by parents who seem perpetually unsatisfied with the progress the child has made or who seem to have unrealistic goals for their child's development.

By talking with parents about the onset of their child's diagnosis, professionals may learn whether they still hope their child will regain the skills he or she had lost at a young age. In learning this, professionals may gain increased empathy and understanding of parents' motivation for their child's skill progression. In some cases, this understanding may help professionals take parents' concerns less personally and work more effectively with them to establish goals that both are realistic and help the child make progress toward the parents' ultimate goals. Additional recommendations for working with parents to establish appropriate goals for their child are offered in Chapters 6 and 8.

Responding to parent concerns from birth. In the cases described above, the changes that parents see as their child develops are painfully obvious. Again, often they represent a change in ability so different from the younger version of their child that the parents sense that something is not right. For many parents, however, their child's development has a more linear regression from infancy, and their child seems to fall a little farther behind where he or she should be each month in language and social domains. The child's behavior has not changed; rather, the child has simply developed differently from other kids all along. Maybe the child's language has lagged behind that of peers for years; or maybe the child's vocabulary surpasses that of other children but the use of language seems stilted, robotic, or very adult. Maybe, despite typical language development, the child has been unable to navigate social interactions.

As one mother stated, her son "could recite a whole book, but couldn't ask me for a glass of milk." Children with these social difficulties might be unable to interact with other children their own age in games that involve imaginative play or do not center on their own interests. They may burst into tears and tantrums each time a peer does not play a particular way, and they might avoid peers altogether and prefer to play on their own whenever they are around children their own age. A mother recounted how her son's teacher shared her son's social difficulties with her:

> She had been mentioning to me all year, "He doesn't really play with the other kids," and for a while I was thinking they're 2, they don't really play together, they parallel play, that's what 2-year-olds do. But obviously she was seeing something in him that was different from the other 2-year-olds. So that had been kind of on my mind, and then I started noticing myself that he wouldn't even really want to parallel play, he wouldn't even want to be near the other kids, which was a change from how he had been in the past.

These same parents might notice the development of restricted interests that at first were quirky but have become increasingly intrusive: fascinations with letters, numbers, trains, movies, or video game characters that seem to surpass the typical fascinations of childhood. The interests dominate conversation and consume the child's free time, and attempts to redirect the child to a new activity can result in outbursts and disruptive behavior. The same mother whose son had difficulty playing with other children remembered his fascination with letters and numbers:

> He was really focused on letters and numbers and the word of the day on *Sesame Street*, which wasn't necessarily a problem in itself except that was really the only thing that he was interested in. . . . If something didn't have letters or numbers in it, he just had no interest.

Another father recounted his son's focus on Thomas the Tank Engine:

There was one time when we went to a picnic with other kids, and [my son] was like many kids on the spectrum: he was really into Thomas the Tank Engine. It was really this big lake, and kids were in the lake and rowing, and he just couldn't get out of this [focus on Thomas]. It really struck me.

For these parents, the gradual appearance of symptoms—not in a dramatic fashion—can make it more difficult for them to attune to the symptoms. While the thought that something might be wrong has crossed their mind, they also wonder whether all this quirkiness is just who their child is, that this is their child's personality as opposed to a diagnosis. They wonder whether delays in language, differences in social skills, and intensive focus on specific interests just reflect their child's natural development and whether at some point the child will catch up to peers and blend in seamlessly. These may be first-time parents who have no sibling comparisons for their child's development. Alternatively, they may have seen some signs but have told themselves that they are overreacting and pushed their concerns away.

In some cases, parents may need someone else, such as a friend, a teacher, a family member, or a pediatrician, to approach them with concerns about their child's development. A mother remembered,

To this day, I will always thank the daycare worker who was brave enough to come to me and say, "I'm really not supposed to tell you this, and I know it's probably hard for you to hear, but I think there is something wrong with your daughter."

For another parent, it was a friend who prodded:

A good friend of mine actually was the one who jerked me into doing something, because at one point she turned to me and asked me if I thought that my daughter had a hearing problem, she said, "Because I'm calling her, and she's not looking." That really got me very angry at the time, but it was really the thing that pushed me into pursuing [a diagnosis].

For parents, questioning their child's development is exhausting. I remember a conversation I had with a dear friend as she was going through the process of assessment to determine whether her son was on the autism spectrum. She told me that she was so exhausted by watching his every move. She said she could not enjoy being with him because everything he did, every word he said, she evaluated to help her decide whether he was developing normally. She felt like she was being robbed of the time she had to enjoy his childhood and to just enjoy him.

When a parent is struggling to make sense of his or her child's behavior, or wrestling with whether the signs are severe enough to warrant an assessment, there is no shortage of people to argue against the diagnosis. Friends and relatives who deny the possibility of a diagnosis can be some of the greatest hurdles for a parent seeking an ASD diagnosis, because the motivation and tendency to explain differences away is high, and relatives can convince a parent that nothing needs to be done and the child will grow out of it. "I felt like something was wrong, but people were telling me that I was wrong and overreacting," one mother recalled of her concern for her son. "People kept telling me I was imagining things, and I was like, 'I'm not imagining this.'"

For parents who are more convinced of their child's difficulties, coming up against family members and friends who are not supportive of seeking a diagnosis can be its own challenge. One parent described how heartbreaking it was to have to "defend" her child's symptoms to her family; they argued that he could not have autism, and though she herself struggled with coming to terms with his symptoms, she found herself defending the presence of symptoms even after a diagnosis was made:

> Once he was diagnosed, then it became the point of telling other people, explaining it to other people, some of whom were very supportive and some basically were still saying, "No, I don't think there's anything wrong, I think he's fine," so being in the position which I really didn't like of having to be, like, "Yes, there is something wrong with my kid, this is why, and . . . these are the problems. He's been diagnosed by a doctor so stop second-guessing me now."

Being challenged by loved ones can make a painful process all the more painful and may ultimately dissuade parents from seeking an ASD diagnosis until symptoms become more pronounced.

Professionals who have contact with a family during this early stage of diagnosis—pediatricians, therapists providing intervention for other developmental concerns, or even therapists for older siblings who are already diagnosed with ASD—can be a tremendous support for families. Professionals should take care not to dismiss parental concerns without careful thought. If a parent is concerned that his or her child is not speaking many words at 18 months, a professional may consider that the range of child language development is broad and that the minimal use of language may not be atypical. However, having the parents seek assessment for language development or other skills will do less harm than good; parents that are sufficiently concerned should be encouraged to seek assessment. If no delay is found, the results of the assessment may put their mind at ease. However, evidence of a delay will provide them access to services that they would not have received otherwise.

Parents will have no shortage of individuals dissuading them from seeking evaluation; professionals should think carefully before adding themselves to that group, because evaluation has very little risk, and in cases where a delay exists, the child will have everything to gain. Practitioners should also inoculate parents against caring family members who nonetheless may try to dissuade them from seeking an evaluation, and provide them with ways to explain to family the importance of the evaluation and the benefit of treatment for the child, using the arguments above about the low risks and potential high benefits of evaluation.

## GUIDING PARENTS THROUGH DIAGNOSIS

Attaining an ASD diagnosis, though easier than it used to be, is not an easy process. The process through which parents must progress to acquire a diagnosis easily breaks down depending on the skills of the professionals they approach. Any practitioner working in the field of child development or ASD, even if not a diagnostician, should have a thorough understanding of the process for seeking an ASD diagnosis, to provide families guidance in the process. Guidance will be especially important if barriers arise, such as those discussed below. Further, practitioners should understand the different assessments available to parents for an ASD diagnosis and be able to guide parents to other professionals in the field who will provide reliable, high-quality assessments, to minimize the confusion of the process and errors in diagnosis.

Recommending pediatricians as first-stop diagnosticians. Once parents have decided to seek an evaluation or diagnosis—which may take some time—often their first stop is the family pediatrician. A professional who is working with a family as concerns about an ASD diagnosis arise should recommend that they consult with the child's pediatrician, if they haven't already. Pediatricians are the sentry of the process, and a lot hinges on their ability to respond to concerns. Fortunately, the increase in incidence of ASD has led to greater standardization of care and evaluation for pediatricians.

The American Academy of Pediatrics now recommends that all children between the ages of eighteen and twenty-four months receive screening for ASD. Many pediatricians use the revised Modified Checklist for Autism in Toddlers (Robins, Fein, & Barton, 2009), a screening tool for ASD recommended by the American Academy of Pediatrics. Parents who note that their child has difficulty with such skills as showing interest in other children, responding to his or her name, or pointing out interesting things may find themselves in a greater discussion with their pediatrician about other concerns they may have, as well as possible options for further evaluation. For children at a young age, referral to early intervention services is warranted, and evaluation will determine the services recommended based on their development.

Many pediatricians are incredibly proactive and conservative, in that they are likely to refer a parent for an early intervention evaluation based on concerns in development. I remember that when my son was 9 months old he showed no interest in rolling over or pushing himself to a sitting position, let alone crawling. My daughter, then

4, had been similar as an infant, and I blamed his lack of progress in that area on my own poor coordination and dismissed it. However, I remember his pediatrician being very concerned and saying that she would be remiss not to refer him for an evaluation for early intervention. She raised my own anxiety about his skills, but ultimately he was enrolled in early intervention within a month and with that support made swift progress. Pediatricians who are attuned to delays in development can be a wonderful support and quickly move the parent along to the services they need.

However, some pediatricians possess their own biases regarding the diagnosis. Some may take the wait-and-see approach, advising concerned families to give the children longer to see whether they will grow out of their delays. I worked with one family whose son did not produce any vocal language at the age of 2; their pediatrician advised them that boys often "talk late" and that he would not recommend a speech evaluation until the age of 3. The responses pediatricians may have can be many. When asked about her child's diagnosis, one parent noted,

> I'm sure you've heard this a million times, but at that time the pediatricians would say, "Don't worry about it. She's your third child, she doesn't have to talk because you guys know what she wants. Do her sisters help?" She said, "Don't worry about it."

Another mother recounted her experience with her pediatrician at the time:

> I noticed when he was about 3 years old that he was kind of going backwards. He was making eye contact, interacting, and then all of the sudden wasn't making eye contact. He was moving by hopping around on his bottom instead of walking, and so I knew something was wrong. I was a teacher, and I had a student with autism, so I went online and I Googled *autism* and looked at information about autism and it seemed to fit. So I made an appointment with my pediatrician, and I went in to see the pediatrician, and they said I was a first-time mom and that I didn't know what I was talk-

ing about, that all kids progress differently, that there was nothing wrong. I just kept pestering and pestering and pestering until he finally agreed to refer me to a neurologist. It was hard to get into a neurologist, and when I finally did I just walked into the waiting room and the nurse said, "Oh, he's autistic isn't he?" . . . It's really concerning that a pediatrician couldn't spot autism and then it was obvious to the nurse in the neurologist's office just simply with walking through the door.

The concern with the dismissive approach of these pediatricians, even if well meaning, is twofold. First, for parents to bring a concern to their pediatrician, they often have to summon a great amount of strength, because they have to admit to themselves that something may not be right with their child. While normalizing fears is a role a pediatrician often has to take on when talking with new parents who are nervous about how much their baby spits up or cries, or how little the child sleeps, downplaying evident delays or resisting standardized screening of core areas of development such as motor skills, language, and social skills is not appropriate. A family who hesitated to bring the concern to their pediatrician in the first place may readily set their fears aside and feel relief that their doctor said not to be concerned. The motivation to seek help again from a professional in the near future will be greatly decreased.

The second issue that arises with pediatricians who are not willing to follow up on a possible ASD diagnosis is that their reticence may result in a delay of services that the child may need. Referring a family for an evaluation of development can do no harm. Many states have an early intervention system in place that comprises both evaluation and treatment in motor, speech, and social areas. If a child has an evaluation done, and the team determines that no evidence of delay exists, the parents may be able to rest a bit more easily. And if the evaluation team does determine that a delay exists, the delay may not be immediately indicative of an ASD diagnosis. Children with speech delays may be referred for speech services, and within a few months they may be catching up with their peers. Their language may have emerged without speech therapy on its own time, but the speech services would have certainly done no harm and in some cases may have benefited them.

For children who are on the autism spectrum, however, early intervention services can be a lifeline. Research shows us that children who receive high-quality early intervention services for ASD treatment have improved outcome over children who do not. For example, a notable series of studies compared children with ASD 18 to 30 months of age who received treatment through the Early Start Denver Model, a program based on developmental and applied behavior-analytic principles, with children of the same age who received community-based intervention. Children who received high-quality early intervention improved more in IQ, adaptive behavior, and diagnostic measures than the comparison group after 2 years of intervention, and these results were maintained when the children were reassessed at 6 years of age (Dawson et al., 2010; Estes et al., 2015).

Again, while it is possible that any delays evident at 18 months or earlier will have disappeared by the age of 3 regardless of early intervention, providing a child with early intervention services safeguards against the possibility that the family may miss a crucial window of treatment if indeed their child does have an ASD diagnosis. In some cases, early intervention is subsidized by the state and is provided at little or no cost to the family; in these cases, aside from the time the family must set aside for therapy sessions, the cost is negligible. Recalling the pediatrician who recommended waiting until the age of 3 to refer the family for further evaluation, at that age the child would have entirely missed his window for early intervention and all the potential benefit it may have offered.

Professionals who hear of pediatricians who discourage evaluation when parents are concerned about specific skill deficits for their child should still suggest alternative routes to assessment and diagnosis other than the pediatrician. For example, when I was told that the family's pediatrician had recommended no evaluation until after the age of 3, I gently recommended that the family still contact early intervention (because no pediatrician referral was required) to have them evaluate the family's needs. As discussed above, I talked with the family about the positive impact that early intervention could have, regardless of whether the child was ultimately diagnosed with a language delay or other developmental disability. Being knowledgeable about other types of diagnosing professionals is helpful for all practitioners in the field so they can provide the best guidance possible to families.

Referring families to other diagnosing professionals. While the pediatrician is often the first stop when asking about an ASD diagnosis, some families may not know that they have other avenues to pursue a diagnosis. Pediatricians and professionals that parents may have contact with prior to a diagnosis should be able to provide them with a list of clinics and other professionals that provide diagnosis using standardized tools and assessment measures. In some states, a referral from a pediatrician is not required to initiate an evaluation for early intervention.

Other professionals who can provide ASD diagnoses include developmental pediatricians, neuropsychologists, and psychologists. The professionals may practice independently or may be part of a larger practice; the ability for families to easily schedule an evaluation, however, depends on several factors. First, the family has to be able to afford the evaluation offered through a specific professional or clinic. Many insurance companies will cover a diagnostic evaluation, but some clinics do not work with insurance, and parents may choose to pay out of pocket for a clinic that has a shorter wait list. Second, and related, many clinics are in such high demand, especially in states with few services or those that work with many types of insurance, that the wait list for an evaluation can be months long. One mother recalled, "We couldn't get in any place. The doctors [our physician] recommended had a 9-month waiting list."

I remember working as a clinician in an ASD treatment program in a large hospital and parents calling for an ASD diagnosis. I felt horrible placing them on a 6-month wait list when I knew how much effort and courage it had taken them to call me in the first place. For parents who feel certain of an ASD diagnosis, this waiting period can feel interminable as they watch the time their child could be receiving treatment slip away. A mother remembered the months of waiting for her child's appointment with an assessment team:

> There was the whole process of trying to figure out where to go and who would do that and who was good and then another wait, I think it was a couple of months, to get an appointment. So there was a frustrating time with a lot of anxiety of not knowing, worrying about it, and trying to figure out what was going on, with nobody besides me really necessarily even thinking there was much of a problem.

This mother called several clinics, was put on several waiting lists, and took the first available appointment at a reputable evaluation site. Listening to her frustration at not finding a site that could move quickly and offer recommendations truly highlighted how frustrating and stressful this waiting period is. Recognizing this, I take no fault with families who jump off waiting lists for the first spot that opens at another clinic, because I would do the same for my children if the opportunity arose.

Practitioners working with families during this stressful time should be empathic and offer suggestions for as many routes to diagnosis as possible so that the family has options and is not waiting on one clinic alone. Additionally, the practitioner may offer other services that may be helpful in the short term without the diagnosis, such as speech therapy and social groups, though access to these services may be limited without a diagnosis due to lack of insurance coverage. Nevertheless, these options should be provided to families.

Explaining diagnostic evaluations to families. Regardless of whether professionals in the field of child development or ASD treatment actually provide the diagnostic evaluations, they should be familiar with the process of diagnosis so that they can best help families understand and prepare for the process ahead of time. Additionally, understanding the components of a high-quality assessment will help practitioners identify and recommend reputable professionals and clinics to which families can turn for evaluation.

The evaluation system is not nationally standardized; a number of different measures are used clinically to diagnose ASD. The gold standard is the second edition of the Autism Diagnostic Observation Schedule (ADOS-2; Lord et al., 2012), a structured assessment based upon social interactions with the clinician (play based for younger children and also conversation based for older, vocal children). The assessment comprises several activities that draw on areas that are known skill deficits for children with ASD. For instance, at the youngest, nonvocal or minimally vocal level, the assessment includes an activity in which the evaluator slowly and exaggeratedly blows up a balloon, counts to three, and releases the balloon to fly around the room. For many young children, this activity would incite interest and excitement; neurotypical children laugh at the activity, count along with the evaluator, make eye contact, and sometimes comment to their caregiver about their excitement, and then request the activity again using gestures or language. However, many of these skills are not present in children with ASD; they may not be interested in the activity or look to share it with their caregiver or the evaluator by commenting, making eye contact, or requesting more. By assessing these specific skills across a variety of activities, the ADOS-2 can provide a standardized score for symptomatology that places a child on the autism spectrum.

The ADOS-2 is frequently paired with the Autism Diagnostic Interview–Revised (ADI-R; Rutter, LeCouteur, & Lord, 2008), a lengthy structured parent interview in which the evaluator asks the parents questions about symptoms that are specific to the ASD diagnosis, such as difficulties with communication development, social interactions with others, and routines or repetitive behaviors that the child often does at home. The information provides the clinician with a wealth of information that, when paired with the observations from the ADOS-2, can often lead to a clearly objective diagnosis for the child.

Many established diagnostic clinics rely on the ADOS-2 and ADI-R for standardized diagnosis. However, because of the time requirement to conduct the ADOS-2 and ADI-R, even separately, and the associated training costs, many psychologists and pediatricians may opt not to use it clinically. Instead, these professionals may rely on short interviews with the parent and unstandardized clinical observation to make their diagnosis. The unstandardized approach leads to inconsistent diagnoses across professionals, especially if a child is considered "high functioning." Take, for instance, the following account of an incomplete evaluation with an assessment team in the parent's school district:

> They took him in for evaluation, and they basically said, "He's fine, we don't see any problems." But by that point I had become even more convinced that everything wasn't fine. Plus, when they sent me the report from their evaluation, it focused almost entirely on his language skills and his cognitive skills, which I already knew were fine—he was advanced in those areas. It said very little about his social skills other than the fact that he made eye contact with the interviewer, which in their minds basically meant, no, he doesn't have autism.

While professionals may agree quickly that a nonverbal child who does not initiate interactions with others but instead jumps repeatedly in place meets criteria for a diagnosis of ASD, the diagnosis for a child with many skills may be more challenging. The scoring of the ADOS-2 is carefully calibrated to identify these children. I completed an evaluation for a child who had gone undiagnosed until the age of 10. He was a very bright boy and could talk at length about topics of interest to him but perseverated on topics and could become highly agitated in school when his routine was disrupted. Professionals called him rigid and anxious, but when I conducted an ADOS-2 with him, the standardized assessment captured several symptoms indicative of ASD: highly formalized speech, preoccupations with topics that were challenging to redirect, and eye contact that was not consistently integrated with his otherwise fluent conversation. The use of the ADOS-2 provided a clear diagnosis of ASD when many professionals before had failed to identify the symptoms of ASD in this fluent conversationalist.

Evaluations that do not fully capture the child's ability and disability can leave the parents in a state of greater confusion. While parents may be relieved to hear an evaluator—an expert in child development—tell them that their child is not on the autism spectrum, often they report that within hours the unsettled feeling that something is not right returns. One father remembered this feeling:

> We scheduled him to be examined by a doctor, and the doctor said she saw no signs of autism, which was great, and we all thought, "Happy, happy, happy!" But that had no effect on what we had seen before. Everything we had seen was still there.

Incomplete evaluations can fuel arguments between spouses, relatives, or friends who disagree with the parent's concern and leave parents unsure of where to turn next. Left with the feeling that things are just not right, parents may end up jumping from clinician to clinician until their child receives a diagnosis.

For parents whose children are not given a diagnosis until later in childhood, as the child I assessed and described above, this prolonged period of uncertainty—which can last for years—can be incredibly taxing and distressing. These parents may be given multiple diagnoses, such as attention-deficit/hyperactivity disorder, anxiety, or depression, to explain their child's behavior, and they may see little to no effect from the treatments developed to treat those diagnoses. Clinicians who see families who have waited for years for a diagnosis should be especially aware of the prolonged period of stress these parents have experienced on the path to attaining an ASD diagnosis.

By better understanding what constitutes high-quality evaluation, practitioners in the field can help parents judge whether their child's evaluation was complete and recommend reevaluation in cases where evaluators did not account for the full diagnostic profile of a child with ASD (e.g., overemphasizing presence of eye contact and well-developed language as indicators that ASD is not present, and not attending to nuanced social concerns). Practitioners who do offer diagnostic evaluations should carefully consider seeking training in gold-standard assessments such as the ADOS-2 and the ADI-R to ensure that they offer standardized evaluation, which will be especially important when evaluating individuals with well-developed language but difficulties with advanced social skills.

## UNDERSTANDING PARENTS' EMOTIONAL RESPONSES FOLLOWING DIAGNOSIS

Many parents can remember the moment they received their child's diagnosis with astounding clarity. That moment often resembles a "flashbulb memory," or one in which the sights and sounds of the moment are captured forever in great detail. One mother described the moments following the receipt of her child's diagnosis:

> When I walked out, my husband went to get the car after [the doctor] just told us [the diagnosis]. I was thinking they were going to tell us something not as bad, not as severe. My husband went to get the car and I was carrying my son and it was so busy and there were all these hospitals, not just one hospital. Everyone was out, and there were these food trucks, and everyone was outside because it was this beautiful day, and I thought, "This is the worst day of my life." I just remember it so clearly, my husband going to the car and me trying to walk towards the parking garage, and it was horrible. It was the worst feeling.

One might be surprised to learn that this mother's child is now an adult. Her recall of the day is as clear as if she received the diagnosis for her son last week. This type of recall is very common. I can talk with parents whose children are 20 years old, even 30 years old, and they can recall the moment of diagnosis with the same level of acuity, and the recollection of the moment often makes parents emotional.

Parents' ability to recall this moment in such detail is not surprising. Detailed, flashbulb memories occur when a person experiences a surprising, consequential, or emotionally arousing event (Brown & Kulik, 1977). Hearing a child's diagnosis of ASD can be very surprising for some parents, and the diagnosis is highly consequential to the parent and child's life. Because of its uncertain outcome and the impact that it has on a parent's life and the life of the child, the diagnosis inevitably leads to emotional arousal and heightened stress. In fact, research has found that parents can suffer from symptoms not unlike those of posttraumatic stress disorder following the diagnosis of their child. A group of researchers found that 20 percent of parents described a high level of posttraumatic stress symptoms, such as having difficulty sleeping, being frequently reminded of their child's diagnosis, feeling watchful and on guard, and experiencing heightened emotions about the diagnosis, sometimes even years after diagnosis (Casey et al., 2012). These research findings indicate how impactful the period of diagnosis is and how lasting that impact can be for parents. This high level of stress persists for a significant length of time, and professionals should be aware of how this can impact parents' mental health.

Though I discuss the impact of the diagnosis of ASD on mental health over time at greater length in Chapter 2, here we examine the emotions that parents commonly experience following their child's diagnosis. Practitioners should be aware of the broad range of emotions that parents may experience so that they can both prepare themselves for parents' reactions in their work with them and understand how these emotions might affect interactions with professionals. Additionally, awareness of the range of emotions experienced by parents can also help practitioners normalize the experience of these emotions for family members. While all family members will experience a range of emotions in response to a child's diagnosis, including siblings and extended family, this chapter focuses primarily on the experiences of parents. Siblings' experiences with their brother's or sister's diagnosis are discussed in Chapter 4, and the experiences of extended family members are explored in Chapter 5.

Validating grief. The range of emotions that a parent experiences at the time of diagnosis is vast. Many experience extreme devastation. Regardless of whether they knew that the diagnosis was a possibility, when parents first hear that their child has ASD, their view of their child and their child's life shifts dramatically. "It was devastating," a mother remembered of her daughter's diagnosis.

> It was shocking. . . . For those days and weeks afterwards I woke up in the middle of the night feeling like somebody had died. It was very hard. . . . Every parent wants their child to be perfect or

close to it, and to find out . . . [your child has] autism and not even really know what that means. . . . At the same time to try to keep your head screwed on so that you can get your child what your child needs, it was overwhelming, it was daunting, it was scary. And it was saddening, it was upsetting, it was devastating.

Parents often liken the news of their child's diagnosis to the death of their child. Their son or daughter as they had imagined, and their dreams for their child's future, are taken away in an instant and replaced with nothing but uncertainty. A mother described this feeling:

At the beginning you feel a great sense of loss. I think everybody I've talked to had the same sense of loss. You have these dreams for your kid: They're going to grow up. They're going to have a good job. They're going to have a family of their own. They're going to be able to take care of themselves. All those things seem like now they're not going to happen. And then worrying, how am I going to care for this kid? When I pass, who's going to take care of this child? Do his siblings have to care for him? What will happen to him when I'm no longer around to take care of him? Will he be able to take care of himself? So you go through the loss of the dreams you had for your child.

As you see from this mother's description, her sudden feeling of uncertainty does not just encompass the next few weeks or months but stretches years into the future. Because children with ASD have varying outcomes as they grow, what can be expected is entirely unknown for the practitioner or the parent. Not only do parents have to question how their child will function in their current day-to-day life, but they also have to consider what this is going to mean long term for their child and their family. As a result, a parent's early reaction to diagnosis is often one of grief and sadness for the loss of the typical feeling of security that comes with raising a child without a disability. "I just couldn't wrap my head around it," a mother told me. "It really just killed me. I just felt like all of my dreams for this boy were gone in an instant, and I grieve it every day. I'm sorry to say it, but I really do. I really do, I grieve it."

Practitioners working with families soon after their diagnosis, and in some cases years after, should be prepared for the sadness parents might experience. Validating and empathizing with this sadness for all parents, regardless of how long ago the diagnosis was provided, will be important. Regularly I meet with parents who tear up when I ask them about their child's diagnosis, and I always take time to pause and validate the sadness they are experiencing by verbally acknowledging how difficult it is to think and talk about their child's diagnosis. Practitioners who share how they often see parents who express similar emotions may be able to normalize the experience of these emotions for parents, especially those who seem embarrassed by expressing sadness to the practitioner. For parents whose sadness seems especially pervasive (e.g., tearing frequently during repeated meetings), practitioners may offer coping resources such as those recommended in Chapter 7.

Recognizing anger. Some parents may also respond with anger about the diagnosis, which first may emerge toward the practitioner who provided their child's diagnosis. "So we went to this [doctor]," a father recounted,

> and we just told him [about our son], and he said, "Oh, sounds like he is autistic." He just dropped that, and then my face must have done something because he immediately backtracked madly. The poor man, it looked like I wanted to strangle him, I guess.

Anger is not an uncommon emotion to experience in times of extreme stress, especially when an element of fear is also present. For example, imagine what happens when two people get in a car accident, and each of them jumps out of the car, screaming at the other. While some of that anger may actually be due to wrongdoing, much of it is in response to the fear and heightened arousal that each person has experienced in a dangerous situation.

For parents, an ASD diagnosis leads to similar stress, because it threatens their life, and their future, as they have known it and imagined it. They may direct anger at anyone who might play a part in the diagnosis of their child: the doctor, their spouse, the well-meaning friend who shared concerns. Unfortunately, this anger, especially in the home, can isolate parents from other people and reduce the support that they receive. The anger may also have a tremendous impact on other family members who are looking to the parents for support but are met instead with anger.

Practitioners who observe this anger can help other family members understand the anger by talking about the broad range of emotions parents experience in response to diagnosis. Additionally, by understanding how anger can be a typical response to diagnosis, practitioners may be less likely to take anger personally when working with the family; the parent may be angry with the situation and the child's diagnosis rather than with the professional. This recognition may help professionals persevere in their interactions with the parents rather than discounting them because of their frustrated responses to the practitioner.

However, one must be aware that a parent's anger is well placed if a professional's approach to sharing the diagnosis is insensitive and hurtful. For instance, the doctor above shared a very impactful diagnosis with the parents in a curt, sudden manner that rightfully incited anger in the father. In my discussions with parents, I often hear them recall the news given to them by clinicians in an unprofessional manner. One mother recalled an appointment with a neurologist for her son: "She was a nasty women and she said, 'I think he is autistic, and I think you have known this all along.' I just slid to the floor." When giving the news of diagnosis, professionals need to be highly attuned to how significant the announcement is going to be to the parents; their future with their child, as they may have envisioned it, will likely become blurred and unpredictable.

Clinicians must recognize the impact of the diagnosis and choose their words carefully and kindly. Clearly detailing the symptoms that have been observed and how they relate to the diagnosis of ASD will be extremely helpful, so that parents are not left to wonder what the diagnosis means. Asking the parents about their initial responses to the diagnosis will demonstrate a great deal of empathy. Further, providing the parents with information on treatment and support will also be beneficial. One parent remembered, "[The clinicians] said she has autism. Here's information on the diagnosis. Here's information on treatment. Here are support groups. I was like, 'Thank you.'" This parent's clinicians recognized the importance of providing information not only on the diagnosis and potential treatments but also on the support that would be necessary for parents in the weeks, months, and years to come. Diagnosing professionals should also consider follow-up conversations with families after the initial diagnosis so that the parents can talk at greater length with the professional after having time to process the diagnosis, and their emotions, and formulate questions about next steps.

Identifying denial. Especially if the child is young, and the difficulties are limited to small impairments in communication and social skills, parents may have difficulty accepting the diagnosis and may instead begin to hope that their child is growing out of the symptoms and that the doctor is wrong. One mother I spoke with remembered that her daughter received a diagnosis of pervasive developmental disorder, not otherwise specified, at 15 months, but at the same time blockages were noted in her ears that affected her hearing. After a medical procedure cleared the blockages, her language began to improve, and for the next year the mother worked to make sure that her daughter received the best speech therapy in early intervention to help her catch up on her language. "They were not focusing on any type of autism piece of it," she told me.

> We went through this for about a year and went back to [the diagnostic clinic], thinking we are going to get a pat on the back, thinking how great we are that we get her the speech therapy and she is hearing now, only to be told they reclassified her into autism, fully, and left the other diagnosis, and really kind of gave us a severe reprimand for not listening to them.

She continued,

> It was just denial, it really was. Again, when I think about it, we were so sure it was her ears, and it was her hearing. . . . So our first

year was, "It's nothing," and it wasn't until that second [visit to the doctor] when I considered that it wasn't nothing. This is not going to go away.

Again, for parents who want nothing more than for their child to grow up as any other child, the motivation and tendency to explain away symptoms—even with a diagnosis in hand—can be very high. Unfortunately, as this mother noted, such a tendency can result in lost treatment for the child.

Practitioners may be able to identify denial in parents following diagnosis by asking them to restate the important points that have been shared during the diagnostic meeting. The professional may also ask parents to share how what they have seen in their child fits the diagnosis that has been provided. Parents who do not agree with the professional may be less likely to recount the main points accurately, or to easily apply the diagnosis to their child. Professionals who recognize this difficulty can emphasize the importance of the next steps for identifying treatment. If parents seem especially opposed to the diagnosis, the professional may share how the treatment could have benefit on specific symptoms parents have noticed, regardless of the diagnosis. By emphasizing the symptoms, rather than the diagnosis, parents may be more likely to seek treatment for their specific concerns. Again, following up with families after the initial diagnosis may help professionals gain an understanding of the parents' perspective of the diagnosis after the parents have had the opportunity to think about it, and gauge the parents' intent to follow through on recommendations for treatment.

Alleviating guilt. The prospect of "wasted time" from delayed services leads to another feeling that is quite common among parents of children with ASD: guilt. For parents who have delayed seeking a diagnosis or enrolling their child in treatment, or for those who knew something was not quite right with their child but were unable to receive an accurate diagnosis until a later age, the feeling of guilt can emerge prominently. "Well, I felt lousy," a father remembered of how he felt after he heard his son's diagnosis. "First I felt bad for him; then I felt bad for myself for not spotting it sooner, for just passing it off as other things and making allowances."

Another mother of twin boys on the spectrum told me how her concerns about her sons' behavior, especially socially, emerged when they were toddlers but that she did not receive a diagnosis for them until one of them was hospitalized for a mental health crisis at the age of 8. "I felt so hopeless and so guilty because he was 8, almost 9 years old before he got diagnosed," she told me. "I remembered sitting up one night looking on the computer researching all this stuff and thinking, 'This is supposed to be diagnosed when they're 2, and it's terrible, he's almost 9 and look what I've done.'" The feeling that the child has lost valuable time in treatment is strong in parents and results in tremendous guilt.

Parents may also carry guilt because of the concerns that they "gave" their child autism. A mother may worry and feel guilty about what she exposed her child to when she was pregnant. Parents may have another person with ASD in their family and feel guilty that they passed along a genetic predisposition toward ASD. A father may feel that he did not spend enough time talking and engaging with his child early in development. Unfortunately, society does little to assuage this guilt for parents. Highly controversial messages about how raising a child can impact the likelihood that a child will be diagnosed with ASD have existed for decades. Early theories on the development of ASD blamed mothers: Bruno Bettelheim, a well-known child development specialist, posited that "refrigerator mothers," who were cold and unemotional when dealing with their children, were responsible for the development of ASD. This work, highly publicized in Bettelheim's 1967 book *The Empty Fortress: Infantile Autism and the Birth of the Self*, instantly cast a shadow over these mothers, claiming they did not care for their children the way they should.

While research has dispelled these outdated theories, parents today are inundated with messages that exposure to environmental toxins, many of which parents knew nothing about prior to diagnosis, can lead to ASD. One need not look far to find the highly disputed claim that ASD develops as a result of early childhood vaccinations. Research (e.g., DeStefano, Price, & Weintraub, 2013; Price et al., 2010) has demonstrated again and again that this is not a valid claim, and the paper originally making the claim has been retracted due to concerns with the design and ethics of the study. Despite this evidence, however, these claims still put onus on parents for the development of their child's ASD: it was a mistake *they* made. Without knowing the true cause of ASD (which we cannot know at this time and may differ for each child), parents are left to postulate all the different ways they could have caused their child's ASD, which leads to overwhelming feelings of guilt.

Practitioners should make attempts to help alleviate parent guilt by explaining the common challenges outside of parents' control that can interfere with the receipt of diagnosis. All the factors discussed in this chapter, such as difficulty identifying nuanced skill deficits, contending with professionals and family members who do not agree with the diagnosis, and difficulty arranging an evaluation for their child, could interfere with the receipt of diagnosis. For parents who are concerned that they caused their child's ASD, practitioners should heavily emphasize that the cause of ASD, at this point, is unknown. They should advise parents not to chastise themselves for purported risk factors of which they were not aware and that may not have had anything to do with the development of their child's condition. Further, practitioners should encourage parents to channel their feelings of guilt toward identifying the steps that can be taken now to best help their child. Recommendations for therapy approaches that may help parents who are struggling with pervasive feelings of guilt, such as those that help them focus on the present moment rather than the past, are offered in Chapter 7.

Welcoming relief. Some parents report that they felt tremendous relief to finally receive their child's diagnosis. Sometimes these are the parents who sensed that their child was struggling in areas of development but had been unable to identify why. They may have been met with doctors or professionals who dismissed their concerns as unrelated to ASD. The frustration that some parents experience in these moments as they worry about their child's development with an increasing concern that something is amiss can continue, in some cases, for years. Some parents report that receiving the diagnosis from a professional means that they finally have a direction: specific

educational approaches are recommended, hours of treatment prescribed, and programs, schools, and services are suddenly available
to them and covered by insurance that had not been before a diagnosis. A mother remembered that what she felt after her son's diagnosis

> was really a mix of anxiety and also relief in some ways. It felt
> like, okay, at least we have an answer, and we can now move for-
> ward. There was a lot of anxiety leading up to it and confusion
> about whether there really was something going on or was I just
> completely being crazy and making this up. So there was a little
> bit of validation on my part feeling, like, "Okay, I'm not imagining
> things; there really is something going on here." And, like I said,
> relief that now we can take concrete steps to address this, we can
> go . . . to the school system and get him in a program. We can start
> doing all these things.

Another mother felt similarly after a series of appointments to assess
her son:

> For so long I knew something was wrong. I just couldn't figure out
> what was wrong. I thought, "Well, what is it? Something is wrong,
> and nobody is telling me what's wrong." I don't want to be told
> that nothing is wrong because I can tell. . . . So I was actually
> relieved when I got the diagnosis because now I know what [it is],
> and we can make a plan. Now we know what to do; now there is
> *something.* I don't care what we call it, as long as there is a plan of
> action we can follow now and I can get into "go" mode.

The feeling of being able to do something active to help their children overcome the challenges they face provides many parents with
a sense of relief after months of being unsure of what to do to best
help them.

Practitioners should welcome the motivation many of these parents will possess in this experience of relief, because they finally
have a diagnosis and can seek an effective treatment for their child.
However, practitioners should also be mindful that parents who have

searched so long for a diagnosis may be especially discouraged when treatment for ASD is not immediately effective or as effective as hoped. Relief does not mean that parents will not experience other emotions, such as grief, anger, and guilt, so practitioners should not be surprised if these other emotions emerge and present challenges in treatment.

Reducing the sense of being overwhelmed. Regardless of the initial responses to diagnosis, and even with a sense of relief that they now can move forward and find treatment, most parents report feeling overwhelmed following their child's diagnosis with regard to identifying the next appropriate steps for their child. Many parents report that the professional who provided their child's diagnosis provided little additional support in seeking appropriate services, aside from recommending what the child should receive. Although recommendations for treatment can be beneficial, telling parents that their child should receive 40 hours of ABA services a week is very different from providing them with state-specific resources on where to find and how to evaluate the available services. A mother recalled how stressful the first few months following diagnosis were:

> I just remember being nauseous, but I also remember a lot of stress and a lot of different types of stress. [The doctor] mentioned 40 hours of ABA, and early intervention is giving you 10, so then you have to go find 30 more on your own, and you have to interview people to come to the house and make sure they are okay, and set up cameras to make sure they are okay with your children, and sit there watching for hours or watching your kid in early intervention, and he's exhausted because you are dragging him to 40 hours a week and he is 2 years old and he has a full-time job, and you have to leave him somewhere crying and you hear him crying, or you're watching through a window. So you have all this stress and guilt and all this.

Practitioners who are working with families as they are just beginning to explore and understand new treatments for their child should recognize how stressful this early stage is. Parents' search for providers who will care for and teach the most precious person in the world to them is incredibly stressful. As a result, these parents may have difficulty grasping all that practitioners explain about new treatment methods, and practitioners must be patient as parents ask questions and the same information needs to be provided repeatedly. Professionals must understand that parents are learning a new language under conditions of great stress and will require support and patience to ensure that they fully grasp what is shared with them.

Parents who are left on their own to search for services for their child on the Internet are bombarded with the myriad treatments available to children with ASD, with little guidance on how to identify which treatments should be pursued. Practitioners should be prepared to provide support to parents in evaluating and selecting effective treatment for their child. Please see Chapter 9 for guidelines on how professionals can effectively teach parents to evaluate treatments.

One mother with an advanced degree in psychology struggled with how best to help her son receive services:

> Even with my background in psychology and with having known . . . a friend who works with kids with ASD, I still found it hard to figure out where to go to get [appropriate services], how to get it set up, and how to interview someone and know if they were going to be a good fit for [my son]. . . . I kept thinking all along that if this was this hard for me, even with all the background knowledge that I have, I can't imagine how difficult it is for parents who don't have that to figure out how to get their kid services, and the right services, with people who are a good fit.

Pediatricians, diagnosticians, and other professionals should have at hand materials that can be provided to families about what ASD is, how to evaluate services their child might receive, guidelines for what treatment is required as part of state mandates, and where to go to find those services.

Resources for families that can be provided at the time of diagnosis are included in the Resources section of this book; professionals should select those that will be most helpful to families with whom they work. While these resources may seem like a lot of information to provide to the parent, a packet of websites and other resources can be quickly assembled to direct parents to the information they need so that they can access it when they are ready. In this way, parents are not inundated with information all at once coming out of the office but have a handful of useful resources when they are ready to begin searching for services.

## CLINICAL TAKE-AWAYS

The intent of this chapter is to help professionals understand the impact that an ASD diagnosis has on a family at the time of diagnosis. The stress that parents experience before, at the time of, and after diagnosis may be the highest they will experience in their lifetime, and professionals need to be sensitive to this. Checking in with parents about their experience, how they are feeling, and how they are handling the situation will go a long way in helping them adjust to their child's diagnosis.

Sometimes practitioners feel that their sole focus should be on the child with ASD, but the child is not in a bubble. The experiences and emotions of the parents will affect how well they are able to respond to practitioner recommendations, and assessing parents' state will not only provide professionals with information about how effectively they are able to follow through on recommendations but also demonstrate to the parents that the professional cares about the family as a whole and help build rapport with the family. Chapter 8 provides an in-depth discussion on establishing rapport with families. The following is a summary of recommendations for professionals at the time of diagnosis.

Practitioners should:

• Understand that the period of diagnosis can be an extended length of time and that the impact is long lasting. Professionals working with parents at any stage of their child's development should be well versed in how they can help parents through the process of diagnosis:

- – Prediagnosis: Help orient parents to appropriate professionals who can provide diagnosis, and help parents troubleshoot common barriers to seeking diagnosis.

- – Diagnosis: Guide parents through the process of diagnosis, evaluate the quality of the diagnostic evaluation, and provide information about the diagnosis sensitively and in a way that is least overwhelming to the family.

- – Postdiagnosis: Demonstrate interest in the parents' early experiences with their child and gauge their goals for their child at the current time.

• Be knowledgeable about the signs and symptoms of ASD if working in any area of child development to aid in the early identification of ASD signs in children.

• Learn how the child's signs of ASD developed to gain a better understanding of the parents' goals for their child and whether they may be hoping to recapture skills that their child may have lost in early development.

• Be prepared for the range of emotions parents will experience in response to diagnosis, which could include grief, anger, denial, guilt, relief, and a sense of being overwhelmed. Empathize with these feelings and normalize them for parents, and also recognize that parent responses to the practitioner may be affected by the emotions they are experiencing in response to diagnosis.

• Be especially attuned to parents' experiences of denial, because this may lead to delayed access to needed services for the child with ASD.

• Assemble a prepared packet that provides parents with useful information related to their child's diagnosis and how to identify appropriate services for their child. Please see the Resources section for examples of information that could be included in this packet.

# CHAPTER 2

# Recognizing Patterns of Parent Stress Over Time

Parents of children with ASD experience greater stress than virtually any other group of parents. For some parents, the level of stress they experience at the time of diagnosis may be the highest they experience in their lifetime. However, professionals should be careful not to make the assumption that parent stress and reactions to their child's diagnosis lessen over time and that life becomes easier as the family falls into the routine of their new life with ASD. Parent stress, and emotions such as grief and anger, will resurge throughout the child's development. For some parents, their stress may remain at an elevated level throughout their child's life.

Parents' stress can have a tremendous impact on their interactions with their family, as well as their ability to serve as effective collaborators with practitioners. Practitioners should be aware of the various factors specific to ASD that elevate parent stress so they can be aware of when stress may be impacting parents' availability in their child's treatment. Additionally, an understanding of parent stress may provide practitioners with a greater sense of empathy when working with families of individuals with ASD. To that end, this chapter provides an overview of stress for professionals and of the ways in which the symptoms of ASD are related to parent stress. The impact of stress on mental health is also discussed, as are the ways in which parents' stress and emotions shift throughout their child's development. Although later chapters in this book provide specific strategies for helping parents cope with their experiences raising a child with ASD, initial recommendations for how practitioners should take parent stress into account when working with the family are offered here.

This chapter focuses primarily on the challenges that parents of children with ASD will face, to provide practitioners with a better understanding of the stress associated with parenting a child with ASD. However, I do recognize that parents also find great joy in raising a child on the autism spectrum. Themes related to the positive impact of parenting a child with ASD are explored further in Chapter 7.

## DEFINING STRESS

Before talking more about parent stress, first consider the definition of stress. Psychological stress emerges when people are presented with an environment that they consider taxing, or that they believe exceeds their own personal resources and thus endangers their well-being (Lazarus & Folkman, 1984). Generally, four types of stressors are discussed in research  (e.g., Elliott & Eisdorfer, 1982; Glasberg, Martins, & Harris, 2006). The first, *acute, time-limited stressors*, are those that are transient in nature and result in instantaneous but fleeting stress, such as that experienced when one is startled by a snake. Although the initial response to the presentation of the taxing event may be a high level of stress, it decreases rapidly once the person is out of danger.

Second, *stressor sequences* are those that occur over a longer period of time in response to a trigger event, such as the death of a loved one or the loss of a job. Typically these events result in a longer period of stress as people adjust to changes in their life that result from the precipitating event. Over time, however, the stress will diminish as the event moves into the past and the person adapts to the changes caused by the event. Third, *chronic intermittent stressors* are those that increase stress but on a variable schedule (e.g., weekly, monthly). For example, when parents manage their child's seizure disorder, they may experience periods of lowered stress between episodes. However, when a seizure occurs, the parents' concern for their child and management of health care will result in an elevated period of stress.

Finally, *chronic stressors* are those that may have been initiated by a discrete event and persist continuously over time. Parenting a child with ASD is best described as a chronic psychological stressor, because the challenges of raising a child with a lifetime diagnosis often are unremitting. Though the level of strain on parents may increase or decrease with the occurrence of specific events in the child's life, a brief review of the literature indicates that parents of children with ASD experience a greater level of stress than do parents of typically developing children. They even experience more stress than do parents of children with other disabilities such as Down syndrome and intellectual disability (Donovan, 1988) or parents of children with chronic physical illness (Bouma & Schweitzer, 1990).

Practitioners working with parents who appear embarrassed or ashamed about the stress or emotions they experience in their time with their child, even long after their child's diagnosis, may share some of this research to help normalize and validate parents' experiences. Many parents may feel that they should be able to handle their child's care without difficulty, but discussing how frequently parents report levels of stress above that of virtually any other parent group may convey to them that their experiences are appropriate and normal. This may in turn reduce negative cognitions they might have about their own ability to cope with their experiences.

Beyond being aware of how the stress of parents of children with ASD compares with others, however, practitioners must also recognize the ways in which this stress can have far-reaching effects not only on the parents but also on their child and their work with the practitioner. Even if a practitioner's primary responsibility is to focus on the child with ASD, he or she should be concerned with whether the mother or father experiences a great deal of stress and the ways in which it might impact the care and treatment of the child with ASD.

## RECOGNIZING THE IMPACT OF STRESS ON PARENT MENTAL HEALTH AND CHILD OUTCOME

The level of chronic stress that parents experience while raising a child with ASD may contribute to the development of mental health concerns. Numerous studies indicate that parents of children with ASD are at a greater risk of problems with mental health and experience greater rates of anxiety and depression than do parents of children with other disabilities (Abbeduto et al., 2004; Bromley, Hare, Davison, & Emerson, 2004; Hartley, Seltzer, Head, & Abbeduto, 2012; Moes, Koegel, Schreibman, & Loos, 1992; Olsson & Hwang, 2001; Yamada et al., 2007). For example, Olsson and Hwang (2001) found that, among families raising a child with ASD, 50 percent of mothers and 21 percent of fathers experienced elevated levels of dysphoria or depression. This is in sharp contrast to the lower rates the same researchers found among families of neurotypical children: only 17 percent of mothers and 15 percent of fathers reported elevated scores on the same depression measures.

Parents who are highly stressed, and especially those with significant mental health issues, may be less able to actively engage in effective parenting or work effectively with practitioners. Further, parents' stress may impact their child's clinical outcome. For example, researchers found that high levels of parent stress counteracted the effectiveness of teaching interventions on child outcomes, such as core symptoms of ASD, educational performance, and adaptive behavior (Osborne, McHugh, Saunders, & Reed, 2008; Strauss et al., 2012).

Professionals need to be aware of the experiences of parents and the resulting stress and emotions that parents face, because doing so will help them better understand parents' participation in parent training and follow-through on recommendations. Imagine, for example, a professional who is working with a couple to help reduce their child's significantly aggressive behavior. The parents have two other children at home, and the child with ASD frequently targets his siblings and is so aggressive that he cannot be brought out in public. The parents' social sphere is highly limited because of the problem behavior. The professional is putting forth his best effort to provide effective strategies for the parents to try but is being met with resistance and little follow-through. The mother, in particular, seems to make half-hearted attempts to implement the suggested strategies and does not collect data on when the behavior occurs, as was suggested by the professional. The professional begins to think of the parents as "problem parents" who do not follow through on recommendations and are not motivated to help their child.

However, this professional needs to think carefully about the parents' current environment. They are faced daily with a child who is highly aggressive and minimally communicative, and they are constantly working to preserve their own safety as well as that of all of their children. They have very little social support, and both may be working outside of the home to pay for the services that they are seeking. Their level of stress is likely incredibly high. The professional should not be surprised to find that one or both parents are struggling with a mental health problem such as depression, which decreases energy level and motivation for even the most important of activities. This context paints a very different picture of the parents: instead of problem parents, they can now be viewed as parents who need considerable help in managing their child's behavior and in identifying ways that they can reasonably implement recommendations in the home, as well as possible individual therapy for themselves.

## UNDERSTANDING THE IMPACT OF ASD SYMPTOMS ON PARENT STRESS

Chapters 6 through 9 of this book offer recommendations to work effectively with parents at home to implement interventions and to address the coping needs of these parents. The important point to remember here is that parent stress can have considerable impact on the effectiveness of intervention at home and, more broadly, on overall child outcomes. Developing an understanding of the variables that can heighten parent stress, such as the general symptomatology of ASD and the long-term care required of parents, may help practitioners better understand parents' responses during parent-professional interactions, develop empathy for parents' experiences, and improve parent-professional relations.

When one considers the diagnosis of ASD, the reasons for parenting stress are unsurprising. The *DSM-5* (American Psychiatric Association, 2013) describes the primary symptom areas for ASD as deficits in social communication and interaction and the presence of restricted and repetitive interests. Each of these symptoms, as well as other related behaviors, will have a unique impact on parents' experiences.

Comprehending the effects of communication. For many children with ASD, communication proves to be a challenge. To gain an idea of what a parent may experience in this realm on a daily basis, think of parents of young infants who do not yet have verbal communication. This period of time for many parents is exhausting; their child is too young to clearly communicate wants and needs, which leaves parents feeling uncertain and concerned that they are not able to meet their child's needs. A baby who cries incessantly for hours on end may leave parents wondering whether the child is hungry, tired, or hurt. Without any answers from the infant, the parent becomes increasingly stressed and uncomfortable and may feel badly about their own roles as parents and their ability to care for their child.

With an understanding of how parents of infants must feel, imagine then an infancy that continues in perpetuity. For many parents of children with ASD, their child never achieves a level of language that allows them to convey their needs and wants to others, and parents are constantly in a state of wondering what their child needs, and whether the child's problem behavior is due to pain, illness, or some other event in the environment that cannot be articulated. A mother stated,

I hate autism. I hate it for him; I hate it for us because he is so involved, and I think that it makes life so challenging. It is so hard to communicate what he is thinking and what he wants, what he needs, and even what he is feeling. It makes it hard to know when he is hungry. I know when he is hungry when he's banging his head. . . . I hate that, I hate that, I hate that.

A father agreed: "The most frustrating thing is that without language, she is unable to tell us her wants, her needs, her pain. That, in a nutshell for a parent, for me, is the most frustrating thing of all."

Even for parents whose children develop language, the language skills may be limited to talking about people and things they see in the environment, but not about more abstract concepts such as feelings and emotions. Even individuals with highly developed communication skills can have difficulty discussing emotions or the social concerns they may face, or they may describe these private events in idiosyncratic ways that a parent is unable to understand. For example, children who are anxious about an upcoming event, such as a school event where they are expected to interact with many other children, may complain that their head hurts, or their stomach hurts, because they are unable to articulate their feelings of anxiety, or they may throw a severe tantrum because of concern about the upcoming event and be unable to explain the reason for the tantrum to their parents.

Like parents of colicky infants, but to an even greater extreme, parents of children with ASD may feel like ineffective parents because they are unable to understand or respond to their child's wants and needs. From research, we know that feelings of efficacy—the feeling that one has the skills one needs to overcome a challenge—result in decreased stress-related concerns such as anxiety and depression (Hastings & Brown, 2002). When parents feel that their child does not have the ability to communicate and, as a result, they cannot understand their child, increased parent stress can result.

The recommendations for practitioners with regard to the impact of child communication skills on parent stress differ based on the practitioner's role in the family's life. To increase parents' sense of self-efficacy, practitioners should refer to the recommended methods for teaching parents skills offered in Chapter 9. Although this book does not provide specific methods of teaching communication to children with ASD (that is left to other texts that focus specifically on that topic), Chapter 9 provides suggestions for how to effectively teach parents the skills they need to help their child, including how to build communication in their child. Additionally, practitioners should recognize that difficulty communicating with their child will be a primary concern for many parents and offer empathy for the complex emotions that parents will experience in response to their child's difficulty in this important developmental area.

Grasping the importance of social skills. Social concerns also contribute significantly to parent stress. Deficits in social skills will affect the development of a relationship between the parents and the child. Everyone who is reading this book has been someone's son or daughter and can likely appreciate the unique nature of the relationship between a parent or caregiver and child. For so many neurotypical children and parents, the really bad days of tantrums, arguments, and misbehavior melt away during times when parent and child can connect through hugs, quiet conversations, shared jokes, and child proclamations of "I love you so much!" and "You are the best Daddy in the whole world!" But what happens when a child does not like to be held or cuddled, has difficulty communicating meaningfully, and cannot interact with parents in the ways in which other children do to help forge that parent-child bond? Parents whose children do not reciprocate easily in relationships can become saddened by the feeling that they are missing out on the relationship.

A common misconception, largely perpetuated by the media, is that children with ASD cannot be affectionate or loving. Some parents of children with ASD have incredibly affectionate children. I had the opportunity to do an assessment for a 3-year-old with ASD. His mother had come to his school for the assessment, and when I brought him into the room where she was sitting, he balked at the door because the room was unfamiliar. But as he scanned the room, his eyes lit on his mother, and he broke into a huge smile and sprinted across the room to hug her. The joy in seeing his mother was obvious, and it brought tears to my eyes to see their connection.

Some parents may have this affection develop naturally with their child. Other parents, whose children are not naturally affectionate, may find other ways to connect with their child, such as through conversations about favorite topics or by playing their favorite activity with them, such as pushing them on a swing. Because the presentation of the parent-child interaction can be highly variable from family to family, it is important to be mindful of how a relationship between child and parent shifts over time, and parents may continue to miss the typical parent-child bond as their child ages. Professionals can help parents identify ways to connect with their child. Even if the activity is unorthodox, activities in which both child and parent can participate together will help parents feel as though they are spending meaningful time with their child.

Challenges with social skills will also impact parent stress as they watch with concern their child's interactions with other children. Parents are protective of their child in social situations and become saddened when their child is taunted, teased, or left out by others. Even if a slight by peers is not intentional, the feeling of anguish that children and teens can experience as a result of peer interactions gone wrong can really upset parents. For parents of children with ASD, the concern about social difficulties is ever present. One father shared, "I know it's ridiculous to have my happiness ride on the ups and downs of each and every play date and outing [my son] has. What I don't know is how to stop."

For a child with limited social skills, parents may worry that their child is missing potential learning opportunities with peers. They may feel excluded from child social events when their child is not invited, such as play dates or birthday parties. Additionally, some of the challenges that can at first be easily accommodated may become more difficult to manage over time. For example, very young children can often be more forgiving or accepting of children with differences in communication or social skills. However, as children age, the discrepancy in skills becomes more apparent, and children become less inclusive. One mother told me about her concerns with peer responses to her daughter's social skills:

> She's got social issues connecting with kids socially, so between
> the communication difficulty with the actual speaking and the

lack of connection with her peers because her interests are so very different and odd to others, she walks into every social situation pretty much at the bottom of the heap. As she's gotten older and become a 10-year-old kid, the social strata become more evident. I think that has in some ways become harder to deal with.

Children with social difficulties may even experience bullying by their peers. Unfortunately, we see countless examples of bullying in the media, and children with ASD are likely targets of the bullying. One study found that 63 percent of children with ASD between the ages of 6 and 15 had been bullied by other children at some point in their lives (Zablotsky, Bradshaw, Anders, & Law, 2014). As any parent, parents of a child with ASD may be saddened or stressed watching their child experience bullying and feel helpless regarding their ability to fix it. Especially because parents will have more difficulty changing the way their child responds to the bully, or altering the behavior that garners interest from the bully, the problem may seem difficult to overcome.

A significant concern for parents whose children have strengths in academic and communication areas but who struggle socially is that these children may be highly aware that they do not fit in socially but unable to figure out how to change their own behavior to effect change in their relationships with peers. When I interview parents during assessments, I frequently ask them whether their child has friends at school. Many parents respond by saying that their child desperately wants friends but is unable to make or keep friends. Some children in this situation can become distressed, and research has found relations between social anxiety, depression, and social deficits (White & Roberson-Nay, 2009) as these individuals experience difficulty making friends, and later, establishing romantic relationships. For parents, watching their child struggle and be left behind in this area can be heartbreaking.

Many practitioners will address parents' concerns with their child's social competency through intensive instruction in social skills for the child. Again, parent training in this area will help them feel that they have the skills to help their child be more successful in this arena. However, practitioners can also help parents identify settings in which individuals with ASD will be accepted without judgment, which can be immensely helpful in providing the entire family with a place where they feel included. Practitioners might help identify activities that offer structured opportunities for social interaction, such as gyms and organized sports that include individuals with disabilities. Karate, for example, offers some individuals on the autism spectrum the opportunity to interact with others in a highly structured manner, provides a common interest with which to interact others, and helps build confidence in learners as they move at their own pace through classes. Activities such as this, as well as creative outlets such as ASD-friendly art studios and theater groups, can provide welcoming outlets for individuals struggling in the social arena.

Navigating the challenges of problem behavior. Beyond communication and social concerns, parents are stressed by the level of problem behavior that their children exhibit. Many children with ASD exhibit restricted interests and repetitive behavior; these behaviors alone can be exhausting, because they limit parents' lives significantly. I worked with one family whose child insisted on sameness and routines. Upon walking into his house, he would scan his house to make sure everything was in place: pillows and stuffed animals arranged on the couch as he'd left them, all of the cabinets and doors closed, some lights on, some lights off. He often asked repetitive questions that required a very specific answer, and he would repeat the question again and again until his parents responded just so.

Other children develop routines that cannot be altered, such as only being able to enter their school building using one specific door, or only being able to drive to the store by taking a specific route.

> [My daughter] was a climber. [She] could scale up a room from one side to the other without touching the floor. So we would sit in the bleachers and [she] would climb up to the top, and jump down to the bottom from the back and then come around and climb it again and jump down. And people would look and couldn't believe I wasn't doing anything about it.

Parents will go to great lengths to preserve these routines. The reason is simple: changes in routine often result in problem behavior. The same child who insisted that his house be arranged in a specific manner or that his parents respond to his questions with a specific statement engaged in uncontrollable, aggressive, and self-injurious tantrums when they were unable to respond as he wanted. An adolescent I worked with engaged in severe tantrums and aggressions when, on the way to school, the number of flags he passed was less than the number he expected (e.g., if a school had not put up a flag because it was raining). I remember waiting out a student's tantrum with his mother and teacher because he'd been told to walk through the left-hand door in a set of two doors at his school, when he always walks through the right-hand door. While some of these trouble spots become highly predictable for parents and they can learn to avoid them, others can erupt without warning, and the parent may have to deal with extreme problem behavior in unsafe or public situations.

In research, the level of a child's problem behavior is often found to be a very significant predictor of a parent's stress level (Abbeduto et al., 2004; Baker et al., 2003; Benson, 2010; Olsson & Hwang, 2001). Problem behavior can result from any number of reasons. As described above, maybe a routine was disrupted. But maybe a child was asked to do something she did not want to do. Maybe the parent was paying attention to someone else. Maybe the child was not allowed to play with a toy he wanted. Or maybe something in the environment, such as a loud noise or change in schedule, disturbed the child. Each child's problem behavior results from a different source, but the result is the same for parents: they spend significant time and energy ensuring that the problem behavior does not occur or avoiding situations where it will disturb or harm others. "I live with a kid who has all these issues, whom I have to watch 24/7," one mother shared. "I've got locks on every window, I've caught him on the roof, he's run away, he's broken into other people's apartments." Severe problem behavior often warrants intervention from therapists who can help treat the problem behavior. One parent shared:

She had some pretty severe self-injurious behaviors. . . . I do think now it was lack of being able to communicate what she was feeling, thinking. She would bang on her own arms and legs pretty severely to the point where she'd be bruised. . . . We eventually came upon a plan where she actually had shin guards, soccer shin guards, but we put them on her arms because that's mostly where she hit herself. It allowed her to do it without hurting herself so that we could give her the space that she needed.

The occurrence of problem behavior can be especially punishing when a parent compares the child with other children the child's age. A mother recounted how she felt when her young child with ASD engaged in frequent elopement, where he would run away from her in public spaces:

A 4-year-old shouldn't be running away from me every time we go to the grocery store. So there was this frustration that I was dealing with behaviors that I shouldn't have to be dealing with, or didn't want to have to be dealing with that other parents with 4-year-olds weren't dealing with.

A parent who frequently faces behavior like this may learn to avoid situations in which the behavior occurs, which may mean spending a lot more time at home where the behavior can be more easily controlled.

For some parents, however, their child's problem behavior robs them of time for relaxation even in their own home, because they need to be constantly supervising their child and be on guard for ever-present dangers that threaten their child, themselves, or other children in the home. A mother remembered how difficult it was keeping her child safe at home:

Trying to figure out the environment at home, it was very, very challenging because he got into everything. He took everything apart. He could never be left alone in a room because he would do something that would potentially hurt himself. . . . He was into everything. If there were books on the shelf, all the books got knocked over. If there was a piece of electronics he could pull apart, he would pull it apart. He just was getting into absolutely everything, so he needed one-on-one attention all the time. He also has never slept well. He was up about every hour and a half, so I was up every hour and a half with him because there was no way I could let him be up without me.

This parent's description of her vigilance with her child paints an exhausting picture: around-the-clock care for a child who may inadvertently harm himself or someone else without supervision. Parents whose children do not sleep well and cannot be left unsupervised lose hours of sleep, and exhaustion can set in quickly. Being on guard and supervising a child constantly will wear a parent down and result in high levels of stress because of the low levels of self-care that can be implemented.

Further, beyond limiting the safety of home life, behaviors such as hitting, kicking, biting, throwing items, screaming, and dropping to the floor in a tantrum can make going out in public a near impossibility. One mother shared,

We always joke that we never go anywhere together. One of us is always home. . . . We go out to dinner together a lot and believe me, [my son] has torn up some restaurants. . . . My husband and I are active in the community, charities and stuff, but he does one and I do the other. We kind of have to take turns. So it's an odd life because we really have to stick close to home. There isn't a lot of freedom, frankly.

Another parent quipped, "We used to have this theory that when you have a child with autism, it kind of makes you have autism, because you can't go to the things that you used to go to if you bring your child." Another parent articulated the toll this can take on a child who truly wants to be able to leave the house:

He's got a lot of behaviors which really clearly limit his ability to get out in the community. . . . It's frustrating for him, and difficult for us. With [him] having a twin there's just an awareness that there's somebody that is free and independent and can open the door and leave and go wherever they want. So it's really complex on a lot of levels.

Challenging behavior can be limiting for parents and for siblings (more about that in Chapter 4), as well as for the child with ASD. In some cases it can lead to physical harm for the child or family and can reduce the family's ability to integrate themselves in the community. Practitioners working with individuals with problem behavior might begin to understand how stressful the challenging behavior can be in their own work with the child. I have worked with staff who are overwhelmed by managing a child's problem behavior in their classrooms or clinic rooms. Think, then, about what the parents of those children must experience on a daily basis when trying to manage problem behavior on their own in a less controlled environment.

Practitioners who stop even for a moment to consider these parental experiences will already be on their way to working more effectively with the family. They will begin to understand the extensive impact that the behavior can have on the family, which will in turn build motivation to provide the family with the services needed to help reduce problem behavior through assessment of the behavior, behavioral intervention, and parent training. Professionals unable to provide these services should refer the family to behavior analysts or other professionals who can competently do so. Often when behavioral interventions are designed, they are done so with the school setting in mind; therapists should consider how the same behavioral intervention will be adapted to the home to help reduce the occurrence of problem behavior in all settings (consider contextualizing the treatment using guidelines provided in Chapter 6).

Additionally, practitioners should be willing to provide an empathic listening ear to parents when they wish to talk about their experiences related to their child's problem behavior. I think professionals often become anxious when parents tell them about a recent occurrence of problem behavior, perhaps because they feel that parents are asking them to fix the behavior. While this may be partly true—no doubt parents want help alleviating the stress of managing problem behaviors—in some cases parents may simply want to share their experiences with someone who will listen and understand what they are experiencing. Allowing parents to share their experiences and validating how difficult the experience is for them will help provide them with support during a stressful time. Providing referrals to sources of social support (see Chapters 3 and 7) that may be able to provide similar sounding boards for parents could also be beneficial.

Acknowledging comorbid conditions. Practitioners must also recognize that individuals with ASD are frequently diagnosed with other associated conditions that can compound the stress experienced by the parents. These comorbid conditions will require additional treatments, professionals, and care that will further tax parent resources, emotionally, physically, and financially. Comorbid conditions may include hyperactivity, executive functioning problems, comorbid intellectual disability, gastrointestinal problems, feeding issues, seizure disorders, sleep disorders, and so forth. In fact, in some of the interviews I completed with parents, the diagnosis of ASD seemed secondary to other conditions they reported. One father remembered receiving his daughter's diagnosis of ASD after a diagnosis of epilepsy:

> It was hurtful, but I went through all the hurt and pain with the epilepsy, the 50 seizures a day. I was sitting in the hospital with her . . . and she would just wake up screaming and have a seizure. That's the most pain.

Diagnosing additional comorbid conditions can be highly difficult for parents and practitioners alike, especially because parents cannot rely on their child's report of bodily pain or discomfort. Challenging behavior that is exhibited by individuals with ASD may actually be symptoms of an underlying condition. One parent stated, "People don't realize that kids with autism also can have a lot of other conditions that typical kids get, and can even make their autism a little more complicated. I think that was one of the most frustrating things." Once these additional conditions are diagnosed, identifying appropriate treatment can be difficult. A mother whose daughter is diagnosed with ASD and other associated medical conditions discussed how difficult it can be to find services that can provide adequate care for all of her daughter's needs: "The hard part is the places that deal with autism can't deal with the medical issues, and the places that deal with medically fragile people can't deal with the autism."

Practitioners should also recognize that associated conditions such as those described above will heap additional responsibilities and care onto parents who may already be struggling to care for a child with significant needs. Acknowledging the very real concerns that parents have about their child's physical or mental health in addition to the ASD diagnosis is important, because it will help parents feel that practitioners are listening to them. Additionally, seeking out ways to communicate with the care providers who address the comorbid conditions for the child (with the parents' consent) will help coordinate care for the individual and minimize the burden of parents' role as liaison between professionals.

Understanding the impact of a lifelong diagnosis. An additional significant dimension of ASD is that the diagnosis is most typically lifelong. As one mother put it,

> At least with my daughter, there's always something new that springs up, and I've seen it with enough other friends that have kids on the spectrum to know that you're always confronting new challenges the same way you would with a neurotypical kid, except it seems to be on a more elevated level.

Most parents who have neurotypical children imagine that their children will live with them and rely on them heavily for the first 18 years and then likely leave home to pursue work, advanced schooling, or travel. Although different stresses occur during this process, the intensive childcare that is required of parents decreases steadily over time as the child becomes more and more independent. For these parents, the requirements of parenthood shift over time, and some parents may be able to enter their later years with children who are fully independent, allowing the parents to pursue interests, work, and travel of their own.

Parents of a child with ASD, however, may find that the intensity of care required for their child during childhood does not remit, and they must provide the same level of support and guidance in adulthood. For example, parents of children with developmental disabilities in general are significantly more likely to have their child live with them into adulthood. Seltzer, Greenberg, Floyd, Pettee, and Hong (2001) report that, among parents in their 50s, 57 percent with children with developmental disabilities still lived with their affected child, compared with 41 percent of parents of children with other severe mental health disorders and only 16 percent of parents with typical children. Parents of individuals with ASD may continue to bathe, dress, and feed their children if the children are unable to develop these skills on their own. They will brush their teeth, drive them the places they need to go, and ensure their safety on a daily basis while they age. As parents of young children know, this level of care is exhausting and leaves little time for parents to care for themselves.

Parents of children with ASD who are able to develop greater independence will still likely have parenting requirements that differ from those of their parenting peers, because difficulties with social skills and communication may still limit their child's abilities. One mother told me about how her son was able to get his own job in New York City as an adult. But, to ensure success, she had to ride the train with him to work and teach him how to walk to his building. She had to meet him on his lunch break to show him where to get his lunch. All of these skills that an individual without ASD may have learned on his own she had to explicitly teach her son to make sure he was as successful as possible in his new environment. Again, the constant care and support required for individuals with ASD, even the most independent, are beyond tiring.

Related, and perhaps more difficult, is the uncertainty of the future. Many parents do not know what to expect of their child as he or she ages. The mother of a young girl with ASD remarked, "[What] I always struggle with is the dreams that you have for your children. . . . She is so young, and also I have no idea what to expect. It's my dreams for her that I might have to let go of." Although parents might assume they will need to provide a greater level of support to their child than other parents will as their child ages, they do not know for sure. This uncertainty makes planning for the future difficult. As one mother said of her daughter, "If you asked me 5 years ago whether she'd be able to do what she can do today, I would have said no way. So how can I say what she's going to be when she's 25? How can I say that?"

While practitioners can do little to lessen the uncertainty and long-term nature of the child's diagnosis, they should recognize that the toll of raising a child with ASD does not necessarily decrease over time. As the next section explains, parents' experiences of stress and other related emotions might rise and fall throughout their child's development and even into adulthood. Practitioners should let go any expectations they may have that parents should have fully adjusted to their child's ASD and its impact on daily life, no matter how far removed in time the family is from the initial diagnosis.

## APPRECIATING THE ROLE OF TRANSITIONS IN PARENTS' EXPERIENCES OF STRESS

Stress and emotions that parents experience do not have a clear pattern during their child's development. From the above descriptions, we can see why stress may remain at an elevated level for many parents as their child develops. This level of stress, however, is unlikely to stay the same from day to day, and the emotions that parents experience about their child's diagnosis will ebb and flow. Chapter 1 describes a number of emotions that parents experience at the time of their child's diagnosis—grief, anger, guilt, relief—but a professional should not expect that these emotions will diminish over time. Rather, these emotions will continually shift, emerging and reemerging as their child ages. Professionals should not be surprised to find a parent who has seemed even-keeled in dealing with his or her child's diagnosis to shift suddenly to a period of grief about the diagnosis. As one parent described her experiences, "I think for us, over time, it's almost like a roller coaster ride." This section describes different events in a child's life that might contribute to these shifts in emotion and stress, so that professionals can be aware of the impact that they may have on the family and the working relationship.

In any child's life, a number of expected transitions occur, generally based on developmental age. Typically, the child enters preschool and, once he or she has reached the age of 5, transitions into a school system, starting with kindergarten. The transition to adolescence can be a rocky one for most families, coupled with the child's transition to high school. Finally, the child graduates high school and moves on to college or the job force. These expected transitions can result in significant stress for parents of children from a logistical perspective, in the sense that significant planning must go into preparing the student for new school settings, teachers, and expectations. Stress can also emerge from an emotional perspective, as the child becomes more independent and requires less support from the parent, perhaps more quickly than the parent is prepared for.

These age-based transition periods experienced by neurotypical children are often mirrored by children with ASD, but for parents they will likely be more logistically and emotionally loaded than what is expected for parents of neurotypical children. Many of these age-based transitions can include a significant change in educational or vocational placement for the child with ASD, and changes in setting offer a host of options to parents in terms of what is going to be best for their child. During these times, parents may be faced with considerable decisions about their child's care that may significantly impact their child's future. All children can be limited by substandard education, but few are as vulnerable as children with ASD. The quality and intensity of educational instruction that a child with ASD receives can greatly impact progress, and parents' advocacy for the best placement for their child becomes a full-time job for many. Recognizing the impact of these significant transitions and providing additional understanding and support during these times will be critical.

Navigating early transitions. The earliest of these placement decisions occurs after diagnosis when parents are first seeking initial treatment for their child. Again, identifying services that are appropriate can be challenging, and identifying whether the program is meeting the child's needs is difficult for a parent who has just learned of the child's ASD diagnosis. A mother or father may barely have an understanding of what ASD is, let alone the needs of a child with ASD and what will be a suitable program. As discussed in Chapter 1, this is an incredibly overwhelming time for parents struggling to understand the special education system within their state, and providing extra support by guiding parents to resources that delineate their child's rights within special education will be immensely helpful.

Unfortunately, initial placement is only the beginning of a long road for parents. If a child has received early intervention following diagnosis, it may be only a year or two before the child is eligible for school services, and decisions need to be made about whether in-district or out-of-district placement will be more suitable for the child. Parents who are convinced that the school district cannot meet the needs of their child face the harrowing prospect of having to convince the school district—and in some cases the courts—that their child would be better served elsewhere. When asked about the challenges she has faced in raising her daughter with ASD, one mother clearly replied

> dealing with the school district and fighting for what she should have, dealing with the constant struggle between school districts wanting to spend as little as possible and us wanting to invest as much as possible in our kid. That's always been a challenge.

This challenge often occurs regardless of whether a family is fighting for an out-of-district placement. A child for whom in-district placement is appropriate can still be caught between different settings within the school. As mandated by the Individuals with Disabilities Education Act, students with ASD must be provided with education in the least restrictive environment. For some students that placement may be a fully mainstreamed position in a public school classroom, where they are integrated with neurotypical peers. Students who struggle to keep up with these peers socially and academically may be best supported by a paraprofessional who can provide extra help and prompting throughout the school day. Students who are not learning at grade level may be taught within a self-contained ASD classroom or classrooms for children with developmental disabilities, and even here there are gradations of education: some students in these classrooms will learn well through group instruction, but others may require one-to-one instruction to make meaningful progress. For all students, the amount of structured social interaction they have with peers will be highly important, because that time will be when they will best learn social skills.

This variety of educational support options within a school presents a good number of decisions to be made by parents and a lot of advocating that must be done for the best placement for the child. I cannot tell you how many evaluations I have done for families who are currently unhappy with their child's educational placement: one child does not have enough time with peers, another child does not have enough one-to-one instruction, another parent feels that her child should be mainstreamed, and yet another feels that his child is falling behind in a classroom and needs an aide or a switch to a more supportive classroom.

Parents must constantly evaluate their child's progress and determine whether the child could potentially make more gains in another setting, which requires a good deal of advocacy on their child's behalf. When parents disagree with a school district, the family, often at great expense, may hire advocates and lawyers. The fear that their child is not getting the education the child needs, the constant pursuit of something better, and the financial cost of this pursuit present a tremendous burden to families. Unfortunately, decisions may need to be revisited repeatedly as the child ages and either does not make progress or makes considerable progress and the suitability of the current program needs to be reevaluated.

Practitioners should keep in mind, when working with parents who are advocating for the best services possible for their child, that the parents will typically focus only on the needs of their child. Sometimes, I find that practitioners compare the needs of one child with those of another and minimize the service requests of a family whose child has a number of skills simply because children with far fewer skills have the same services or less. Practitioners must understand that parents will always push for what they feel is best for their child and may not use other individuals on the autism spectrum as a frame of reference—nor should they. These parents should not be viewed as insensitive or selfish but, rather, as intensively focused on the needs of their child. Sometimes interactions with parents can be negative as they push for services the district or program cannot or does not wish to provide. During these interactions, practitioners who view these parents as highly motivated by care and love for their child, rather than oblivious to the needs of other children and staff, may find themselves engaged in more understanding and constructive conversations with the family.

There is another possible transition that many parents of young children dread: the child's transition to residential placement. As one father described, "The hardest decision in my view a parent can make is to send your loved one away. . . . I can't tell you how much pain it was." Parents are often more prepared to send their child to a residential placement in adulthood, as it parallels the process of having a neurotypical child leave for college or work. In contrast, sending a young child to live in a residential placement feels unnatural for many parents. However, when parents are faced with considerable behavioral challenges that cannot be safely controlled in the home, they may make the difficult decision to send their child to a placement that can provide around-the-clock care.

One of my first jobs in the field of ASD treatment was working in a residential home for children 5 to 8 years of age. Even then, still a college student, I could not help but imagine the pain the parents must experience sending their child away from their home. Some of the parents lived states away, and though they visited their young children as often as they could, they trusted us to care for their children and manage their high levels of problem behavior safely. Even parents who lived locally sometimes struggled to get any sign of recognition from their child when they visited. While many parents may experience relief in no longer providing daily care for their child or managing problem behavior, the guilt of not being able to care for their child and the worry and concern about others' caretaking abilities and the well-being of their child may be ever present.

The father above sent his daughter to live in a residential placement when she was 8 years old. He described how challenging and unsafe her behavior could be:

> In the car she was biting, she was out of control. She was so out of control, the best way to describe her was that she was possessed. When she would get in that demon position, you couldn't do anything with her. She was dangerous. It got to the point where if you were in the car with her—and this happened numerous years and still to this day—when she gets out of control she attacks the driver. Instead of just harming herself, along with the driver, you could get into a car accident and do damage to innocent people.

This uncontrollable behavior, at home and in the community, led him to make the decision to find a residential placement for her. "I was going there every weekend and taking her home for weekends," he told me.

> When we would get her, she was so happy to see us, and then when we left her she wouldn't get out of the car. We had to fight with her. . . It's such a demoralizing feeling, saying goodbye to your daughter.

Perhaps more than any other professional working with young children with ASD, practitioners who work with parents struggling to make this difficult decision for their child or who care for young children in residential placement should be cognizant of the unbelievable level of stress and complex emotions that the parents will experience. Checking in frequently with the parents about their emotions and experiences during the transition will be helpful, as will connecting parents with others who have made similar decisions so that they can provide support for one another. Practitioners must take care to devise ways to maintain connections between parents and child, such as sending parents frequent updates and pictures of their child in residential care, as well as making use of technology to allow visual contact when visits are not possible. However, practitioners should take their cues from parents, who may find these forms of communication to be subpar proxies for in-person connection. Offering parents a variety of options for how to connect with their child will sidestep any inadvertent negative outcomes of these well-intended services.

Addressing the transition to adulthood. An area that has received considerable attention is the transition from secondary school programs to adult programs, whether they are vocational, academic, or residential. Considering possible paths for each child with ASD begins early, often as early as 14 years of age, and parents must begin to work with professionals to help guide their child to the most successful program in adulthood. A mother of a young teenager stated,

> The transition piece is now the piece that's in my brain. I worry about it a lot. There's no place to go. There's such a shortage. He is in that huge hump when [ASD] exploded, so when he transitions, massive amounts of individuals are going to be looking for jobs, supported placements, adult programs, and residential placements at that same time. We're going to have to be then what we did [when he was younger]: we made his own home program. I hired people, trained people. We set it up; I did it myself. I sort of feel that's the boat we're going to be in.

For adults who are unable to work independently, the support is much less available than for children and adolescents; in many states both state funding and programs are scarce. One mother bemoaned the lack of available programs for her adult son: "The piece that almost makes me lose it is the idea that in a state with this much money, there isn't a place for him. I'm 60 years old so that's a worry." As parents age, providing their children with a setting to maximize their independence and potential to contribute to the community by working in a vocational or similar setting is a primary goal, but identifying programs that meet the varied needs of their children can be challenging. As children with ASD age, parents find that few options exist and often are left to support their child at home. While tenable in the short term, the high level of care required for adults with ASD may be more than an aging parent can physically handle. In these cases, evaluating the options for residential care for individuals who need it can be especially difficult, because parents need to identify a program that they trust to ensure their child's safety and care. Emotionally, handing care off to other individuals after providing care so intensely for literally decades can be difficult. "I can't imagine her not living with me," a parent of an adult with ASD shared. "There would be this huge hole. But my hope is that if and when the time comes, when I have found a place where I believe she'll truly be happy, that I'll be able to let her go."

At this point, practitioners should all be knowledgeable about the transition services that are available within their school district or state, or at least be able to direct parents to the state department that manages adult disability services. Further, any program for children with ASD should have a fully outlined plan for how an individual will transition out of the program upon reaching adulthood and the efforts that will be put forth to identify an appropriate placement for the individual following graduation. Considerable emphasis should be placed on identifying adult placements that are well suited for the individual's skills. Job sampling, in which the individual tries a number of different positions or jobs prior to graduation to help identify best placement, will be beneficial before the time of transition arrives.

For parents whose children are able to continue on to a vocational setting or college, increased fears about the child's ability to function independently after years of close supervision by teachers and job coaches loom. While all parents are faced with emotional turmoil when their children leave home for college or work, imagine the concerns of parents of children with ASD. They have to be concerned not only about their children's academic or vocational success but also about how the children will manage socially and take care of themselves. College, for example, requires a level of independence not asked of teenagers when they are living at home; they must meet all requirements and obligations of their own accord, summoning their own motivation to attend class and coordinating their schedule so that they do not miss important class meetings, assignments, and events. Socially, roommate situations can be a challenge, and the abilities to turn to other members of the student body for help and direction ("How do you get to Smith Hall?" "What is the assignment for tomorrow?") and to collaborate in class and other activities are necessary for any college student. Expectations that their child will be able to handle all of these new responsibilities can be hard for parents.

A parent shared her experience in sending her son to college. Academically gifted, he excelled in high school and was accepted to several colleges. He and his family chose a university with a "small college feel" a few states away. But, as his mother shared,

> I dropped him off at the campus, and it was just wrong, wrong, wrong from the beginning. He went with a . . . focus program where he hung out with some kids the first week before school, and it was all socially oriented. It was the worst way he could've started because he just didn't fit in. By the time we got him into the dorm, he had a roommate, and he was just a deer in headlights, and I knew it was bad. I took a look at all the other guys in the dorm, and I said, "My kid is not like this." . . . So we went through this horrible process of him doing well the first semester and every semester he would get further and further behind and . . . needless to say, he went on leave.

Fortunately, we are seeing more and more colleges and universities develop programs that provide wonderful support for individuals on the autism spectrum as they make the transition to college. At my own university, the college support program for individuals with ASD provides orientation activities such as learning to navigate the campus and ride the bus system and building important skills such as communicating well with instructors and working with other students, as well as an adapted roommate system, social skills groups, and a peer buddy system in which students on the spectrum are paired with other college students who fill a supportive role for them. A program like this is a lifeline for parents who are sending their children with ASD off on their own for the first time; feeling as though they are individually cared for and looked after, even in a large university setting, can go a long way in alleviating parent fears. The family described above found a similar program for their son in another university:

> He was able to walk to [the university] and start taking classes part time, and there came a time when [the university], bless their soul, started a transition group, a social group, and a counseling group for their students on the spectrum. . . . And I really think that saved his life. I really do.

Again, professionals can help parents by working with families to identify programs such as this that will support individuals with ASD. Additional resources for college transitions are listed in the Resources section.

Minimizing the impact of a change. An added complication of all transitions is that new placements, even within the same program, lead to changes in teachers, supervisors, or caregivers who work with the child. At first glance, this may seem to be inconsequential for professionals—neurotypical children in public schools change classrooms and teachers each year. However, the educational and behavioral needs of individuals with ASD can make these transitions particularly difficult. Different schedules and classroom or program routines will affect the child as well as the parent. Increases in problem behavior, at home and at school, may be observed as the child adjusts to the new setting and new staff, which we know has an impact on parent stress.

Additionally, the parent may struggle to understand how a new teacher or new treatment team works and how to best establish a communicative relationship. Some parents whose children are mainstreamed may have to acclimate to a new teacher each year, and conveying the teaching methods and approaches that have worked best with their child may be difficult, and in some cases may not be accepted by the new teacher. I have heard many stories of children's problem behavior skyrocketing when transitioning to a new teacher, resulting in referrals to self-contained or out-of-district placements, only to find that the following year a transition to a new teacher and classroom results in reductions in the problem behavior. Patterns such as this indicate that the environment, including classroom structure and teacher expectations, have considerable effects on behavior.

For parents whose children are in self-contained classrooms or out-of-district placements, transitions may not occur every year but instead every 2 or 3 years as the student ages out of the classroom. This type of transition can be particularly difficult for parents because they have to leave a teacher or treatment team with whom they have an established, long-term relationship. Building up therapeutic relationships with new therapists in the new setting is hard work for parents, and leaving behind the relationships they have developed with teachers or caregivers they have learned to trust with their child's care is emotionally and logistically challenging. One mother shared how difficult these transitions can be for this reason:

> We have so many people that come and go out of our lives. . . . I don't think people understand how hard even a classroom transition is for all of us. . . . I have to develop new relationships with people all the time, and it takes a tremendous amount of energy, *tremendous* amount of energy. It makes me tired even thinking about it: "Oh my, there is so much that you don't know yet, there's so much that I have to tell you, there's so much you don't know about me and how I work," that I have to sort of establish that all over again. . . . And it's hard. I've heard people complain about how parents get less involved as their kids get older, but . . . I think that they get really tired. It's hard to keep investing.

In all transitions, parents may also feel that valuable information about their son or daughter has been lost in the transition; new teachers may not know about certain problems the student has faced in the past and what has been used to overcome that problem. Here, the recommendation to all professionals is to glean as much information as possible about the student from previous educational and treatment teams. Even if professionals intend to reevaluate a student and develop a new education and treatment plan, the team should be knowledgeable about what was done in the previous placement so that they can actively discuss these treatments with the parent and articulate reasons for moving away from the plan, especially if it was effective.

Validating emotional reactions to transition. Beyond managing the logistics of all of these transitions, many parents may experience increased stress or resurgences of grief or sorrow during these transitions because of the reminders that they present about their child's diagnosis. Being reminded of their child's diagnosis, the long-term nature of the diagnosis, and the goals they once had for their child that may not be reached can be especially emotional for parents. One mother remarked,

> When he was younger, every birthday was devastating. One thing you can tell people, oh my God, beware, birthdays are not happy days for a lot of us. . . . They're a reminder of everything, particularly when they're little, that they're not doing.

These feelings of disappointment and grief may resurge each time parents experience a new transition and remember the goals they once held for their child. When a child transitions to adolescence, the parents may imagine the goals they hoped the child would have accomplished by that point—especially those typically accomplished by other neurotypical children—and again grieve the loss of the child they once thought they had. Again, when the child reaches adulthood the parent may experience sorrow that their child is not as independent as other adults at that age. These reminders can occur during times of transition that give parents opportunities to look back at what their child has accomplished and to mourn what has not been accomplished.

For example, when children are young and approach the age when they may be mainstreamed in a public school inclusion classroom, where children with ASD work and play alongside their neurotypical peers, parents may experience increased anxiety or stress about whether their child will be eligible for this setting. Some parents may desire inclusion for their child, and when they are told that their child does not possess the skills to be successful in this setting and would be best served in an ASD program, parents may be devastated. With all the progress in ASD treatment over the past few decades, we frequently hear stories about children who receive an ASD diagnosis but then make considerable progress during early treatment and, in the end, are virtually indiscriminable from their peers. Some of these individuals make so much progress that they are able to write about their experiences in books when they are older.

Because so many of these stories become mainstream via television and the Internet, some parents with a child diagnosed with ASD may hope their child can achieve the same goals: that their child will be the one who will look like his peers when he is older, that their child will be the one who writes the book about how she successfully overcame the challenges she faced in childhood. When parents with these hopes are told that their child will not be successful in mainstream settings, they may feel in many ways as though they are being handed a second diagnosis. They are being told that their child still has ASD and will have ASD for the rest of his or her life. One mother recounted this feeling:

> I remember initially feeling, "Okay, he's pretty high functioning." At that time, people say, "Well, he's high functioning . . . you know the stories, he may fall off the spectrum," and so on, and [I felt] a lot of hope with that, and a lot of disappointment that that did not happen.

Times of expected transition also offer moments when parents may compare their child with other children the same age. My own daughter attended a preschool where children with ASD were included in her classroom for various activities and provided with opportunities to practice social skills with peers. When my daughter turned 5, she joined her classmates in "graduation," where all the students graduating and moving onto kindergarten, or the next classroom in the center for children with ASD, donned caps and gowns and performed for the parents. While I was thrilled to watch my daughter bask in the success of finishing preschool and moving to a new, exciting school, I could not help but consider how different that experience must be for the parents of the children with ASD, comparing their children (who would remain in the center) with the 5-year-olds preparing to move on to kindergarten. I reminded myself that these parents may see the graduation as a major milestone in their child's life regardless and be proud of their child for completing preschool, but I could not help but wonder what the parents of the children with ASD were thinking and feeling that day.

Comparisons such as this often prompt powerful reminders of the challenges the family faces with the diagnosis and can be experienced at any time by parents. Parents who know children of a similar age as their child grows and watch those children learn to talk, pretend, and socialize with their peers may feel grief that their child is unable to do the same. One mother remarked,

> I see the other kids getting ahead of him and I see him playing with younger and younger kids. And then I see strides and I think, "Oh, today he is okay" and then, "Oh no, he's not okay," and it's just exhausting.

Such reminders can often come up unexpectedly, such as this mother's story:

> One day a couple of years ago, my son and I were walking, and all the boys his age were out on my neighbor's front yard playing football and being the gangly tangle of boys that they were, shouting, yelling, laughing, throwing football, and no parents there. They were just out, without any supervision, having such a good time, and it just hit me so hard, because my son would be there, he would be in that. If my son didn't have autism, he would be on that front yard I would be at home; he would be happy and playing, and those would be his friends. He'd be doing that. Walking by with my son, we were so outside of it. It's hard, the visual, like something

gets pulled away that we would never, ever, ever get to be a part of, like this train that left.

Parents who have other children in the family or close relatives the child's age may be faced with regular reminders of what their child could have accomplished by a certain age if not for ASD. A mother remarked, "[My daughter] has a sister who is thirteen months younger, so it makes it that much harder because I keep looking at her younger sister and saying, 'What if?'" While these siblings can be wonderful role models and playmates for their brothers and sisters with ASD, the constant comparison can be trying for parents.

In addition to practical recommendations for how professionals can help guide parents through transitions, practitioners should also be mindful of increases in parent stress and intense emotions that parents can experience during these times. Normalizing these experiences for parents by talking with them about what the practitioner has seen in other families who have gone through similar transitions may be helpful, as may be putting parents in touch with other families who have undergone or are undergoing the same transition. Most important, however, professionals should be aware of the possibility of surges in stress during these periods and be sensitive, supportive, and empathic (using approaches provided in Chapter 8) when working with parents during these times.

## ACKNOWLEDGING THE COURAGEOUS PARADOX

One area with which I see parents struggle again and again is in working not only to recognize their child's limitations but also to continually push their child to achieve more than expected. Many parents of children with ASD experience what is termed the "courageous paradox" (Hartshorne, 2002, p. 268), in which they tell themselves that, if their children never make progress, they will accept them as they are, but at the same time they never give up hope that their children will improve beyond all expectations. This position that parents must take can be difficult when they encounter professionals who might not have the same hope. One mother remembered,

> You have these hopes, but then you have the professionals who shoot down your hopes. I find it extremely disturbing when I go back and think about it now. "If the child is not speaking by now the child will not speak," a top neurologist told me that, and it's not true. Because [my daughter] does speak, and her speech didn't come until much later.

Continually hoping for progress and the best outcome can be a challenge for parents when faced with professionals who are focused on the child's current skills, who want to meet the child at his or her current level, and feel that pushing a child faster than he or she is ready will result in problems with skill acquisition or problem behavior.

For example, strife between parents and professionals often emerges when parents have particular goals in mind for their child that exceed those expected by the professional. Parents who push for reading goals for their nonverbal child when few prerequisites for reading are in place may be met with resistance by professionals who are concerned that the functionality of reading appears limited when other important independent skills have not yet been acquired. I have heard parents say to teaching teams, "You never listen to my ideas anyway, so I am not going to tell you what I want." These situations arise when parents' goals do not match those of the instructional team, and care needs to be taken in these situations to repair the parent-professional relationship. Parents who do not feel as though professionals are listening to them will be highly stressed and appear uncooperative, largely because they do not agree with or support the goals being taught, or feel as though the teaching team is not moving quickly enough nor maximizing their child's education. A teaching team putting their all into teaching skills will feel unappreciated in their work. A rift can quickly develop in relationships such as these that can be difficult to repair.

In these situations, professionals must work to validate the parents' concerns and the goals they have in mind for their child. While professionals may feel that some parents may seem to be in denial about their child's disability, they must also consider that the goals parents have for their child may come from a place of hope. They must respect that parents' wishes stem from love and concern for their child and from the view that if they do not advocate for their child, nobody will. Practitioners must also understand that letting go of goals for a child can be incredibly stressful and sad for parents, and conversations about this must be approached sensitively.

If professionals are concerned that the parents' goals are beyond the child's reach at this point in time, they should sit down with the parents and find common ground. For instance, both professional and parent can agree that they would love to see the student read in the future. The professional should then work closely with the parent to lay out the necessary prerequisites for the skill and, with the parent, identify what skills the student has still to learn. Together, they can then identify the next skill that can be taught to bring the student closer to the desired, common goal. Additional steps for building and maintaining strong communicative relationships with parents are discussed in Chapter 8.

## CLINICAL TAKE-AWAYS

Parents of children with ASD are highly stressed compared with other parents, and this stress is related to their child's symptoms, the unpredictability of the disorder, and the specific transitions and experiences related to raising a child on the autism spectrum. However, professionals must also recognize that many parents develop significant strengths in managing their stress and that specific coping strategies and other protective factors can help reduce the stress they experience. Practitioners are highly encouraged to read more about parent strengths and the positive aspects of parenting a child with ASD in Chapter 7. The following list summarizes recommendations for practitioners working to understand and navigate patterns of parent stress.

Practitioners should:

- Recognize that the stress experienced by parents of individuals with ASD is higher than that experienced by virtually any other parenting group. Sharing this research with parents may help normalize their experiences.

- Understand that high levels of parent stress can have a negative impact on parent mental health, as well as the parents' ability to engage meaningfully in treatment for their child:

  - Problem solve ways to help parents participate in treatment when other factors, such as stress and mental health concerns, may interfere.

  - Provide referrals to individual therapy for parents with significant mental health concerns.

- Counteract the impact of deficits in communication and social skills and the challenges of problem behaviors on parent stress by teaching parents skills to address these areas, using recommendations in Chapter 9.

- Empathize with parents' challenges related to deficits in communication, social skills, and adaptive behavior. Listen empathically to parents' reports of their child's behavior to provide them with support and understanding.

- Identify activities that parents and children can enjoy together to increase meaningful interactions.

- Collaborate with families to identify structured social activities that may reduce the family's isolation and provide the child with opportunities to build social skills.

- Provide referrals to professionals who can effectively assess and treat challenging behavior, and provide recommendations for how to address problem behaviors specifically in home and community settings, not just in school.

- Acknowledge the presence of comorbid conditions and connect with other health providers to reduce the burden on parents to act as a liaison between professionals.

- Prepare for increases in parent stress while they are planning for a significant transition, such as early intervention or transitioning to adult services. Practitioners working with young children transitioning to residential care should work closely with the family to identify ways to maintain connection between parents and the child.

- Collaborate with families to establish a transition plan to adulthood early by providing opportunities such as job sampling for individuals with ASD or researching college programs that will be highly supportive of individuals on the autism spectrum.

- Connect with previous treatment teams and teachers during transitions to share information about effective strategies for teaching and managing challenging behavior; this will minimize the loss of valuable information about the student during the transition.

- Recognize that parents will continually advocate for their child and may push for goals that seem out of reach to the professional. Viewing these goals as originating from a place of hope rather than denial can help professionals work more effectively with parents to arrive at objectives that make progress toward a shared goal.

# CHAPTER 3

# Appreciating the Effects of ASD on Parents and Their Relationships

Chapters 1 and 2 discuss the impact of specific symptoms of ASD on the parents' stress and mental health and how transitions and other events in the child's life will impact parents. Many parents also experience concomitant effects of the ASD diagnosis that take a considerable toll, including the impact of the diagnosis on parents' own dreams and goals, their relationship with their partner, and their social life. Some of these effects may not readily come to professionals' minds because they are focused on the child's behavior and skills. However, recognizing the impact of the diagnosis on these important dimensions of parental life will help practitioners better understand and be sensitive to parents' experiences. Additionally, although marital and career counseling will be outside the purview of many practitioners' responsibilities, awareness of these dimensions of family and personal life may help practitioners provide more sound referrals and recommendations as concerns arise.

To begin, it is helpful to think about your own life before you had children or the experience of someone close to you who has become a parent. The transition to the role of parent is regularly chronicled and discussed in parenting columns in newspapers, Internet blogs, and online parent groups. Although the birth of a child is an amazing, wonderful transition, in many ways it is just really, really hard. Much of this has to do with the parents' loss of their own individual life and identity from before they had children. Parents who once had time to go out to their favorite restaurants regularly, sleep in late on weekends if they wanted, toil at their jobs until the evening hours to stay on top of projects, and share quality time with their significant other are thrust into a world in which they often do not have the time or the ability to do those things.

Caring for their child suddenly becomes the most important part of their life, at the expense of many of the things they loved about their life before they had a child. These parents love their children unconditionally, and take joy in many of the moments spent with their child, but raising a child is hard, draining work. Even regular day-to-day tasks, such as helping a child with homework, managing a toddler's tantrums, keeping to a strict naptime and bedtime schedule, and all the work that goes into keeping a child healthy, when piled upon the demands of the household, the workplace, and the parental relationship, can begin to feel overwhelming. It is not a bad parent who looks back on his or her old life and longs for those times, or becomes sad that life has changed so dramatically.

Now, if you can, imagine that one or more children in the family have ASD. Those regular day-to-day tasks mentioned above are common but often occur to an extreme. Some children with ASD need help not just with homework but with each part of their daily routine, from brushing their teeth and putting on their shoes to communicating with others. Tantrums may not end in early childhood but may persist into adolescence as the child grows and becomes more difficult to manage. Concern about a sleep schedule extends to concern about the entire daily schedule and ensuring that inflexible routines are not interfered with, to reduce problem behavior. The slew of doctor's appointments, therapy sessions, and careful administration of treatment far exceeds what is required of a typical parent. Juggling all of this, on top of the demands of the household, the workplace, other children, and the parental relationship, seems not just overwhelming but downright impossible.

Mothers and fathers will respond differently to their child's diagnosis and the demands it places on their own life. They often take different roles within the family as they work to manage the needs of their child. This chapter summarizes the ways in which parents will differ in their experience of raising a child with ASD and how those differences can impact the parental relationship. Further, I discuss how a parents' social support evolves over time after their child is diagnosed with ASD.

Throughout this chapter, I consider differences in how fathers and mothers react to their child's diagnosis of ASD, but I must be clear that there is no one way of responding for all mothers or for all fathers. Every mother and father is going to respond differently, and the way they respond may differ from what I describe here. The discussion below is drawn from the stories shared by parents for this book, as well as from research. I do not mean to overgeneralize or perpetuate stereotypes of men and women. Additionally, in this chapter I discuss at great length differences between mothers and fathers, but I want to point out that not all families comprise a male-female parental unit. Some families raising a child with ASD include two fathers or two mothers, or single mothers and fathers, or extended family. The research on such family structures is limited, and we need to be cautious applying to these families what we know about mothers' and fathers' differential responses to diagnosis over time.

## DIFFERENTIATING MOTHERS' AND FATHERS' RESPONSES TO DIAGNOSIS

Chapter 1 discusses the ways in which parents might respond to their child's diagnosis of ASD. However, those descriptions were generalized across parents and not specific to mothers and fathers. In truth, research indicates that mothers and fathers may respond differently before, at the time of, and after diagnosis. Practitioners should be aware of the differences between how parents respond because differences not only may affect family functioning but also will impact parental involvement in treatment as the child ages.

Normalizing conflict. I find that in some families mothers and fathers seem to have been on the same page at the time their child was diagnosed. When considering their child's behavior before diagnosis, the parents were in agreement on pursuing an assessment, responded to the diagnosis in a similar manner, and worked together to identify treatment. However, far more often I hear from parents that they differed in how they adjusted to their child's diagnosis. Time and again, mothers and fathers share that it was more difficult for the father to come to terms with the child's diagnosis and to be convinced of it. One mother shared,

> My husband . . . didn't want to believe that there was anything wrong with our son, so there was a lot of disagreement in the family. He was saying, "Oh, he's a perfectly normal boy. Why are you looking for trouble?"

Similarly, another parent shared, "We just didn't see eye to eye on this, and he really didn't accept it."

When parents have different views on the diagnosis of their child, friction can begin to emerge. This tension can make the period of diagnosis especially stressful for both parents, because they cannot rely on their usual source of support. However, as previously detailed, the period of diagnosis is one of the most stressful periods for parents, and it is not unusual for parental conflict to emerge during times of stress.

I will use a personal example from my own life to illustrate the relation between stressful life events and marital strain. My husband started a new full-time job after a long period as a stay-at-home parent. This transition coincided with my own miscarriage of a pregnancy. The stress from the change in our routine, with both of us now working full-time, and my own emotional and physical responses to the loss of my pregnancy resulted in a considerable shift in our relationship. Though we were usually on the same page, with minimal arguments, I suddenly felt as though we did nothing but bicker with each other. The tension in our relationship on a daily basis seemed to trickle down to our children, which resulted in increases in problem behavior from them and more areas of conflict for us. I began to worry about the health of our relationship. About two months after my miscarriage, we had a weekend getaway. During this time, away from work and away from our children, we fell back into our old healthy habits of lengthy conversations, humor, and increased physical affection. I was so relieved to see, in just those few days, that our relationship was still intact and healthy, and I learned that under considerable stress our relationship can be strained. As time passed and we settled back into our life, our conflict dissipated.

The short of it is this: periods of extreme stress may result in periods of conflict, but this conflict does not necessarily indicate that the relationship is not strong. Many parents emerge from the stress of the initial period of their child's diagnosis and are able to create a balance in their relationship that is healthy and cooperative. One mother shared how her relationship with her husband has evolved since their son was diagnosed:

> So, I think my husband was pissed at me a lot at first because he didn't want to hear what I had to say, so I think in the beginning we had a lot of friction. He was pissed at me, because I was kind of figuring it out a while before him, so I had come to terms with it. He was really devastated by it. But we have gotten to be a very good team, and I think that he is a lot of the time more proactive about things than I am.

When parents share with professionals the concerns they have about the health of their relationship during the period of diagnosis, practitioners can help normalize the conflict they are experiencing by discussing the significant stress both parents are likely experiencing and sharing how parents commonly experience conflict during this time. Additionally, practitioners should be able to talk knowledgeably about the ways in which partners may differ in coping with the diagnosis, as described below.

Appreciating differences in coping. In addition to difficulty coming to terms with the diagnosis, mothers and fathers may cope with the diagnosis very differently. While some parents may face the emotions head-on, others may engage in self-preservation by distancing themselves from the care of and planning for the child with ASD. A father remembers his early response to his son's diagnosis:

My wife took it better than I did. I ostensibly took it well, but I just didn't really deal with it. I remember there were times where I would put my headphones on and put really hard music on really loud, and it would physically drown the thoughts in my head. It took me a long time to realize that you look in the rearview mirror, and all of a sudden your behavior at a certain time makes sense, and I was not dealing with it.

This father distanced himself from his son's diagnosis and his related emotions by avoiding talking about the diagnosis with others. In contrast, mothers are more likely to seek out social support and want to talk about their emotions with others (Gray, 2003; Pelchat, LeFebvre, & Levert, 2007).

Parents may also differ in approaching their child's diagnosis by focusing on their own emotions or by approaching the diagnosis as a problem to be solved. These types of coping are discussed more in Chapter 7. Mothers are more likely to engage in emotion-focused coping, while fathers are more likely to engage in problem-focused coping (Pelchat et al., 2007; Thoits, 1995). These approaches to coping with the diagnosis differ considerably, which still leads to conflict. In a conversation with me, one father shared, "[Our daughter's diagnosis] hit my wife a lot harder than it hit me. I am not as emotional." In a separate interview, his wife expanded a bit on the topic:

I would just say that my husband was all the way on board, fully involved, and fully invested, and active and sort of aggressive—all of the things you would want to be when managing a situation. I don't want to say much more about that, but it didn't bring us closer together, and I'll leave it at that.

These views demonstrate two parents who are actively involved but in different ways: she worked to emotionally process what was happening with her daughter, while her husband became very active in researching the diagnosis. While both were actively involved, it seems that neither was able to support the other as each would like.

Another father shared his view on the proactive approach that some fathers may take in response to their child's diagnosis: "I sort of assess what is there, and do what I can, and I make a plan and go forward. That is a good way to approach things, but emotionally it leaves stuff behind." This quote seems to highlight the discord between the first couple: by researching and identifying programs and making plans for treatment, the husband found a way to avoid dealing with his emotions about his daughter's diagnosis. For his wife, who needed support in processing her own emotions, the difference in their approach was challenging.

The reason for fathers' need for emotional distance in response to diagnosis is not completely clear. First, we know that men in general are more inexpressive in their coping styles than women are (Thoits, 1995) and that men are generally more likely than women to suppress emotions when faced with a stressful event (Gray, 2003). Additional reasons for the distancing may be due, in part, to the symptoms of the diagnosis itself. Men often connect with their children, especially boys, through physical play. If their child is not able to enjoy play as other children would, as can often be the case with children with ASD, fathers may have difficulty identifying other ways to connect with their child and so may be more distanced from the child and family (Pelchat et al., 2007).

Additionally, as discussed in Chapter 2, most parents when they have children have dreams about how they will grow and develop. A diagnosis of ASD may indicate that a child may not be able to achieve those dreams, regardless of the child's level of functioning, and this may be a considerable blow for the father. My own pilot research (Fiske, 2009) indicates that fathers may be particularly affected by having to let go of the goals they had for their child. Especially considering that the child with ASD is commonly male, culturally fathers in particular may have visions of passing down family heritage and of their son carrying on their family legacy and following in his father's footsteps in career and in leisure activities, such as sports or other hobbies. Because of the cross-gendered experience, with boys mothers may have a better ability to see past this imagined future. Additionally, because mothers take on a greater share of the childcare responsibilities and are more commonly with the child on a daily basis (discussed later in this chapter), they may be better able to see the child's small steps and growth and focus on those moments. Fathers may not witness these moments, because of the division of labor that develops in the household, and they may be more focused on what they have lost with their child.

Differences in parents' focus on emotions as part of coping can result in strife between partners. Again, normalizing the difference in coping strategies between parents, as outlined above, may help them better understand how they differ from their partner and that their partner is coping in what might be considered a typical manner. However, this understanding will not necessarily help parents who are seeking emotional support from partners who are emotionally distanced. Practitioners can provide these parents with alternative sources of emotional support (e.g., other parents, therapists) that can be helpful during stressful times. Additionally, fathers and mothers may benefit from individual therapy that helps them strengthen skills in effective coping strategies. Specific recommendations for therapy approaches that might be beneficial for parents are included in Chapter 7.

## ACKNOWLEDGING CHANGES IN DIVISION OF LABOR

The stress experienced by parents during and after a child's diagnosis can result in mental health concerns, most commonly anxiety and depression, but parents do not experience mental health concerns at the same prevalence rate. Research indicates that mothers not only are more likely than fathers to experience greater stress when raising a child with ASD but also are more likely to experience other mental health concerns such as depression than are fathers (Dabrowska & Pisula, 2010; Moes et al., 1992; Olsson & Hwang, 2001).

One potential reason for the increased stress of mothers, relative to fathers, is the caretaking role they so often have in their family. In general, when a couple has children, the parents' division of labor begins to fall along traditional gendered lines, with mothers taking the larger share of household labor, indicating that the role as parent is more central to their identity than to fathers (Katz-Wise, Priess, & Hyde, 2010). This gendered division of labor is particularly evident when a child in the family is diagnosed with ASD because of the intensive care required by the child. Although this is not always the case—I have worked with a number of families with a stay-at-home father as the primary caregiver and the mother working full-time—in my career and in research, the parent who stays home with the child with ASD is most commonly the mother. Even if mothers work outside of the home, they are most commonly the parent who takes on primary childcare responsibilities and attends meetings and appointments for the child when both parents cannot be there (Gray, 2003; Lee, Harrington, Louie, & Newschaffer, 2008). The mother commonly takes on the role of care coordinator and advocate, which essentially amounts to a full-time job with a significant level of responsibility and stress, but with no pay. One mother shared,

> I think almost by default, partially because of my background [in psychology] and partially because I'm a stay-at-home mom so I'm with them all the time, I'm the one who takes him to all the appointments. I'm the one that researches treatments for autism, I'm the one who that talks to his therapists about what's going on, and what he's doing, and how we can help him. I try to relay some of that second hand to [my husband], but he doesn't have the background that I have, and he's not with them all the time, and it's all second hand. Sometimes I feel like I'm alone in trying to manage what my son needs because [my husband] just doesn't understand what he needs.

The role of the default parent in a family frequently occurs regardless of whether both parents work out of the home; often one parent (typically the mother) takes on the larger share of responsibility when it comes to managing their child's care and treatment. From a professional's perspective, fathers are often conspicuously absent from school meetings. Professionals frequently assume that the mother will attend the meeting and are surprised if a father attends.

I also see fathers participate in research projects or in support groups less frequently than do mothers. I received an e-mail from a friend of mine following his attendance at a local support group for parents of children with ASD:

> Went to a really terrific support group meeting last night for parents of kids on the spectrum—helpful and enlightening to us in many ways. And I was the only man in the room. I'm told this is unusual, that men do come. Still, I was shocked. The woman who ran the group, who was terrific, praised me for coming to the meeting. I like praise as much as the next person, but my honest reaction was, "Of course I came! He's my son!"

Conflict can emerge between caregivers when one perceives an inequity in division of labor. While talking about the frequency with which traditional division of labor emerges in families can be helpful for parents, encouraging a discussion about the division of labor and ways in which each partner may be able to shift responsibilities to better equalize the load each carries may be useful. For instance, the partner who does not take on the task of advocating for and coordinating his or her child's care may not recognize how taxing the role is, and dialoguing about these responsibilities may help build appreciation for the parent's role and increase willingness to divide household tasks more equally.

## RECOGNIZING THE IMPACT OF ASD ON PARENT CAREERS

Some parents find that accommodating the high needs of a child with ASD must lead to sacrifices in their career. For example, a family whose child has been diagnosed with ASD and enrolled in early intervention may find that the intensive daily needs of the child, such as parent participation in early intervention sessions and transportation to other related services if not provided in-home, require sacrifices. Especially in the younger years, the demands of childcare

are extensive, and the child's participation in therapy may require a level of care and transportation that cannot be offered when two parents are working. Because of this, if a family is able to afford it, one parent may either stay home or work part-time. Although a portion of this population is fathers, most commonly it is the mother who chooses to leave her career for childcare (Cidav, Marcus, & Mandell, 2012). Much has been made of the plight of the "stay-at-home mom" in the media, and not without merit. Spending all day, every day, with one's children is a tiring responsibility for the average parent. Caring for a child with ASD on a daily basis, and being the point person for all therapists, doctors, teachers, insurance companies, and other professionals, is exhausting.

The demand of being the primary caregiver for the child with ASD can be exacerbated by the fact that the parent who stays home with the child may be setting aside years of schooling and a rewarding career to best support his or her child. Years of education and training for the job may feel wasted, and parents who take on this role may feel as though they will never achieve what they set out to do when they were younger. That feeling of loss of their own professional goals may at times be just as stressful as the emotions they feel about their child's diagnosis. Because one parent must continue to work, the parent who stays home or has made some other career sacrifice may feel considerable resentment toward the working parent that continues to grow professionally.

Additionally, leaving the workforce for an extended period of time can make it difficult and scary to reenter, even when it seems as though a balance between work and home might be possible. A mother shared her experience with leaving the workforce:

> I've been home with the kids since [my older son] was born, by choice, but am currently trying to get back to *something*. This is hard for many reasons, but [my son's] diagnosis and schedule is making it even more complicated than it would otherwise be because I have to work any potential schedule changes and childcare arrangements around his therapy, school, and appointment schedule. Of course, all of those things are modifiable to some

extent, but for a kid on the spectrum, as you know, that level of disruption to his schedule is its own concern, and I certainly don't want to pull him out of things that are working for him if I can help it. In some ways, I can hardly even fathom how we would ever manage to have both [my husband] and I working full-time and still get [my son] to all of the services and appointments he needs. Obviously, many people make this work, and I am sure we will, too, and of course this is something that all parents struggle with, but like so many other things, the ASD diagnosis and associated services just add that one more layer of complication to everything we do.

When one parent decides to stay home, the other partner has the difficult task of working enough to cover the family's significant financial needs. This working parent also has to make sacrifices. Some working parents may find that they are unable to take on work responsibilities that would allow them to progress in their field (e.g., increased hours, travel) due to needs of the family. Additionally, because of the financial needs of the family, that parent may feel unable to work less in order to spend more time with the family. As a result, especially if the work is outside the home, this parent may feel out of touch with the daily care and responsibility related to raising a child. This parent may be unable to attend therapy sessions, important meetings for his or her child's academic or vocational planning, and meetings with professionals who offer advice on what to do with the child. As a result, this parent must rely heavily on his or her partner to explain and teach what has been missed.

In these cases, professionals must remember that a parent's continued absence from meetings or therapy sessions does not indicate that he or she is not devoted or invested in the child's development; rather, work requirements may be such that attending meetings in the middle of the day may be difficult. The stay-at-home mother above shared,

It's not like I think [my husband] should take a day off from work to come to every single appointment we have because that would be ridiculous, but it just makes it difficult because he's only ever getting the information second hand.

For this family in particular, identifying ways to include the father in meetings was an important goal, and he did begin to attend more meetings. The mother shared,

> That a was big step for both of us because he feels like he's more involved and I feel like he's more involved and interested in and keeping up on things and understanding what's going on, and so I think that has helped.

This anecdote is important, because it indicates that not attending meetings about the child not only impacted the mother, because she felt she was alone in getting the information about her child, but also made her husband feel less involved in his child's progress. Finding ways to include both parents in treatment planning can go a long way to building up a team approach to care within the family. For example, offering follow-up phone calls with both parents after school or home visits and conferencing parents into important meetings via phone or video when they are unable to step away from the office may help reduce a parent's distance from both treatment and the family.

Of course, one must remember that some parents are financially unable to have one parent stay home. The cost of ASD treatment, if not covered by insurance, is astronomical. One study estimated that the lifetime costs of raising a child with ASD are $1.4 million if the child does not also have intellectual disability, and $2.4 million if the child does (Buescher, Cidav, Knapp, & Mandell, 2014). This figure takes into account not only the necessary treatment for a child with ASD but also the lost parental income that often occurs when a child with ASD requires intensive care. Although great gains are being made across the country regarding coverage for necessary ASD treatment, some parents may still have to pay out of pocket for the treatment they or professionals deem necessary. Research indicates that the annual cost of caring for a child with ASD is almost 15 percent of reported income (Montes & Halterman, 2008). For many families, this expense necessitates two working parents, and when this is the case both parents may struggle in balancing the needs of home and the needs of their child. They may feel as though they inadequately address both work and home and that their career and home life both suffer for it.

Constantly being pulled in different directions is a considerable challenge for working parents. A working mother shared,

> I work. [My son] has a caregiver, but if he has difficulties, I still have to leave work early and work at home, which I luckily have the ability to do. I can work part of the day at home at least. So if there's an issue, I always have to pick up the phone and rush home to make sure that he's safe and the caregiver is safe and all of that.

This mother paints a picture of being divided between work and home and constantly feeling on call for both. Mothers who work outside the home indicate that they work fewer hours overall and feel the quality of their work suffers because of their divided attention (Gray, 2003).

The difficulty separating work life from home life can be a challenge for parents, and the balance requires flexibility on the part of both employer and parent. A father remembers his experience in striking the work-family balance when his son was first diagnosed:

> I was this person who was traveling a lot; me and [my wife] were spending a lot of time apart. When [my son] got diagnosed, we kind of got together and said, "We're going to do this together, and we're going to do everything." So I stopped traveling. I went to my job and said, "I can't travel anymore. You can either give me a job where I don't have to travel, or I'll leave and go somewhere else." So they said, "Okay, you can work from home 100 percent, you don't have to travel anymore," which is nice. It allowed me to be involved in [my son's] life more. They always tell you to stop and smell the roses, and maybe I wasn't doing enough of that, and when this happened, we did. And [my wife] and I became a lot

closer from that I think, and obviously, I'm glad that the last 13 years I got to spend so much time with [my son].

A job with this much flexibility is the ideal for parents, but finding employers that offer this much flexibility can be difficult. In the face of this, schools should be sensitive to the stress that parents may experience when the care required for their child conflicts with their responsibilities at work. For instance, some individuals with ASD have comorbid health conditions that require extended absences from school, or for parents to pick their child up from school frequently due to illness. In these times, parents may seem frustrated and exasperated with staff members who request that the parent come get the child or keep the child home. Professionals must recognize that these parents may be dealing with external pressures from their job and have concerns about losing their job due to the care they take on for their child. While professionals should not bend health requirements (i.e., agreeing to keep a sick child at school), they should be sensitive to the hardship parents experience in these positions and respond with empathy and understanding when possible.

## GRASPING THE IMPACT OF ASD ON THE PARENTAL RELATIONSHIP

Parent response to diagnosis will have a considerable impact on the parental relationship, for many reasons. When you think about parents, you think of two people who are joined by a common life. They share the same house, raise the same children, and face the same home-life challenges on a daily basis. As a result, a parent's significant other can be the biggest form of support he or she has; nobody else will have gone through what they have gone through, with respect to that specific family. This holds even truer when the parents are raising a child with ASD. Very few of their friends or family members will be able to understand what they face on a daily basis, so two parents can be an incredible support for each other. As one mother noted,

We both have those days we come back from something with our daughter and we say, "Wow, that was really hard," and the other one, even though they weren't there, they know what it's like, and they're *there*. So yeah, I'm lucky.

At their best, parents can serve as a sounding board and support for the biggest hurdles that the other parent will face, although the relationship will be tested.

Embracing positive effects. Though conflict does arise, I am pleasantly surprised to hear from many parents that the experience of raising a child with ASD has had a positive impact on their relationship. The stressors faced by parents force them to rely more heavily on each other and develop skills in communication and support that strengthens their bond. A mother articulated how autism affected her relationship with her husband:

I think it bonded us more. [My husband] does have stresses in terms of alone time, of course, and our daughter does not sleep through the night. So, it's like having a newborn for this long. But I do think it brought us closer.

Another mother quipped, "I think we've gotten closer, because it brings out the worst in you." Both of these parents acknowledge the stress that they experience raising their children, and how that stress can cause their own behavior to change in a negative way as they work to cope with the struggles they face. But, they also acknowledge that because their relationship has survived the worst, it has been strengthened a bit more. Additionally, parents often note that the qualities of their partner help balance out their inability to manage tough moments. For example, one mother shared about her husband,

He's much more patient than I am. There are definitely times when I'm flying off the handle, and I do because I'm not always a patient person. Our balance is a good thing because sometimes I say, "I can't take it, honey, I just can't take it." And he'll say, "Alright, I'm stepping in."

Similarly, another parent noted, "I think we just came to the acceptance that we can each have bad moments, or get depressed, but we can't do it at the same time. We kind of joke about it saying, 'It's my day, or my hour.'"

I have also heard parents acknowledge that they observe qualities in their son or daughter with ASD that remind them of their partner. One mother shared how this observation impacted her relationship with her husband in a positive way:

> I think because of the similarities between [my husband] and [my son], dealing with things with [my son] and learning about things with [him] helped me understand [my husband] a little bit better, which is in some ways good.

Ultimately, it is wonderful to hear from parents who truly feel that their relationship has stood the test they have been faced with. "We have a really good marriage," a mother shared,

> and I think it has brought us closer together. I just thank God every day that I am married to him and that we are going through this together, and that he is [my son's] dad. I think that [my son] is the luckiest kid to have him as a dad. He is just a terrific man, and brilliant and wonderful, and I love him.

Statements such as this are especially reassuring when parents also acknowledge how difficult and unpredictable their life is: "So our relationship is as good as it can be with a clearly difficult life. We're looking forward to being alone, in rocking chairs reading books in our old age. Will it happen? I don't know."

Listening to parents such as those I interviewed helps clarify that practitioners should not make the assumption that parents of individuals with ASD have a strained relationship. Practitioners may quickly but erroneously arrive at this conclusion based on, for example, lack of a parent's involvement in therapy or meetings or parental differences in opinion about the child's treatment. Despite the challenges that parents will face, many find that their relationship is strengthened over time and that they are able to maintain a loving relationship while raising a child on the autism spectrum.

Recognizing conflicts. Even the strongest of relationships will be tested. Many of the parents above who testified to the strength of their marriage also identified periods in their child's life, from diagnosis to adulthood, that have negatively impacted their relationship. No matter how strong the relationship, small cracks will begin to appear with the introduction of a stressor, and a diagnosis of ASD within the family is one of the most significant stressors a parent can experience.

As discussed in this chapter, each parent has a different reaction to the child's diagnosis over time. Parents often note that their partner's reaction was far different from their own, and problematically so. This is often the case when one parent is not on board with the diagnosis, while the other works hard to understand the diagnosis and take all the steps necessary for caring for the child. This can leave one parent feeling extremely isolated as he or she navigates unknown waters alone. If this pattern persists, each parent will be missing a crucial form of support that may be needed, and their relationship will suffer over time.

Additionally, the new division of labor that is established following diagnosis can also take a toll on the family. If one parent takes on most of the childcare, that parent may have considerable burnout and resent the parent who gets to leave the house every day for work. Similarly, the parent who works all day may feel resentful and guilty from not wanting to spend every minute at home helping with the household and the family. If both parents are working, dividing up responsibilities for childcare or household can be another battlefield. If one working parent takes on the lion's share of the childcare and household upkeep, the resentment between partners may grow.

Further, raising a child with ASD offers up more conflict zones than many typical relationships. Research indicates that parents of children with ASD have more arguments and conflict than do other parents (Brobst, Clopton, & Hendrick, 2009). As one would expect, parents of young children often face conflict with each other as they work to establish rules and a family culture. Small decisions about whether a family should sleep train their child or whether their child needs to finish dinner before he or she leaves the table can become a hotbed for parents who have clear positions in opposition to each other. Increased child independence means that parents will have fewer decisions to make for their child as the child learns, for better or worse, to make decisions on his or her own. In the family of a child with ASD, however, the long-term care required of a child means that decisions about the child's daily life long remain a part of the parents' domain. Where will the child, now an adult, live? Who will care for her? Should he be allowed to be on his own? A parent remembered the impact on her own family:

> I definitely know there were times where I said to myself, "I can see how families break up over this," because everything is very, very trying. If you have a disconnect on how many hours of services you want to get your kid, whether it's too much for your kid, whether we shouldn't be fighting with the school district over the kid, whether we should not put the kid in a sport, whether we are getting too much therapy, whether we're getting too little therapy, whether we have tracked down enough different therapists and made the right decisions. There's just so many pieces that, if you can't compromise, it's just another burden that you have to deal with. If you have any breaches in the dam, you can have problems in the relationship.

Parents who are having considerable difficulty communicating with each other and reaching agreement—or even civil disagreement—in their care for their child with ASD should be encouraged to seek the help of a therapist who specializes in couples therapy. Valuable lessons in how to communicate and compromise can be learned in the context of therapy. Though some families will dismiss the idea outright, a referral to a reputable therapist is recommended when parents share significant conflict with the practitioner.

Of course, all of this conflict can be hard to manage if parents are not able to care for their own relationship. As I mentioned, in a period of increased conflict my husband and I recognized that our relationship was as strong as ever once we were able to take a short break from work and our children, but I fully recognize that for many parents time away like this (even for a few hours!) can be difficult to attain. All parents, when they have children, are told to make time for the parental relationship, to schedule date nights, time to talk, time for intimacy. When as adults we have so many time-sensitive responsibilities, care for the parental relationship is often one of the first things we drop. As one mother shared,

> The stress of having two kids, period, is hard, and then you add in all of [my son]'s issues and doctors and appointments on top of it, and I think it makes it really hard because we have no time to talk to each other or be with each, other than "I need you to do this, I need you to do that" kind of thing.

Parents of individuals with ASD usually tell me that they just do not have the time to care for their relationship with their partner. Babysitters for children with ASD are difficult to come by, because finding someone who is qualified to care for a child with such intensive needs, and who also knows the idiosyncrasies of the specific individual, can be an immense hurdle for parents. A mother illustrated this challenge:

> So the only disagreement [my husband and I had], if you even want to call it that, [was] I think he would have liked me to look for more respite care for her so that we could have spent more time together, and I wasn't as willing to just leave her with anybody.

With no time without children, finding time for conversation and intimacy during the routine of daily life can seem impossible. When the rare moment comes along, often both parents are too exhausted to take advantage of it. A mother expressed,

> I don't think it's at all unusual for families with an autistic child, because the child just needs so much attention, for the spouse to feel neglected. [My husband] was neglected, but I didn't have any other choice. You've got to do what you've got to do.

When parents feel limited in their ability to spend quality time with each other, practitioners should encourage them to find ways to carve out time at home. While dinners out and weekends away are ideal, in some cases experiences like these are difficult to arrange. Instead, suggest parents make time for each other in quiet moments at home, perhaps after children are asleep. Small touches that feel special, such as ordering take-out or turning off the television, can highlight the importance of this time. These moments, set aside in the week, allow parents the opportunity to talk with each other and connect meaningfully, if only for brief periods.

Understanding the prevalence and impact of divorce. In some cases, relationships under pressure become very strained and often irreparably so. In past years, it was thought that divorce rates for families of children with ASD were significantly higher than the rest of the population, as high as 80 percent of couples. Recent research, however, indicates that the divorce rate among parents of children with ASD is actually no higher than that of parents of other children (Brobst et al., 2009; Freedman, Kalb, Zablotsky, & Stewart, 2012), but that the relationships are more marked by arguments and conflict (Brobst et al., 2009).

However, divorce does occur, and when I talk to parents who are divorced, they most frequently cite their child's ASD diagnosis as the specific reason that their relationship crumbled. "[The diagnosis] totally destroyed my marriage to his dad," one parent remarked.

> He couldn't handle [our son]'s disability, and he couldn't handle his own failures and his own mental health issues, so our marriage just totally collapsed. So from fairly early on I was really on my own in the whole thing.

Another parent pointed to the division of labor in the relationship as a reason for her marriage's dissolution. When asked how autism had affected her relationship, she responded,

> Well, ours went right down the tube. My marriage ended. We got through the school district thing, and I felt like it was all on me. I

did not have the support of my husband, and he worked a lot, and perhaps that was his way of dealing with it.

When parents divorce, one parent may be left to shoulder the brunt of the childcare on his or her own. Additionally, that parent may also have to work to maintain financial security. All that has been discussed in Chapters 1 and 2 in terms of the strain of raising a child with ASD, especially when coupled with other demands such as work and other children, may now fall to one person. Alternatively, two parents may struggle to share childcare responsibilities and make significant decisions for their child's education and care while living separately. Professionals should be particularly mindful of parents who are parenting on their own, including divorced and single parents who were never married, and of the reduced resources that they have in their life to help support the load of parenting a child on the spectrum. In addition to the constraints on their time, these parents may also have decreased social support because of the loss of their partner, and helping them identify other social supports will be of paramount importance.

## CONSIDERING THE IMPACT OF ASD ON PARENTS' SOCIAL NETWORK

Compounding the toll on many parents' marriages is the reduced social network that many of them have. Most people notice that when they make a significant transition in their life they lose many of the friends that they had. For example, college students who move into the job market may feel that their social support has dwindled, because they no longer have activities, classes, and experiences in common with their friends from college. Although some true friends may remain, without the context of college many relationships will end. Similarly, when people have children, they often note that their social network decreases, as relationships they have with friends who do not have children become harder to maintain. Time available to care for these relationships lessens, they have fewer commonalities in their lives, and friends have difficulty continuing to offer support to each other because they do not have a great understanding of the challenges each person faces. However, as their children age, the parents often begin to make new friends among a new social group: parents of their children's classmates or other people that they have met through work or other local activities.

Parents of children with ASD have experienced this shift in social networks twice since having children. First, they may lose touch with friends when they become a parent. They may begin to rebuild a social network among other parents or family members that they have, but the ASD diagnosis can set this back tremendously. They are faced with the same challenges in building new relationships again, but at an extreme level. Common events where parents of neurotypical children often rebuild their social network after having children, such as children's play dates and birthday parties, may not be accessible for parents of children with ASD. Social gatherings such as these can be difficult for these parents to attend because of their child's problem behavior or discomfort. They are also less likely to be invited to events due to their child's behavior.

Connecting with parents or family members who have children without ASD can be extremely difficult, as others simply may not be able to "get it." One mother described trying to tell a group of mothers whose children did not have ASD why her son was diagnosed:

> Some of the other moms were like, "Oh, well, you know, all the kids do that, all the kids are really interested in one thing for a while." It's hard for me to explain, yes, that's true, but it was different with him. It's even hard for me to put that into words, so I understand why they don't get it.

Finally, many parents of neurotypical children find that their friendships may dwindle when they have children but that they are able to maintain relationships with other professionals they work with. A similar support may be found for parents of children of ASD, as one father pointed out: "I have a long-time friend at the company. She no longer works there; she's recently retired. I would talk to her a lot, and that was helpful."

Though this connection with other individuals can provide parents with substantial social support, parents—particularly mothers—who have to leave the workforce to care for their child with ASD will not have access to peers in this professional forum.

Even when parents do find another like-minded person to connect with, they have very little time to devote to building and maintaining new relationships. Additionally, maintaining a relationship with others who have children without ASD can be a painful experience for parents whose child is not making the same gains as other children. Similarly, the friends may be less likely to share their own experiences or concerns about their child with the parents of children with ASD because they do not want to seem ungrateful, or too proud of their child who does not have ASD for fear of offending or hurting their friend. One mother noted how she often views her friends' children in a different light than they do:

> The one thing I've noticed is that if I have friends or relatives . . . that have typical children and I think they do something great and I notice the parents don't go, "Oh my God, that was the most amazing thing I've seen," it drives me nuts. I appreciate what other people's kids do so much. I think, "How are you not going crazy?" I don't know if that is necessarily jealousy, or I think that sometimes people don't realize how great they have it, because they take it for granted.

Dealing with thoughts and emotions like this on a regular basis with friends who do not have a child with ASD can be taxing and lead to rifts in what were once strong relationships.

Parents will retain some friends: those that stand the test of time. Many parents refer to their child's diagnosis as a great litmus test for whether a friendship is true; those friends who remain steadfast and present in the family's lives and are not driven away by the lack of connection, fear of the diagnosis, or awkward nature of get-togethers become the truest of friends. A mother describes how her collection of friends grew as her child aged:

> There was a weeding process: I had some friends that I was friendly with, but they went because they didn't get it or they couldn't meet

me in my world. . . . A few close friends just really stepped up to the plate, and I think those people were always there for me.

Some parents, however, will be left with a limited social network after their child is diagnosed that is hard to rebuild. Initially, this loss of friendships and a support network can be incredibly isolating, especially if parents are not able to turn to their partner for adequate support. Finding others to talk with about the parenting experience can be an effective coping strategy (see Chapter 7) but is certainly difficult without an established social network. Though the number of children with ASD has certainly increased in recent years, parents of children who are recently diagnosed may have difficulty finding how to contact other parents who have similar experiences. Other parents of children with ASD are not a readily available, accessible community, especially when all of these families face challenges getting out into the community to meet other people. Practitioners can help parents connect more easily with others who can provide social support using information provided in Chapter 7; ideas for sources of support follow.

Over time, parents ideally will begin to establish a network that can help support them in their experiences. Their relationships come from a variety of sources and will differ from family to family. Some families may find support in their own extended family, including grandparents, aunts, and uncles; more information on the significant benefits of these relationships is provided in Chapter 5. However, some parents are unable to derive support from their extended family and create a support network with others. For example, a family may develop strong bonds with other families of children with ASD or developmental disabilities as they involve their child in different programs and support services and meet other parents there. A father noted,

What we ended up doing, and probably what a lot of people do, you end up making the family somehow. [My son] is in the Special Olympics, and the families there, they're our family now as opposed to the family we had, like my brothers, sister, and stuff like that. I think over time with your caretakers and with a community that you build up, they become your family. I think more so than . . . your real blood family.

Multiple parents who talked with me spoke very highly of their child's involvement in Special Olympics, especially that the organization allows them to meet other families and develop long-term relationships with them, bonding over a central activity. Frequent events pull families close together on a regular basis, allowing them to develop strong relationships. The father above continued about his experience with Special Olympics:

> They're understanding of disabilities, so that helps. I think overall they're just positive. They feel like [my son] is a family member; they treat him like that. [My son] has his first friends. He may not understand the word *friend*, but people at Special Olympics view him as a friend. I think it just makes you feel like a family. . . . They care about him, that's the big thing. . . . And we can see that. It makes [him] happy.

Similarly, social support groups, or groups of parents of children with ASD who come together to talk about their experiences, are a lifeline for many parents. In these groups, a range of parents come together to share their concerns for their children and their proudest moments, and they are met by a group of parents who have all had very similar experiences. When I was writing this book, I invited groups of parents to talk with me about their experiences. During these meetings, I was struck by how much support they were able to offer one another. Regardless of the age of the child—some parents had children still in early elementary school, and some had adult children—or the child's skill level, all parents could relate to one another's experiences and offer words of solace and support. And even if no support was offered, all the parents felt that they could share and offload their most difficult of experiences and know that at least one other person in that room would understand.

Parents who have difficulty leaving the home because of family demands or finding childcare to attend parent support groups may also find solace in support groups offered online. I belong to one online group that is primarily for parents of children with disabilities but also allows professionals to join. The parents who post in this group regularly ask questions about early intervention or assessments, but just as often they post comments about their daily struggles parenting a child with a disability. The wonderful thing about this is group is that no sooner does a parent post than several other parents reply with a resounding chorus of, "Me too!" "I know exactly what you mean!" and adding suggestions for strategies that might help. Although many of these parents do not know each other outside of this forum, they still find that the group is a safe place to look for support in their daily life.

Families may also find support in those who go out of their way to help individuals with ASD: the teachers and caregivers who work with the families. One mother remarked, "People who were our early caregivers became part of the family and stayed part of our family. . . . They're married and have families now, and they're my extended family." Those professionals who take the time to get to know the family as a whole, and truly demonstrate care for not only the child with ASD but for all the family members, can be a significant source of support for parents.

As professionals, we should not underestimate the social support that we, too, can offer to parents. Some parents have built their network of support out of their child's past teachers and respite care workers. While building a relationship as close as this is not always advisable or easy to do, all professionals should keep in mind that while we are not all parents of children with ASD, we can offer considerable support to parents (ideas for this are discussed further in Chapter 8). By providing a listening ear for parents, and sharing the experiences of other parents with whom they have interacted, professionals may be able to provide parents with a feeling of support that reduces their sense of isolation.

## CLINICAL TAKE-AWAYS

Practitioners must take care to not make assumptions about the household roles and coping strategies of parents based on their gender. Some parents may take on nontraditional roles within their family and not fall in line with the research summaries presented in this chapter. All practitioners should consider the broad range of impacts a child's diagnosis of ASD has on parents' careers, division of labor, and relationships over time when assessing the support they need. A summary of recommendations for practitioners working to address the impact of ASD on parents' careers and relationships follows.

Practitioners should:

- Normalize conflict between parents by sharing the frequency with which it occurs, even among parents of neurotypical children who are faced with decisions about child-rearing.

- Be aware of the different coping strategies used by mothers and fathers as demonstrated in research. Mothers more commonly focus on emotions and emotion-focused coping than do fathers, who are more likely to distance themselves from their emotions and engage in problem-focused coping. Sharing these general differences may help parents better understand their partner's response to their child's diagnosis.

- Help parents identify sources of emotional support if they are unable to get that support from their partner. Examples include support from other parents of individuals with ASD and from therapists. More information on building social support is provided in Chapter 7.

- Encourage partners to dialogue about inequities that arise in their division of household and childcare duties, to help build appreciation for each other's roles and increase motivation to redistribute responsibilities.

- Be creative when finding ways to include parents in meetings that may be difficult for them to attend because of work responsibilities, such as having them call or video conference into the meeting, or holding the meetings at times when they can attend.

- Never make assumptions about parental investment or devotion to the child based on attendance at school events or meetings. Rather, be sensitive to parents' concerns about job loss when they are struggling to attend meetings for their child or seem frustrated with staff requests to keep their child home when he or she is sick.

• Avoid making assumptions about the quality of the parent relationship based on parent involvement or conflict; many parents share that their child's diagnosis of ASD has brought them closer together despite the conflict they experience in their relationship.

• Make referrals to couple's therapy when a parent expresses concern about excessive conflict within the parental relationship, to focus specifically on building communication and cooperation between parents in all aspects of their relationship.

• Encourage parents to be creative in identifying ways to make time for each other if they have difficulty caring for the parental relationship. For example, organizing at-home "date nights" can help parents connect with each other if only for a brief time.

• Recognize the increased burden of care that is placed upon divorced and single parents and be sensitive to the increased requirements related to work and childcare that these parents must take on.

# CHAPTER 4

# Providing Support for Siblings

Parents' lives have been shaped by many influences prior to the birth of their child with ASD. Although their children play a leading role during their adulthood, prior to having children parents were influenced by their own parents, siblings, extended family, friends, and colleagues. Thus, for many parents, their early development unfolded unaffected by ASD. In contrast, the development of siblings of an individual with ASD will co-occur almost entirely with the development of their brother or sister on the autism spectrum. Therefore, their early childhood, adolescence, *and* adulthood will be largely affected by their sibling's diagnosis and required care.

Often professionals will assume that growing up with a brother or sister with ASD has a negative impact on the neurotypical sibling and that the outcome for siblings is poor. However, the research on siblings' experiences and outcomes is mixed and inconclusive. In general, growing up with a brother or sister with ASD offers benefits and challenges to the sibling, and in the long run siblings of individuals with ASD do not seem to fare any worse than siblings of neurotypical children. This chapter summarizes the impact an ASD diagnosis can have on the sibling and offers recommendations on how to effectively include siblings in ASD-related treatment.

## MAPPING THE DEVELOPMENT
## OF THE SIBLING RELATIONSHIP

The sibling relationship is unique in many ways. For those of us who have brothers and sisters, that relationship is often the longest we will have in our lives. Many of us either cannot remember the time before our younger siblings were born or, if we were the second or later child, siblings were always present during our childhood. Because siblings are often close in age, they will age and grow old together. Though siblings may not remain close, they may still be the longest relationship each has had.

In addition to the length of the relationship, many traits and experiences are shared by siblings who grow up in the same household. If born from the same parents, the siblings will share the same genetic material and may have a tendency to develop similarly. And, if they grow up in the same household, the siblings are exposed to the same experiences growing up, with their parents, with other members of the family, and in their neighborhood. As such, siblings can be wonderful supports for one another as they develop. They become natural playmates and, as they age, can develop into wonderful confidants.

Neurotypical siblings develop into playmates early. By the time the youngest turns 2 he or she begins to play together cooperatively with older siblings. The relationship will shift over time, with considerably more strife between siblings in their adolescent years. However, as siblings age, their relationship becomes more egalitarian, and they can provide considerable support for one other in adulthood if they choose to do so. This can be especially beneficial as siblings struggle with new stressors in adulthood, such as creating a family and adjusting to their own role as parent, and supporting aging parents. Siblings who are able to refer back to their childhood and work from a common ground can find considerable support in a brother or sister.

Consider, then, the difference in a sibling relationship when one of them has ASD. Neurotypical siblings may have brothers or sisters who cannot speak or care for themselves independently or, at the other end of the spectrum, who have difficulty navigating social relationships and may rely heavily on their siblings for interaction. Regardless, the dynamic of the relationship shifts considerably, and siblings without ASD may end up taking on different roles and responsibilities in the family than is expected of their peers. This chapter first describes the development of a sibling's understanding of ASD and then describes the ways in which having a sibling with ASD can impact the neurotypical sibling's relationship with that brother or sister, parents, and peers. Finally, I summarize the ways in which siblings cope with growing up with an individual on the autism spectrum and offer suggestions for how professionals can provide support directly to siblings.

## CONCEPTUALIZING SIBLINGS' UNDERSTANDING OF AUTISM

Understanding the development of siblings' comprehension of ASD will help highlight some of the issues that arise as a child ages. Harris and Glasberg (2003) asked sixty-three different siblings about their understanding of ASD and how ASD affects their life and their brother's or sister's life. By analyzing the responses of children at different ages, a picture emerged of their understanding of ASD over time. At 6 years old, siblings have a poor understanding of ASD and how it relates to their lives. Children at this young age tend to define ASD based on what they can observe. For example, a sister's understanding of her brother's ASD may be that he goes to a special school, or that he cannot talk, or that special teachers come and play with him after school. An adult sibling shared her recollection of her early memories of her sister:

> I feel like you kind of know growing up, "Okay, there's something different. She's going to a different school and she's getting a different program," and all of that. I think some of it is a good thing because it was just what it was. I didn't think anything different. . . . By the time I was old enough to know anything was different, it was just how it had always been.

If siblings know the word *autism*, they might liken it to a virus that is contagious and can be "caught" from other people. In other words, a 6-year-old's understanding of ASD is unsophisticated.

Harris and Glasberg (2003) found that 7- to 10-year-olds do not fare much better in terms of defining ASD and may still have little concept of the impact that ASD has on their lives. At this point some may have siblings with ASD who are younger than them and just barely diagnosed. I remember one 7-year-old sibling I worked with whose brother was only 3 years old. At that time it was clear that she did not understand what ASD was and how it affected her family; to her, her brother was still a baby, with no language and little interaction with her. Explaining what ASD was to her at the time was difficult and unnecessary, because its impact on her at the time was unclear. As a teenager, this same sibling remembered her earliest memories of her brother when they were younger:

> [I remember] the noises and repetitive behavior and things along those lines. Especially as we would go out places he would be, I don't want to say odd, but he acts differently in public, and it's kind of embarrassing for me.

As siblings age, they begin to develop more specific definitions of ASD and have a better understanding of how ASD impacts their life long term. A 12-year-old may be able to recognize that his brother's diagnosis is based in the brain and that it has a large impact on his day-to-day life. And adult sibling recalled,

> As [my brother] progressed through elementary school the social differences started to pop up to me. He wasn't making as many friends; he had a hard time playing with other kids. He interacted in a different way with my friends than their siblings did.

These preteens can begin to articulate how ASD impacts their life: what it is that they cannot do because their brother or sister has ASD, such as having friends over to their house or going out to see a movie with their family. They may be more likely to compare their family with other families and identify differences between what they have to deal with compared with their friends. An adult sibling recollected her realization that her family was different from others when she visited a friend's house and saw how her friend interacted with her sibling: "[I thought,] 'Why don't you give your brother a shower? I don't get it.' Then I was like, 'Oh, not everyone's brother has autism. . . . Oh, wow, *we* are the different ones.'"

Teenagers have a much better grasp on how ASD affects their life long term. Siblings at this age can begin to articulate their plans for involving or not involving their brother or sister in their adult lives, the care that they may have to provide, and how having a brother or sister with ASD will affect where they choose to live and how they create their own family. I discuss these considerations as siblings transition to adulthood later in this chapter.

Practitioners should be knowledgeable about and carefully consider siblings' developmental age and understanding of ASD when working with families. This understanding will help contextualize how siblings respond to their brother's or sister's behaviors and how they conceptualize their role in their sibling's life, now and in the future. Additionally, when parents ask how to talk about ASD with their neurotypical children, practitioners should direct parents to helpful resources on siblings' development of understanding, such as the text authored by Harris and Glasberg (2003).

## APPRECIATING THE IMPACT OF ASD ON THE SIBLING RELATIONSHIP

As children, many siblings with ASD find that they have a disappointing playmate in their brother or sister (Harris & Glasberg, 2003). As I watch my two oldest children play together, I often think of this. At the ages of 5 and 3, they develop elaborate play scenarios in which they are puppies playing together, or a doctor taking care of a baby, or a policeman catching a robber, or a mommy taking care of her son. A box becomes a bus, the chair becomes a house, and their father and I get pulled in as supporting cast. Their play, if uninterrupted, can go on for hours.

However, in families with a child with ASD, the play that neuro-typical siblings might initiate with their brother or sister may be unreciprocated, as the sibling with ASD may not have developed the skills necessary to engage in play, or the play may be of poor quality and lack interest for the neurotypical sibling because individuals with ASD have difficulty engaging in the pretend play. A parent described the play between his two daughters, the younger of whom was diagnosed with ASD after a period of seemingly typical development:

> [My older daughter] would attempt to play with [her younger sister], and [her sister] really didn't give her the feedback. You know, ignored it. I have tapes when [my younger daughter] related—they would take a bath together, they would play together. I tell [my older daughter], "You have to treasure those times because you had them, even though it was brief, where you felt like you were the big sister and had a relationship."

Interestingly, when I interviewed neurotypical siblings about their younger years with their sibling with ASD, they were less likely to recollect missed opportunities for play and instead recalled missing out on another common feature of the sibling relationship: fighting. A teenager talked about the lack of conflict between her and her younger brother:

> When you look at other people and their siblings . . . they always get in fights and things along those lines. I can't really do that. I don't have the opportunity to really get into a fight with my brother because he can't fight back. Because we don't get into fights it's weird because we don't get to have that experience that you should have with a sibling.

This sibling is right: conflict is a natural part of sibling development, and just as with play, siblings can begin to work out many rules of social interactions within the safety of the sibling relationship. Arguments allow siblings to establish their own personal limits and values, determine right from wrong, and learn to sort through conflict independently, without the help of an adult. Research finds that sibling dyads engage in less overall interaction when one sibling has ASD than another disorder such as Down syndrome (El-Ghoroury & Romanczyk, 1999) and experience less conflict (Kaminsky & Dewey, 2001).

Having a brother or sister with ASD also impacts relationships between other neurotypical siblings in the family. These siblings can be an incredible source of support for one another as they grow up and have to adjust to transitions in the family's home life. As one sibling noted,

> I think it was helpful to have another sibling [without ASD]. There are definitely families in which there are two children, one with [ASD] and one without, and I feel that it would have been harder to go through it alone. Although it wasn't our everyday conversation, when something was going on, if we didn't feel like we wanted to talk to our parents about it, we had each other to talk about it. So I feel like it was helpful to have another sibling.

*Defining sibling roles in the family.* As described above, because of differences in skills demonstrated by siblings with ASD, some neurotypical siblings may take on additional responsibilities and caretaking roles in the family that differ from those typically seen in other households. These roles may disrupt what is typically expected of children based on birth order. "[My son with ASD] still needs more attention than [my daughter] does," one parent told me,

> and so she often takes on the role of caregiver of him, even though she's 15 months younger. She's always had to be the older sibling even though she's younger. When he had trouble putting on his clothes, she would help put on his clothes, and she would help button his clothes, and she would help put his shoes on. If he wanted to eat soup and couldn't get the soup to his mouth, she would feed him the soup. She's always been his little mommy, also helping to take care of him, instead of getting to be a kid herself.

In addition, siblings of children with ASD often fall into the role of teacher for their brother or sister, whether older or younger. Another parent talked about her son's relationship with his sister on the autism spectrum:

> I think [my son] recognizes the family anxieties and stresses . . . over her development and has taken it upon himself to be a helper in any way that he can. . . . He's taken on a little bit more of a responsibility role where he's very, very often sitting down and saying [to my daughter], "You're not doing this right, here's what you have to do," or "Here's how you do it." He's taken on a teaching role. He's actually very patient. He knows what makes her tick, and he wants to be involved.

Another adult sibling shared how she has tried to help improve her sister's communication:

> I have a friend growing up from high school [who] is deaf and . . . from him I know some sign language. I tried to teach her signs, and it's hard for her to grasp onto signs, but she 100 percent knows how to finger spell out all the letters.

Practitioners should recognize, however, that not all siblings will take on caregiver or teacher roles within their family—either they are not expected to by the parents, or they do not want to take on that role. I talked with a wonderfully honest sibling who clearly artic-ulated her role in her family:

> My role is just to be his sister. I've never felt obligated nor have my parents pushed me to take care of him. Because that's not what I want to do. I feel like I should kind of have that choice, because a lot of siblings, they have to take care of their brother or sister, or they want to go into a field like that. That's just not what I want to do. I want to remain or maintain that sibling relationship with him, but I don't want to have to feel obligated to have responsibility over him.

This perspective, shared by the teenager and supported by her parents, is an important one to be aware of when working with families. Although many siblings are eager, or at least willing, to take on additional caregiving responsibilities in the family, some may not want those additional responsibilities, instead desiring to foster as close to a typical sibling relationship as possible.

Helping siblings navigate problem behavior. Though some conflict between siblings is expected, parents and professionals must begin to recognize when the problems of the sibling experience exceed that of typical sibling relationships. A mother told me about how her son and daughter interact:

> Eight-year-old girls bother their 10-year-old brothers. Most 10-year-old girls bother their 12-year-old brothers. That's just how it goes. But then there's the added piece, like in public [my daughter with ASD] is doing X and that's not okay with him, where a neurotypical kid wouldn't do that, you know.

This parent recognizes that although siblings often become annoyed with one another, the behaviors that siblings face when their brother or sister is on the autism spectrum are not typical.

When viewing the sibling relationship, the professional should recognize that, in addition to the limitations that social and communication deficits will have on the sibling relationship, the dyad might also be affected by problem behaviors. Some siblings with ASD may engage in aggressions, self-injury, or disruptions. Another mother described her daughter's frustration with her multiple brothers on the autism spectrum:

> I think she is frustrated at times, especially when they go into her stuff, and her makeups and creams, and play with it and dump an entire bottle. My son likes to watch water and nail polish [go] right down the drain. . . . He will destroy [her makeup], and I say, "I'll buy you a new one. You have to understand he didn't do it on purpose. You left them out; you have to be a little bit more diligent. I'm sorry, but that's the way life is; you have to learn to make adjust-

ments." She has had to make more adjustments at an earlier age than your typical children.

This behavior described by the mother is not uncommon in households; toddlers and young children are known to get into and destroy things that belong to their older brothers or sisters. However, if you consider that this teen's brothers are adolescents, the behavior seems far less typical. Her mother describes teaching her daughter to adjust her own habits to adjust to having siblings on the spectrum, which is all too common for neurotypical siblings.

Siblings must also be aware of and adjust to behaviors that are specific to ASD. For example, rigid and routinized behavior can be a particular challenge for siblings to work around. I describe a family in Chapter 2 in which the son with ASD had an extreme insistence on sameness in their house—pillows and stuffed animals arranged just so, some lights on and some off, and so on. His older sister and younger brother had adapted and knew which lights in the house needed to remain on or off and where particular toys needed to be kept to avoid their brother's tantrums. Another sibling recalled her brother's behavior when they were younger:

> I think that what stands out to me when he was a younger kid was just having to tiptoe around the rigidity. . . . I think we accommodated his preferences a lot. I remember almost in a physiological way the stress that I would have. . . . He always went to bed at a specific time, and if we were out when that happened, like we were out late, it was a really big deal.

Severe problem behavior becomes a particular challenge for siblings. I have met siblings whose siblings are so aggressive that the family's life—and that of the siblings—revolves around tantrums. Siblings are sent upstairs to their room not because they have done something wrong but to protect them from their brother or sister during a tantrum. I have had siblings watch as brothers and sisters cause considerable damage to their family's house and to their own belongings. Many siblings carefully go through their day avoiding activities that might trigger problem behavior. I remember one sibling, years ago, telling me that she had to eat her dinner by herself in her room because the food she ate could send her sibling into a tantrum.

Siblings remember not only the problem behavior but also how they helped control their brother's or sister's behavior as they grew up. One sibling recalled,

> [My brother] was going through a phase of spitting on people, banging his head. He broke some bones in his head; he had to wear a hockey helmet. . . . He bit his arms, he has all scars on his forearms, and his knuckles are a little bit deformed. I remember him doing it, and he still has that callus in his forehead; sometimes his hair doesn't grow as much on one side. . . . He would hit his head with his wrist, and I'd try to put my hands between his hands and his head quick before he'd hit himself, stuff like that people never had to do.

This sibling choked up as she told me this story, with good reason. Taking on the responsibility of preventing her brother from physically harming himself is a stressful, scary position.

Another sibling remembered having to control her brother at school as a child when nobody else could:

> He was also in drama club because we wanted him to be involved in afterschool activities with us so that he can make friends. And he just had an episode, and he started pulling hair; he was running around. The school didn't know how to deal with it. So I was in about the fifth, maybe sixth grade, and I had to be out chasing my brother. I had to call my mom because the school wasn't dealing with it. The aide was crying.

The challenge of having to step into these difficult situations as a caregiver and a child is both stressful and formative for siblings of individuals on the autism spectrum.

When the child with ASD in the family has considerable problem behavior, practitioners should always counsel parents to talk about the behavior with their other children. The next section discusses how siblings can be included in discussions of how to address their brother's or sister's challenges, but practitioners should recommend that parents talk openly about problem behavior with all their children, no matter their age. Given that problem behavior may be one of the most salient symptoms of ASD for even the youngest siblings, talking with them about what they observe and how they feel when the behavior occurs will open healthy communication before problems arise. Additionally, parents can talk plainly about what to do when the behavior occurs, especially if the behavior might harm the child with ASD or the sibling. What does the parent expect of them? What will the parent do to keep everyone safe? Having a plan for how to respond to problem behavior will help siblings feel more confident and safe when the behavior occurs.

## INCLUDING SIBLINGS IN TREATMENT

Many of the concerns that arise for siblings of children with ASD, such as the difficulty they have interacting with their brother or sister, how to help teach (if they want to take on that role), and the challenges they face when their sibling engages in problem behavior, can be addressed by including siblings in the treatment for their brother or sister with ASD. However, professionals who have been charged with providing treatment for the child with ASD may not include the neurotypical siblings. Siblings are highly attuned to the attention their brother or sister gets from other caretakers, especially if those caretakers are providing support within the sibling's house. One sister shared her view on siblings' experiences in general:

> They feel so passed over [by professionals] and not included. It's not the case across the board, but I think that's a sentiment that I've heard from a number. Just ask. "I know a lot about him, ask me anything." . . . Looking back on it, I really would have appreciated if someone [asked], "How are you doing?"

Practitioners can also check in on siblings by asking the family specific questions related to the siblings' understanding of ASD and how it impacts their life. For example, a practitioner might ask parents of two brothers, one of whom has ASD, such questions as, Does the sibling ever talk about his brother's diagnosis? What does he say? What is his understanding of autism and what it means for his brother? What kind of things does he like doing with his brother or by himself? Are there other things he would like to be able to do with his brother but doesn't know how? How is he feeling about his family these days? Does he have concerns about his brother, parents, or his own life? Posing these questions to parents, worded sensitively, can help direct parent attention to the sibling without ASD. Asking these same questions of siblings can help them feel that someone cares about their role in the family and can better elucidate their view of their brother or sister, which can ultimately inform the support the practitioner provides.

The support provided to siblings can take on many forms. As the sibling above noted, one way to include them is to simply ask siblings for their input when providing treatment to the brother or sister with ASD. In some cases, a sibling's input could be very helpful; he or she may have a different view on a problem behavior or a different take on a skill that would benefit the family. At the very least, including siblings in conversations about family treatment can help make them feel that they are part of the team. A sister remembered how she admired a therapist who always got her input when working with her brother:

> I think that was good just because you can see how the siblings act together, and how they can work the treatment around that. I would be brought in with my brother, and then later they would have an interview just with me. I think that works because you can just see exactly what the sibling thinks and how the kids are back together.

Similarly, informing siblings of the treatments that will be implemented in the home is also a respectful, inclusive move for professionals. One sibling remarked,

If you're reinforcing [one of my brother's behaviors] at home, I should be told, because I have to be a part of that reinforcement. If you don't, if not everyone is on the same page, then the behavior is not going to stay. Also, don't discredit someone who's really young, because [siblings] are totally observant and really know what's going on.

Siblings can also be incorporated directly into the treatment for the individual with ASD. Research has investigated ways to include siblings in activities that practitioners might not think about. For example, Celiberti and Harris (1993) successfully taught 7- to 10-year-old siblings of preschoolers with ASD to get their brother's or sister's attention during play by giving simple instructions, prompting when necessary, and providing social praise. This simple intervention improved play interactions between the siblings even 4 months after the training ended. Ferraioli and Harris (2011) taught siblings with ASD to establish joint attention—an important skill in which children use eye contact to share an experience or event with others—with their brother or sister with ASD. Following training, the investigators found that the children with ASD not only responded to and initiated joint attention more frequently but also imitated their sibling more frequently during play. These research examples illustrate how siblings can be incorporated into treatment as both a teacher and a playmate.

Activities such as those mentioned above give the opportunity to engender positive interactions between siblings and to develop skills in children with ASD that may help them become more independent or proficient in skills in other settings. The importance of including siblings in treatment is twofold. First, it can offer tremendous potential gains for the child with ASD. Here is a peer, often similar in age, who is highly familiar to the child with ASD and often present in the environment. Teaching a child with ASD skills—play skills, social skills, or even academic skills—by including a sibling makes the work highly applied and increases the likelihood that the skill taught will be maintained in the home setting. Second, this approach can also be highly beneficial for the sibling. As has been mentioned, siblings with ASD can be very disappointing playmates.

Including siblings in treatment can give them a chance to interact with their brother in a sister in ways they have done not previously and to establish a sibling relationship more similar to that seen in other families. A sibling recalled the work therapists did to include her in her brother's treatment:

> I would try to play games with him. I remember bouncing balls with him, I'd push him on the swing, just random little stuff like that. . . . But [we would work on] a sibling relationship they'd kind of get me to have with him or I'd want to have with him.

I remember one of the first times that I included a young boy in his brother's treatment sessions. I was teaching his brother to follow an activity schedule, and it occurred to me that I could include the older brother in the sessions and teach them to play together. Each time a new activity showed up in the schedule, we would figure out how to incorporate the older brother in the activity. When a farm set appeared in the schedule, I taught the older brother how to make sounds with the animals so that his brother could imitate him. The first time he did it, saying "moo" and placing a cow in the barn, and his brother copied him, he looked at me with the biggest smile and said, "I didn't know he knew how to do that!" Building up that relationship became so important. We eventually included activities that the older brother enjoyed, like playing baseball. His younger brother needed considerable help with this activity, and for sure the game was not as thrilling as a baseball game with his peers, but his older brother smiled and cheered the whole time we played like it was a major league championship. Helping build up that relationship and positive interactions between siblings can be so important.

In terms of determining when to integrate them into their brother's or sister's treatment, siblings advise that professionals take the lead from them. "Be respectful of what the sibling wants," a teenage sibling suggested.

> If they don't want to be included in what [the professional] is doing with the person with autism, that's okay. And if siblings want to have a relationship with the consultant or the therapist or who-

ever, that really makes it easier on the sibling because it just makes them feel more included and more open to helping.

But, she continues, professionals should take cues from the sibling and only start working with neurotypical siblings when it seems that they are open to the idea and more comfortable with the new professional.

> There are [professionals] that immediately wanted to have a relationship with me, and I was like, "Whoa, I need some time to adjust to a new person in my house," because there have been so many of them. That's another thing. If you have a family in this situation, they have people coming and going from their house all the time, and [professionals] need to be aware that that's the situation.

Regardless of how professionals integrate siblings into treatment, they should acknowledge the significant role that a sibling plays in the family, especially if he or she takes on additional responsibilities or works hard to be the best playmate possible for the child on the autism spectrum. A sibling who works in ASD treatment as an adult shared the story of a family she met following an assessment she had done. The older brother, about 9 years old,

> pulled up a little chair, and he sat next to me, and he crossed his legs, and he listened to everything I said and nodded along. And whenever his brother or sister would knock something over he would get up and make sure everything was okay, and then he'd sit back down. He was just phenomenal, just absolutely phenomenal. The family was leaving, and I pulled him aside, and I said, "I want you to know that you're an amazing kid. You're an amazing brother." And he stuck his chest out, got all proud, and he said, "Thank you."

A simple expression of admiration and appreciation for the role the sibling plays in the family can have a tremendous impact and make siblings feel as though they are present and part of their family's experience. This adult sibling shared simple words that she felt would make a difference to a sibling: "Just know that somebody thinks you're amazing."

## UNDERSTANDING SIBLINGS' RELATIONSHIPS WITH PARENTS

As one would expect, having an individual with ASD in the family can have a considerable effect on the relationship between other siblings and the parents. The effect can be felt both ways; both parents and siblings openly share how ASD has impacted their relationship. The primary way they feel their relationship has been affected is in the level of attention that parents are able to give their children who are not on the autism spectrum. A mother commented,

> I'm sure [my daughter's ASD diagnosis] has taken time away from [my son] because she requires so much. It's inevitable. I do what I can always to take quiet time with him or make sure that he's getting his fair shake, but I'm sure as soon as you sit down with a calculator and add up the numbers and the amount of time I spend thinking and doing for her versus thinking and doing for him, she's triple the time easily.

Most parents will state that they have tried their hardest to not let ASD affect their other children, but ensuring this is incredibly difficult. The demands of raising a child with ASD are vast, and parents may be balancing all of the therapies and treatments required of their child with ASD, as well as the support needed in home to help the child with tasks they cannot complete themselves. Even the best-intentioned parents will find that a large amount of their time is spent caring for the child with ASD and that their neurotypical children receive comparatively less attention. One parent recalled,

> I think early on [my son's ASD diagnosis] pulled me away from [my daughter]. . . . I think I was so sad, so worried, and so preoccupied.

I felt like I was present, but I'm sure it wasn't to the degree that I could have been. [His ASD] was just perpetually and constantly on my mind.

Countless cartoons and comedians have highlighted children's desire for attention from their parents when they are younger; images of parents worn down by incessant cries of, "Mommy, Daddy, look at me!" easily come to mind. Children can be highly attuned to the attention they get from their parents and the extent to which another sibling gets more attention than they do. A teenage sibling remembered her younger years with her twin brother on the autism spectrum:

I had to fight for the attention. And now that I'm older, I understand that they have to pay more attention to him. He needs it. I can be independent and he can't. But it still gets to me a little bit that I have to fight for their attention.

For the most part, the teenage and adult siblings I interviewed indicated an understanding of the reasons that their parents had to allocate more attention to the sibling with ASD, but many were still quick to point out that they did wish they had more time with their parents. A sibling shared,

[My parents] didn't do a ton of checking in with me because they knew by and large I was doing well. I think, looking back on that, I totally understand how that's the case. I really assumed that role without questioning it very much. But I wrote my college essay on basically that: understanding that [my brother] needed more than me and I was happy to take less but that sometimes I wish I had more.

Regardless of siblings' understanding, parents often report feeling considerable guilt that they are unable to give the same amount of attention to all of their children and are unable to participate in all of their children's lives in the way that other parents can. A mother shared,

I think it's probably more my guilt at this point, feeling like I didn't spend enough time with [my other children] and I wasn't always there for them. I couldn't get to every game, and I couldn't be their Girl Scout leader.

Another mother noted relief that she had an upcoming doctor's visit for her son without ASD to follow up on some developmental concerns:

I am looking forward to going and sitting with the doctor and having a conversation just about [my son] because I feel like I'm not, in some ways, paying enough attention to him . . . because there's just so much else going on all the time.

In some cases, the division of attention can make parents feel as though they are missing out on important events or concerns in their neurotypical child's life. One mother shared her feeling that she neglected her daughter's dyslexia while she focused on her son's ASD:

[My daughter] must have suffered because she didn't get the right intervention at the right age. Me being a former teacher, I feel really guilty that I wasn't on top of her, because she was getting by and everybody was saying, "Oh, it's fine, it's fine." It wasn't fine. And I knew it wasn't fine, but I didn't have the energy or the time to champion for two kids. So I championed for my son because he was on fire, and I let my daughter slide because she was just simmering.

When her daughter approached her with suicidal ideation because of her poor performance in school, this mother realized what she had been missing and immediately worked to find a new educational placement for her daughter. But the guilt that she reports at this time is considerable. Practitioners should be aware of families that seem spread too thin. In this situation a single mother was caring for two children, one with ASD, and teachers and professionals should be cognizant of the siblings without ASD and provide as much support as possible to ensure that these siblings do not get inadvertently passed over. In this situation, the mother was doing everything she could to support both children, but she is only one person and able to do only so much. Professionals need to be aware of all family members at times like these.

Some siblings, even at a young age, recognize the toll that raising a child with ASD has on their parents and work their hardest not to add additional concerns to their parents' plate. These siblings may take on the role of being the "good child," because they recognize how many challenges their parents face with their brother or sister with ASD. To minimize how much their parents have to care for them, they work to become the best they can be, in academics, in extracurricular activities, and at home. When asked about the role she filled in her family, an adult sibling recalled,

> To be good. . . . I feel like I tried to always not cause trouble, because I knew how much mom worked. My parents are divorced . . . so it was just me, mom, and [my brother]. When I was younger . . . I kind of always thought, just let me always try my best . . . in everything: do the best, get good grades, don't get in trouble, stuff like that. Then it kind of shifted; I would try to pick up whatever [responsibilities] I could, like give him a shower, help him in the bathroom. Whatever I was capable of I just kept adding on.

Siblings like this demonstrate genuine care for their parents' well-being and concern that they do not want to add additional stress for their parents.

Siblings also take great care in remembering the efforts parents made to maintain a sense of normalcy for them, such as making sure that they were able to participate in extracurricular activities just like their friends. "I played sports all year round," an adult sibling recalled. "Any time there was an activity, [my mother] would sign me up. She never wanted me to not be able to do something because of [my brother]." Siblings also point out the special time with parents that is set aside just for them. These small outings or getaways can make a big difference in strengthening connections between parents and siblings. A teenage sibling talked about how her parents often had to allocate attention to her younger brother with ASD:

> They would have to put me on hold. Which I understood, but it was hard at times because I needed something, too, or I wanted something, and he was kind of a priority in those kinds of situations. But at the same time, my mom would always find time for me, to get a babysitter for [my brother] . . . and we'd go do something. That really strengthened our relationship because there was always time for us to go off and do something and talk about him, or complain, or whatever it was.

Although this sibling recognized that her brother might draw her parents' attention at times, she highlighted the importance of special time with her mother to reconnect. Her mother talked about her commitment to spending this time with her daughter:

> It was a huge financial stress, but I put childcare in place . . . and I could go to her school events without him, I go to her recitals without him, because I feel she deserves my full undivided attention at certain times. . . . I always went away with [my daughter] each summer and had [my son] with caretakers so we could do a little bit of something together, be away, and have her have that experience like other kids her age were having, like vacation. It wouldn't be big and fancy or anything, but she would do something she wanted to do.

Much like practitioners should recommend that parental partners find time to spend with each other, they should also suggest that parents find moments in which they can give their other children undivided attention. Even a few moments of undivided attention can provide the opportunity to communicate and connect in the midst of a busy family life. For instance, my older daughter likes to play what she calls the "happy/sad/mad" game at night before she goes to bed; I ask her questions about things that happened in her day that made her happy, sad, and mad, and she then asks the same questions of me. This small routine, which lasts about 5 minutes, gives me the opportunity to check in with her and learn about her day and what she is thinking and feeling, and it leaves us both feeling better connected just before she falls asleep. Other activities such as reading a book together before bedtime or slipping out for a quick breakfast together at a restaurant can help provide neurotypical siblings with the sense that the parent is focusing on them and also allow parents the opportunity to check in with their children about recent accomplishments or concerns in their family, school, or social life.

As siblings age, this time together and sharing in the care of their family member can lead to a special bond: "Sometimes I feel like we are peers," an adult sibling noted.

> I'm the daughter, but I also kind of feel like we are in it together. Especially now I'm in my twenties I really feel like that. She's not totally on such a different level than me. A lot of ways we are the same.

A mother agreed, talking about the positive impact of her son's diagnosis on her own relationship with her teenage daughter: "I also think it's made us really close. I think being a single parent, and she was kind of like an only child, I felt like it was [my daughter] and I taking on the world." Just as parents in a relationship can rely on each other for social support because they have had the same experiences with their child, parents and their neurotypical children— especially as the children grow into adulthood—can offer significant comfort to each other, sharing an empathy for each other unmatched by others outside of the family.

Additionally, siblings will grow to have a better understanding of their parents' experiences and sacrifices, which can lead to a closer relationship between siblings and parents. A sibling shared her now adult perspective on her parents:

> At this point, . . . most people's kids are done with college or finishing college, and everyone's out of the house, and now they're back to just husband and wife doing their thing, going on vacation,

things like that. . . . My parents don't necessarily and may never have that freedom. In one sense they may enjoy having [my sister] around, but in another sense I'm sure they equally see that their peers are all pretty much "free," and they're in a spot where if they want to go have dinner with their friends, they have to arrange for me or someone else to come be with [my sister].

Increases in siblings' understanding of their parents' life over time can positively impact the parent-sibling relationship, because the increased level of siblings' empathy for their parents may decrease the demands and criticisms they place on their parents over time.

## ACKNOWLEDGING SIBLINGS' RELATIONSHIPS WITH PEERS

The behavior of a sibling with ASD can also have considerable impact on a neurotypical sibling's social life. As discussed above, because of the demands on parents' time, siblings may have fewer opportunities to spend time with peers because parents are unable to transport them to events they would like to attend. In addition, some siblings report that they never have friends over to their house. Their hesitance may be due to several concerns. One sibling noted that she did not invite friends over because "I didn't want to put that on my mom" by adding additional demands on her mother to ensure that her brother was well behaved, or even dressed, in their own home.

Siblings also noted concerns about having to explain their brother's or sister's ASD to their friends. One sibling shared, "[ASD] requires a lot of explaining. Particularly, I think, because he is so relatively high-functioning that he doesn't have an obvious disability." Explaining why their brother or sister behaves in a certain way or does not respond to peers in the same way as other children can be a tough task for many siblings. They may face this challenge already if they share a school with their sibling, or when they are out in the community, but they may not want to willingly invite that responsibility into their home lives. Concerns about how peers and others perceive their sibling, themselves, and their family may be pervasive and color the sibling's experiences with the brother or sister.

For other siblings, their brother's or sister's problem behavior may make it uncomfortable for peers to visit. "I've always been very tense around my brother, especially when my friends are around," a teen-age sibling shared,

> because I don't know what exactly he's going to say or do. So that's the thing. Big thing. . . . When my brother was younger, he would pull my friend's hair or make comments that were inappropriate. He doesn't do it so much now . . . but all that they remember are those behaviors. It's hard to forget, and when they're around him now, it's still a little uncomfortable for me.

Concern about how these behaviors will impact their social network will be at the forefront of many siblings' minds when they consider having a friend to their house.

Notably, siblings also point out that their brother or sister with ASD can act as a test of a friendship to determine whether the peer is the type of person that they should keep in their life. Because of how different their family situation can be, siblings note that finding friends who can support them through their experiences is impor-tant. A teenage sibling shared how her brother is a great litmus test for the quality of a friend:

> I used to be really embarrassed of him, so I wouldn't really want people to come over. . . . If they did come over, I would be, like, "My brother has autism, just ignore him," stuff like that. I would apolo-gize for him. As I got older, I realized they're my friends—if they don't want to accept how my life is, I don't want to be friends with them. . . . None of my friends responded negatively whatsoever, and that made me feel I had a really close group of friends that I could always talk to and trust because they accepted every part of my life.

Siblings can benefit from connections with other peers who have similar family experiences, especially if they have difficulty finding support from others who can understand their family life. One form of connection is to have siblings gather together in a support group specifically for siblings of individuals with ASD. I have worked with many sibling support groups, where siblings gather to learn about ASD, how to play and interact with their brother or sister, and how to effectively communicate with their parents. Perhaps one of the best effects I have seen develop through the sibling group is simply their recognition that they are not the only ones who experience growing up with a brother or sister on the autism spectrum. One of my favorite moments in running sibling groups is starting the initial meeting by asking the group members to raise their hand if they have a brother or sister with autism. The looks on their faces as they raise their hands and realize everyone else has raised their hands, too, is priceless.

A sibling who participated in our sibling group when she was only about 7 years old remembers very little of it, but she recalled, "I kind of remember thinking, 'Wow, this is six other [siblings], too. It's not just me.'" The children make quick connections, talk about similar problems they face in their families, offer support to one another, and sometimes develop friendships that last beyond the sibling group. Another sibling stated the importance of talking with other siblings of individuals on the autism spectrum:

> If I met someone with a brother or sister who also had behavioral problems, it was nice to connect to someone who knew exactly what was going on, because my friends don't really understand his behaviors. They can't really connect [with me] on the same level as someone who knows exactly what's going on and lives with it every day.

Providing support in sibling groups, however, presents with challenges. As families struggle to balance the needs of the child with ASD with the needs of neurotypical siblings, attending sibling groups sometimes becomes impossible. Prioritizing social groups is difficult, especially if attendance requires travel time. In these cases, other ways of connecting siblings may be identified. For example, some programs develop sibling pen pals who can write to each other about their experiences. With today's technology, the possibility of setting up phone calls or video conferences with other siblings could offer potential benefit. Professionals should consider some of these options, included in the Resources section at the back of this book, and suggest them to families to provide additional support to siblings.

Parents may also find that involving the entire family in communities accepting of individuals with disabilities can have a positive impact on siblings as well. For example, one sibling shared her experience when her sister was involved in Special Olympics:

> That's just an amazing atmosphere and environment for people with all kinds of disabilities, but also that's the kind of place where you go and [my sister] can do anything, she can take her shirt off and run around and it would be fine, it's normal. That's kind of cool to see. I think probably as a kid [I thought], "Okay, maybe this is not so weird of an experience. There are other families like us."

In essence, having siblings spend time in communities where their brother or sister is easily accepted may help minimize some of the negative emotions they experience toward their sibling and expose them to support from others who have had similar experiences.

## UNDERSTANDING SIBLING ADJUSTMENT

Just as each child with ASD is unique, each sibling adjusts differently to having a brother or sister on the spectrum. I have met siblings who cover the range of all possible responses to having a brother or sister with ASD. A number of factors can influence a sibling's reaction over time to a brother or sister on the spectrum. One factor is the symptoms expressed by the brother or sister and the impact that they have on the neurotypical sibling. Challenges with communication, social skills, and problem behavior can all impact the sibling. Because of limited independence on the part of the child with ASD, some siblings help care for their brother or sister by helping them with things that they cannot do themselves. The extent to which the symptoms of their brother or sister's ASD affect their own life will moderate the effects of the diagnosis on siblings' reaction. However, some emotions are common to many siblings. These emotions are frequently experienced among all siblings, but they may be heightened when one sibling has autism.

Recognizing challenging emotions. Some siblings describe a feeling of embarrassment in situations that involve their brother or sister on the spectrum. Feelings of embarrassment are not uncommon in families—embarrassment about how a brother, sister, mother, or father is behaving—especially as children reach adolescence. But when a sibling has ASD, the source of embarrassment is different from that experienced in other families, which may exacerbate the feeling of embarrassment. One mother remembers feeling particularly concerned that her daughter would be embarrassed by her older sister with ASD when growing up, because she had watched other siblings of children with disabilities:

> It was so clear to me that these siblings were ashamed of their sibling with autism; they were embarrassed. Even some of the parents, they were . . . embarrassed to go out in public with [their children with autism]. . . . I swore when I was pregnant with [my younger daughter] that she was going to accept [her older sister] for who she was. I got her involved in every little thing . . . and I explained to her at a very young age that this is who [her sister] is and it's not her fault. . . . I made her part of the thing.

Despite the efforts of the most well-intentioned parents, however, embarrassment is difficult to avoid and is often recalled by siblings of individuals on the spectrum. An adult sibling recalled eating out at restaurants with her brother:

> He would order literally off the menu. He'd read it exactly how it was written, which I think took people by surprise and then that added to them not knowing what he was talking about. . . . Every time he would try to order they'd say, "Oh, sorry, what?" And I

would just feel this like giant wave of anxiety because he would get so upset.

She continued,

> I still have those feelings because the social stuff is the most salient to me now, when he does things or he misses cues or people try to make small talk with him if we're in a store or something and he doesn't. I think, knowing something about myself, I get very socially anxious about not wanting to offend people or wanting to be polite and act the right way, and he just blows right past that.

As has been discussed, some siblings may experience emotions such as jealousy or resentment toward their sibling for the perceived extra attention or special treatment their brother or sister gets from parents and other caregivers. Jealousy is common among all siblings, because they frequently compare what they have—attention, toys, food—with that of their siblings. All parents are familiar with the all-too-common phrase, "That's not fair!" when a sibling perceives that another has received an unfair share of anything. As parents of children with ASD are quick to point out, inequity happens more frequently in their families than in others. As one mother noted,

> We worked really hard to make sure that attention was distributed as fair as possible, but [my daughter] knows when the wind is blowing [in the direction of my son with ASD], and it tends to blow that way a little bit more often.

In response, siblings may experience jealousy or resentment toward their brother or sister. One mother noted that her own daughter expressed her jealousy plainly:

> I don't think I treated my daughter any differently [than her brother] or did anything differently, but now I remember she wrote a letter, probably when she was about 8, that she wished she had autism because then I could treat her like I treat [her brother].

Other siblings may experience feelings of anger toward their brother or sister with ASD. For these siblings, whose lives seem to revolve around their brother or sister, childhood presents them with challenges that their peers do not face. A mother shared,

> My daughter, it still affects her. . . . When they are together, there is still this anger that I see in her, and frustration with him that I wish wasn't there. It doesn't affect . . . the rest of her life. She goes off and has a perfectly good life, and she is strong and independent. . . . She has very little tolerance for the things he does that I think he can't help doing.

A teenage sibling openly shared the feelings of anger that she sometimes feels toward her younger brother. For instance, she recalled a trip to a bookstore with her mother and brother when she was in elementary school, where she overheard two women talking negatively about her brother's behavior. "'Wow, I didn't know they had monkeys here,'" she told me they had said.

> I was so embarrassed, and I just wanted to scream at him to shut up. . . . At the time I was so upset; I was furious with him. I was like, "Why do you have to be like this?" Now I'm thinking back, I was little; it was an appropriate response to that situation at that point, but now I'm furious at the people who said that.

This teen's description of the event with her brother perfectly captures how feelings of embarrassment can quickly turn to anger toward the brother or sister on the spectrum. While adults can view this situation and recognize that the anger should be directed at the insensitive women in the store, a young child may not be able to take this perspective. Feelings of anger directed at the sibling with ASD are common.

In some cases, a sibling's anger can grow to encompass more than just his or her experiences with the sibling on the autism spectrum, especially when neurotypical siblings are young and unable to make clear causal relations. For example, some siblings may not be able to discriminate things they cannot do because they have a brother or sister with ASD, such as having friends over, from what they cannot do because they are a young child. A sibling whose life is impacted by his or her sister's ASD because she cannot do some activities that interfere with her sister's therapy, or because the family cannot take on the extra commitment, may become angry when parents present rules common in childhood, such as having to go to bed at a specific time or not being able to wear makeup. The sibling may misconstrue these additional limits as related to having a sibling with ASD (because it seems that so many rules are put in place because of the sibling with ASD) and as a result may become even angrier about having a brother or sister on the spectrum. In these cases, helping the child understand the general rules of being a child, and how they are often common across families, can be a positive step for families and professionals.

Some siblings may report feelings of guilt. They may feel guilty that they are often embarrassed by or angry at their brother or sister. In the children's book *Beezus and Ramona* (Cleary, 1955), Beezus shares her concern with her mother that she does not always like her younger sister, Ramona. Her mother tells her that her feelings are understandable and that she is not expected to like her sister all of the time. Teaching such lessons to brothers and sisters of children with ASD can help alleviate feelings of guilt. Siblings may also feel guilty that they do not want to help their parents care for their brother or sister with ASD. One sibling shared her perception that siblings should take the role of caring for or babysitting their brothers or sisters on the autism spectrum.

> I felt that I should do that, but at the same time I didn't really want to. I felt guilty, obligated that I should. But as I . . . talked to more people about it, I realized that it's my life.

This teen highlights the importance of hearing adults reinforce her choice not to be involved in caretaking for her brother. Acknowledging and affirming that siblings are able to make a choice in that role will be immensely helpful in reducing sibling guilt.

Practitioners should recommend that parents keep open lines of communication with siblings about the emotions the siblings are experiencing in response to the dynamics of their family and their brother's or sister's behavior. Especially when parents feel that siblings are excessively upset or angry, they should talk with them about what might be contributing to these emotions. However, parents should also be comforted by the knowledge that the emotions experienced by siblings of individuals with ASD would still be experienced—though not with the same triggers—if their brother or sister did not have ASD. That is, feelings of anger, jealousy, and guilt can arise in neurotypical sibling relationships. Further, parents should let themselves off the hook and not try to "fix" all of the negative emotions that siblings experience. Sometimes, despite parents' efforts, these emotions will still emerge, and siblings have to learn how to cope with them when they become overwhelmed.

However, if siblings seem unable to develop strategies to cope with these emotions on their own and emotions such as anger and sadness seem to form the majority of the siblings' emotional experiences, practitioners should be prepared to recommend individual therapy for the sibling. Sibling support groups can also provide benefits from interacting with other siblings with similar experiences and helping siblings learn effective coping skills.

Embracing positive outcomes and emotions. Though siblings may report negative emotions associated with having a brother or sister with ASD, they also note several positive outcomes of their relationship with their brother or sister. For example, some research indicates that siblings of ASD have a high sense of self-sufficiency because they are often required to act more independently than their peers (Macks & Reeve, 2007). Relatedly, siblings of individuals with ASD may have a greater sense of competence and self-confidence and better self-esteem than their peers (Orsmond, Kuo, & Seltzer, 2009; Verté, Roeyers, & Buysse, 2003). This may be due in part to the increased responsibilities that they are asked to take on and in part to comparing themselves against their siblings who may be less independent.

Additionally, siblings can experience a great sense of pride in their brother's or sister's accomplishments. A sibling shared such a moment:

> I was at [work] when I found out that [my brother] got into college. And I cried. I'm going to cry now. I was just so tremendously proud of him. He's a person who perseveres really, I think, in spite of so many obstacles that, if it were me, it would really knock me off course.

In these moments siblings convey such a sense of true love for their brother or sister with ASD. One adult sibling shared, "I always so unconditionally loved him more than anyone else in my life, and I feel like more than other people [love their] siblings."

Resoundingly, siblings share that their brother or sister has made them a more patient, accepting person. "I think if anything, [my brother's ASD] has made me more open to accepting different people and sympathizing or empathizing with people who have issues themselves or issues in their families also," one sibling shared. Another sibling mused,

> I don't judge people as much as I feel like I could have if I hadn't grown up with someone with autism. Because I know how it feels when we walk down the street. My brother is doing something weird, and people are gawking at [us]. And I just don't want to put that on anyone else.

Adult siblings often share that this level of acceptance and compassion has positively impacted their work in their own profession. For example, one adult sibling noted,

> I work in family medicine. . . . I think that [having a brother with ASD] shaped me into a more caring person, accepting person, so that when I'm seeing patients and they're telling me about different things, I feel like I can relate to people a little bit easier on a level like that.

Another adult sibling shared how her own experience shifted her view of treatment in her own career:

> I always make sure to check in with families. . . . I think it's easy to get very focused on the child or whoever the identified person is. And I think that I always sort of have an eye for . . . how is everybody *else* doing? And how is everybody else dealing with this, and what do the interactions look like? I also definitely make sure to ask and check in about siblings. I don't know that that's a normal or typical thing for people.

Siblings are also able to share moments of joy that they have experienced with their siblings. "He's hilarious," a sibling stated of her brother.

> He remembers everything. So, if there were any happy moments in our memory, he can pinpoint the exact time and just bring you back to it. I think that's one of the best things about him: he can just bring you back to any happy moment. He is just so funny, that's the main thing I love about my brother.

Another sibling, when asked to describe a time her brother brought her joy, thought for a long time before giving her answer:

> It's just the little stuff we did together. . . . Sometimes I would push him on the swing and play with him for a while. When he's responsive, and when he goes along with [me] in that kind of way, it feels really good because it almost mimics that sibling relationship that I wish I had.

## PREPARING SIBLINGS FOR ADULTHOOD

Up to this point, I have primarily discussed the experiences of siblings with their brother or sister with ASD during childhood. As siblings age, however, many will have to consider the role they will play in their brother's or sister's lives as an adult. Parents and siblings must both consider that siblings will likely be the longest-living family members able to provide support for the individual on the autism spectrum and plan accordingly. Some siblings will not have to consider a guardianship role for a brother or sister who will be able to live and make decisions independently. Still, siblings have to consider how they will be a part of their brother's or sister's life as they age. One sister shared,

> I always want to be close by. I don't know exactly in terms of distance what that means. But I want to be able to get to him, and I want to be able to be there to help him. I think that he's starting to share a lot with me, and I see that our relationship will continue to grow. I think I'll continue to be a support system for him.

Other families will have to consider who will take guardianship of the individual with ASD when the parents are no longer present. In my experience, I have seen an enormous range in siblings' views of their life with their brother or sister in adulthood as they consider these options. I have met siblings who openly tell me that they want nothing to do with their brother or sister when they are adults, or that they cannot wait to move out of their parents' house and live on their own. These are siblings who have felt especially challenged growing up with a brother or sister with ASD. For some siblings, these plans may change over time as they grow into adulthood and their feelings toward their sibling shift. For instance, a teenage sibling shared her tempered view of caring for her brother as he ages:

> I don't want to assume a caretaker role or really be a guardian when my mom isn't there anymore. But I want to be there for him, and I want to help make decisions of some kind. I want to still be his sister, but I don't want to have him living with me or have the responsibility for his financial things or life needs. I want somebody else to be in charge of that, but I want to have some sort of say in what goes on, because he's still my brother.

Frequently, I have met siblings who have made plans to care for their brother or sister into adulthood regardless of whether their parents have set that expectation for them. An adult sibling shared, "I do know and recognize that at some point, [my parents] will be no more, and I'll be [my sister's] primary person. That's fine. I really wouldn't want it any other way." Considering guardianship of a sibling has a significant impact on siblings' view of their adulthood. They will have to shoulder the financial concerns of caring for someone on the autism spectrum in adulthood, but they will also have to consider where their brother or sister will live—with them or in a residential home—and how that will impact their own family life. An adult sister shared her view on caring for her younger brother as they age together:

> I just want him to be totally comfortable and happy all of the time. As much as I can, I'll do anything to make that happen. If I meet someone he has to love [my brother] a ridiculous amount. I'm expecting a lot. I'm bringing a lot to the table, and I'm expecting a lot. I'll never send him anywhere. It will always be the two of us.

The responsibility of caring for a brother or sister with ASD may be divided if multiple neurotypical siblings are available to help provide care in adulthood. Having other siblings who can help provide support for the sibling with ASD can reduce the impact of the care required from each sibling. A sibling laughed about her family's plans for caring for her sister with ASD in adulthood:

> We always halfway joke about this because technically it's written . . . that my older sister controls the money [for our sister's care] and I control [our sister with ASD]. So I get to inherit [our sister] and she gets to inherit the money.

Again, the presence of additional siblings in adulthood will provide a sounding board and a listening ear when needed as they grapple with decisions and situations that their peers will not understand.

Deciding when to have a conversation about the future can be difficult for families. Often, parents of younger children will avoid talking with siblings about the future, even if the future seems relatively predictable. As one mother pointed out,

I'm not going to tell him, "Someday when I die, you're probably going to be her primary caregiver." I'm not putting that on him at 12 [years of age]. I do say, "You're her big brother. I do expect you to always help," something more general.

One teenager, however, expressed a desire to talk more with her parents about what will happen as she and her neurotypical brother grow into adults with their brother with ASD:

The future, [my parents and I] don't talk about it very much. Some-times I wish we talked a little more about that, because I don't really know what's going to happen, how it's going to work with my [other] much older brother. I would talk to them; I don't think they would be uncomfortable talking to me about it. I guess it's weird for my parents to talk about it because it's their kid and you think that your kid is just going to grow up and be independent. But now there's someone who can't be.

As professionals work with families on planning for the transition to adulthood for the individual with ASD, they should encourage parents to initiate a conversation with their other children about the roles they might play as they grow older. The conversation should begin with open questions about the siblings' perspective on how they want to be involved, and highlight the importance of everyone caring for one another as siblings as they age. Teenage and adult siblings will likely then be able to participate in a meaningful conversation about guardianship and finances, and if and how they will be involved in those matters in adulthood.

## CLINICAL TAKE-AWAYS

Siblings' experiences with their brother or sister with ASD are unique, and they will encounter a broad range of emotions and responses to the effects ASD has on the relationship with their sibling and with their parents. Unfortunately, little can be predicted about how siblings will respond to the challenges that arise. In the face of this uncertainty, practitioners should be prepared to help parents learn to effectively respond to developing concerns for neurotypical siblings, and to help identify forms of sibling support such as linking them with sibling support groups and including them in their sibling's treatment. Recommendations for practitioners follow.

Practitioners should:

- Understand the progression of siblings' understanding of ASD, as the awareness of the symptoms and impact of ASD will change with age. This understanding can help practitioners guide parents in how to effectively talk with neurotypical siblings about their brother or sister with ASD.

- Encourage parents to talk with siblings about problem behavior their brother or sister exhibits and how siblings should respond when it occurs.

- Ask siblings for their input when working with the brother or sister with ASD, both how they feel about their brother or sister and their thoughts on specific behaviors or treatment plans. Asking for input will make siblings feel included and part of the treatment team.

- Identify ways to facilitate activities between siblings based on the skill level of the child with ASD and the interests of neurotypical siblings.

- Take cues from siblings on the extent to which they want to be integrated into their brother's or sister's treatment.

- Help parents identify times to connect with siblings, even if only for a few moments at a time. These opportunities will strengthen the parent-child bond and potentially help parents identify sibling concerns before they become problematic.

- Recognize the impact the diagnosis of ASD will have on siblings' relationships with their peers, and offer recommendations for local sibling support groups as well as other support options that may not require family commitment and travel.

- Facilitate conversations between parents and siblings about the siblings' role in caring for their brother or sister as he or she approaches adulthood.

# CHAPTER 5

# Integrating Extended Family in Care and Treatment

For many families, the extended family will play a considerable role as parents raise their children. When I conduct assessments for children with ASD, I am unsurprised to walk to the lobby to greet the family and find not only the child and the parents there but also grandparents and sometimes aunts and uncles. These relatives can be key players in the care and treatment of the child with ASD, so practitioners should be knowledgeable about their role in the family. This chapter describes how relationships among family members generally evolve as a new generation of children enters the mix, and how these relationships are affected when a child is diagnosed with ASD. I discuss the ways in which family members can provide much needed support to parents of children with ASD and offer suggestions throughout that practitioners should consider when working with this constellation of family members.

## DEFINING THE ROLES OF EXTENDED FAMILY MEMBERS

Historically, the function of a family has changed dramatically over the years. While family members were once a structure based on societal norms and laws, as gender roles and rights have shifted the family has become a unit not based primarily on lawful obligation but rather on companionship and love.

No members have experienced a greater shift in their role in the family than grandparents, who are often the first family members that come to mind when one thinks of extended family. The matriarchs and patriarchs of the family, these individuals hold an esteemed place. As life expectancies climb, grandparents now fill their familial role for many years longer than in the past. Often, they will have the opportunity to develop strong relationships with their grandchildren and may even watch their grandchildren grow to adulthood (Bengtson, 2001).

I recognize that in some families the relationship between grandparents and parents is strained—these relatives might even be estranged—and that the general statements I am about to make about these family members will not apply to all families. However, for many families, grandparents can be a great source of companionship and support for their adult children. Their years of life experience, including those spent raising their own children, place them in a unique position to offer advice and solidarity as their adult children face the challenges of adulthood and parenthood. Grown individuals who have lost their parents or who do not have parents capable of filling this caring role often mourn the absence of this important source of support in adulthood.

Grandparents also develop a unique relationship with their grandchildren that has benefits for both. Grandparents can derive considerable life meaning from spending time with their grandchildren and passing along their wisdom and family history to their youngest relatives (Hastings, 1997; Seligman, 1991). Time with their grandchildren provides them with the opportunity to "relive" their time as parents, practice old parenting skills, and engage in playful interactions that they would not experience otherwise. For grandparents, this time can be especially enjoyable and unmarked by the same level of stress that parenting can bring, because they do not hold the same parenting responsibilities as their adult children do. I have often heard that the best part of being a grandparent is reveling in the joy of young grandchildren but then being able to hand them back to their parents at the end of the day.

For grandchildren, grandparents can offer a special relationship different from that with other family members. When I was working on this chapter in a coffee shop one day, the door opened and a little boy, about 2 years old, walked in with his grandmother. His grandfather had been waiting for him, and when the little boy saw him his face lit up and he ran to him, recounting his morning—a trip to the library with his grandmother—with a combination of single-word and two-word phrases. The excitement he expressed upon seeing his grandfather was obvious, and listening to the banter between them reflected their fun, playful relationship. Grandparents can provide a source of considerable companionship and support for their grandchildren as they grow.

The time spent with these older family members can offer grandchildren another adult from which to gain knowledge and advice, love and care. Because the parents are not responsible for child-rearing in the way that parents are, the relationship can develop without the same concerns (sometimes much to parents' chagrin) for boundaries and discipline. Grandparents' positive relationships with grandchildren have been shown to have protective effects on grandchildren, especially those of at-risk children. Grandparents can help alleviate some of the stress that parents experience, which can considerably lessen the impact of parent stress on children (Hastings, 1997).

In addition to grandparents, aunts and uncles can also offer support to their adult brothers and sisters and their family. The level of support offered will largely depend on the quality of the relationship between the adult siblings. Brothers and sisters who have close bonds in adulthood can provide considerable support for one another and, if they live close, also offer tangible support such as childcare. Siblings who raise children together have the opportunity to share in the parenting experience as they care for their children and perhaps also their aging parents. As mentioned in Chapter 4, the sibling relationship is unique and can be a primary source of support in adulthood. And these members of the family can establish a special bond with their nieces and nephews. My own children look forward to visits with all of their aunts and uncles, remembering distinctly the excitement that each relationship brings based on the personality of the relatives: one aunt is very musical, an uncle is very playful, and yet another has creative ideas for activities. Special time with any of these relatives—grandparents, aunts, or uncles—can be highly valued by children.

## RECOGNIZING THE IMPACT OF ASD ON THE EXTENDED FAMILY

When a child in the family is diagnosed with ASD, the entire extended family dynamic will shift as everyone adjusts in their own way to the diagnosis. First and foremost, the direct dynamic between the grandparents and their grown children, the parents of the child with ASD, will be significantly impacted. For grandparents, the ASD diagnosis can have a particularly strong effect because it brings to the forefront not only their concern for their grandchild but also their concern for their own child. At all times, practitioners must recognize that the love and concern parents demonstrate for their child with ASD will be mirrored in grandparents' concern for their own grown child. Watching their adult child have to adapt to what can be a demanding parenting role, and considering how best to provide support to them, can be incredibly difficult and draining for grandparents. Although aunts and uncles may not have the same parenting role for their adult brother or sister, they may neverthe-less experience similar concern for both their sibling and the child with ASD.

Grandparents and other family members may feel powerless as they watch parents cope with the daily challenges that ASD can present. They may develop significant concerns about the well-being and development of the child over time but, because of their position in the family, have less impact on or information about the child's development than do the parents. Grandparents who want to be very involved may find it frustrating to be held at arm's length by their adult children and to have to wait to learn information about their child's progress second hand. As practitioners consider the family dynamics between parents and their family members, and deter-mine how best to include family members should they want to be involved, they should consider the impact of ASD on all relationships in the family, beginning with diagnosis.

Navigating the challenges of diagnosis. Diagnosis can be a significant period of difficulty for all relatives. Grandparents of individuals with disabilities often note many of the same emotions as parents when they first learn of their grandchild's diagnosis: shock, devastation, anger, and loss (Scherman, Gardner, Brown, & Schutter, 1995; Vadasy, Fewell, & Meyer, 1986). Just as parents have imagined their life with their child prior to diagnosis, grandparents may have imagined the role that they will play in their grandchild's life as he or she ages. They may think about the life lessons they had hoped to pass on to their grandchild, and the ways in which they would establish a close bond over time. However, the announcement of an ASD diagnosis—a diagnosis that may limit their ability to interact effectively and connect meaningfully with their grandchild—may cause grandparents to mourn the loss of this relationship.

Practioners must be aware of the impact of the ASD diagnosis on the family members. Grandparents, aunts, and uncles can be considerably affected by the diagnosis and may experience emotions of grief or loss similar to those experienced by parents. Extreme feelings may limit their ability to provide support to the parents and to be active participants in providing care for the child with ASD. Practitioners should understand that failure to provide support or care may be the sign not of a disinterested relative but, rather, of one who is potentially grieving and having a difficult time accepting the diagnosis and his or her new role in the child's life. Providing family members with referrals to sources of support for their own experiences, such as Internet resources, grandparent support groups, and therapists, may help address some of their struggle with emotions.

In some cases, grandparents and other relatives may be aware of and concerned about the symptoms of ASD long before the diagnosis is given. As parents themselves, grandparents may view their grandchild compared with their own child's development (or that of other grandchildren) and note delays in social skills and communication before parents. As discussed in Chapter 1, bringing these concerns to parents may sometimes be met with opposition: parents may not agree with the grandparents' assessment of their child's skills and may resist suggestions to seek evaluation. For grandparents who are concerned for the welfare of both their grandchild and their child, the period leading up to diagnosis can be particularly stressful and confusing and can lead to family conflict. However, the benefit of having grandparents work as advocates of diagnosis is that, when the diagnosis is made, they are prepared to be supportive of parents and understanding of the diagnosis because of their early suspicions.

On the other hand, a considerable number of grandparents will also experience denial leading up to and following their grandchild's diagnosis (Möslä & Ikonen-Möslä, 1985), which can lead to considerable conflict within the family. One mother recalled of her family,

> They were all in denial. Everyone thought I was crazy. Everybody said she was a late speaker, she was an only child. . . . It was this whole thing of I was overreacting. "It's not true," [they'd say.] "The doctor doesn't know the future."

This denial may emerge in part because the grandparents are unsure of how to cope with the challenges facing their grandchild and their adult child or how to manage their own sense of pain and loss. Additionally, often extended family does not see the child on a regular basis, so they may have missed some of the signs that parents may regularly see that indicate a diagnosis of ASD and think that the parents are overreacting to their child's behavior. "Stop borrowing trouble" was the phrase one mother said her father used when she talked to him about the possibility of her son's diagnosis.

Grandparents, for whom ASD can be a relatively new term, may struggle to understand what ASD is and how the diagnosis applies to their grandchild. These family members may instead attribute the grandchild's behavior to weaknesses in their child's parenting skills and assert that their own parenting skills are the answer to the problem. One mother recalled,

> When [my sons] were early diagnosed, my mother-in-law was convinced that if my sons spent a month with her, that she would be

able to get them to talk. "The doctors don't know what they are talking about," [she'd say]. My sister-in-law was convinced [the reason they behaved as they did] was because I let them watch too much *Teletubbies* and *Blue's Clues*. That was the reason they have the autism.

In a surprising number of interviews, parents reported that relatives offered corporal punishment as an effective means of changing the child's behavior. A mother recalled her mother-in-law's reaction to her child's behavior: "'I had five children,' [she said], 'and I never had a problem because I instilled discipline, and if they didn't do what I wanted, I beat them. If you just beat your kids more you wouldn't have these problems.'"

Parents are also up against biases against diagnosis and family concerns that the diagnosis will stigmatize the child. "Why do you need to keep attaching labels to these children?" one mother-in-law asked of a mother I interviewed. In past generations, appropriate services were not connected to diagnosis in the way they are today, and the importance of diagnosis may be poorly understood by relatives. A mother recalled the difficulty she had getting her mother-in-law to accept her son's diagnosis of ASD:

I think what she was having a problem with was the label; she didn't want to label him. For whatever reason, people don't like to label things. I sort of look at it as he is who he is, it doesn't really matter what we call it. The label gets him services that he needs.

Another additional problem is that, for some grandparents, acknowledging a diagnosis can highlight something that they may have missed in their own child's development. Parents who have symptoms similar to their child but were never diagnosed may bring up guilt or concern in grandparents that they missed the diagnosis in their own child-rearing and created a more difficult life for their child by not seeking services. Additionally, their own child's success in life may make it difficult for them to acknowledge the diagnosis in their grandchild. A mother acknowledged the similarities between her son and her husband and how it may impact her mother-in-law:

[My son is] very similar in a lot of ways to [my husband]—I saw that a lot at the time. I think that's what [my husband]'s mom was seeing as well, and partly why she was pushing back a little bit on accepting the diagnosis because it was, "Well, [your husband] is exactly this way and he turned out fine." Of course I agree—I married him. I agree that he turned out fine. But he will tell you that he had a lot of struggle socially when he was a kid, and so my big thing was I want to make things easier and smoother for [my son] if we can.

For a positive spin, she continued to discuss how the similarity between parent and child can also help the grandparent interact effectively with the grandchild:

I think [my mother-in-law] is really good with [my son], and I think she gets how he's different, because I think he's a lot like [my husband] was when he was a kid, so she knows how to deal with him.

Regardless of the source, the denial that grandparents and other family members may experience in response to a child's diagnosis can be especially difficult for parents of children with ASD. As discussed, social support can help reduce the stress experienced by mothers and fathers of children with ASD, and when their parents, brothers, or sisters do not agree with the diagnosis, parents may lose a substantial form of support in their lives, contributing to their stress. Practitioners may be able to help parents navigate the denial of their family members in a number of different ways. Practitioners can be extremely valuable in validating parents' concerns. In the face of so much opposition from family, parents will feel relieved to hear that someone sees what they see and supports their view of their child's development. Practitioners can also provide parents with recommendations for resources about ASD that they can share with family members to help them better understand the parents' perspective.

Practitioners can also extend invitations to family members to participate in assessment and treatment sessions. This is especially beneficial in families of diverse backgrounds, as discussed in Chapter 6. Family members may be more likely to listen to the opinions of a professional than those of the parent. The professional would have the opportunity to articulate the signs and symptoms of ASD and explain how they manifest in the family's child. A discussion of the importance of a diagnosis with regard to accessing services may help family members see the diagnosis as a means to an end and take the emphasis off of any stigma they perceive with the assignment of a diagnosis.

Fortunately, many relatives are able to overcome these initial feelings of denial (Möslä and Ikonen-Möslä, 1985) and become powerful sources of support for the parents. A mother recalled,

> My mother-in-law, before the diagnosis, was pretty sure we were bad parents because she saw things that didn't have the name to go with it. But from the moment of the diagnosis, they were very supportive, and up to this day they are very complimentary about how well he is doing and our parenting skills that help bring him along.

Grandparents and other family members who are supportive can also help validate the concerns that parents have about their child's development and open lines of communication between family members. This connection can offer considerable support for the parents. A mother shared,

> I think since [my son's] diagnosis he's gone through more periods where it's been more obvious to [my parents] that there is something a little bit different in him than other kids. That was sort of gratifying to me to see too. Again, "It's not just me, I'm not making this up. You see it too, right?" My mom is always coming home with, "I've read this article about something" or "I found this resource that might help you." They just get who he is, and they don't try to make him a typical 4-year-old.

Moving family toward adaptation. After the period of diagnosis, all nuclear and extended members must begin to adapt to the challenges and joys of raising a child with ASD. The interactions between family members as the child grows will be a source of considerable support, but also of potential stress, for parents of individuals on the spectrum. Even following diagnosis, family members may have considerably different views of the child with ASD and the ways in which ASD impacts the family. Family members may not fully appreciate the ways in which ASD impacts the nuclear family's life, because often they are not living with the family. For example, a study by Harris, Handleman, and Palmer (1985) asked grandparents about their views of the impact of ASD on the nuclear family. Notably, none of the grandparents was living with the family, and they did not have as many responsibilities for the child with ASD as did the parents. When asked whether they agreed with the statement that "things have gotten worse" in the family since their grandchild with ASD was born, maternal grandmothers were likely to respond more positively than the child's mother. That is, they were less likely to indicate that the ASD diagnosis had a negative impact on the nuclear family. Likely, grandparents do not have a full appreciation for the scope of impact of the ASD diagnosis on the family's life.

A mother recalled the months following her son's diagnosis: "I was very isolated. I don't think [my family] meant it meanly; I don't think they understood, and I don't think it was priority, maybe because they didn't understand how profoundly it impacted my life every day." One mother I spoke with bemoaned her parents' lack of understanding of how ASD impacts the family's everyday life:

> [My parents] didn't understand how schedule oriented [my daughter] was. She still is to this day. Don't come over unless you're on a schedule. No surprise visits. We don't do surprise visits; we need to put you in the schedule.

Because the parents do not live with their granddaughter, they likely do not appreciate the significant impact that changes in schedule can have for her and, transitively, for her parents. Seeming obliviousness to these parental concerns can indicate a less than full appreciation for the pervasive impact ASD can have on family life.

Family members may also have different views of the child's

capability, which can work both for and against the parents. Research indicates that although mothers and maternal grand-mothers can often agree in their view of the child's capabilities, responses between fathers and paternal grandparents are often more discrepant. For example, paternal grandparents can either over- or underestimate their grandchild's skills compared with fathers (Glasberg & Harris, 1997). Again, discrepancies such as these can create conflict among family members when expectations are placed on the family that they are not capable of meeting. As one mother shared,

> We also have a problem because sometimes we wanted to do stuff with other people, and they are not as accommodating. We wind up not going, and it looks like we chose not to go, but really we couldn't go because there were all these factors that needed to be in place for us to go on vacation with them. We couldn't [get them in place], and they didn't want to bend a little bit, so we couldn't do it.

When family members have expectations that are unrealistic, parents can be placed in an awkward position of having to adapt to these expectations or explain that the expectations are unrealistic.

The impact of child behavior on family interactions can also be stressful for parents and impact the relationships with extended family members. A mother remembers,

> I got an invitation a few years ago for a wedding on my husband's side of the family. [My daughter] was not invited to the wedding. ... [The invitation] said "no children," but don't forget that we have other children in the family that are older than [my daughter], but their children were invited. I wasn't going to bring her anyway. ... I'm not out to ruin someone's wedding. I know what my child does.

This mother felt particularly hurt that her child was not invited to the wedding as others were and that she was not allowed to make the decision for her family not to have her daughter attend. Moves such as this within a family can strain relationships and cause the parents to feel unwelcome and untrusted.

The occurrence of problem behavior can be especially problematic when talking about interactions between the child with ASD and his or her cousins; interactions between these youngest family members can create distance between their sibling parents. A mother shared how her own child's problem behavior impacted her relationship with her siblings' families. "Nowadays [my son] is much better, but when he was little [my siblings] did not want to spend too much time with him because [his behavior] was upsetting to their kids."

When appropriate, families can benefit from professionals who provide the parents with tools on how to communicate more effectively with family members. From my experience, in their child's treatment parents often discuss the ways in which their own implementation of strategies can be interrupted by grandparents, or how their child can be "set off" by the insensitivity of family members at family gatherings. Providing these parents with steps for how to communicate effectively with these family members could help improve their relationships with other family members, and potentially improve the child's behavior with extended family members. A mother remembered the ongoing difficulty she had with family members and how her clinician helped her manage the conflict:

When [the family] did get together at family outings, events, somebody would always do or say something to instigate one of the boys having a meltdown. And then it was my fault. [Our therapist] got to one point where she was right; I look back and I'm so thankful for her. She said, "You need to stop going. Stop taking them. Tell [your relatives] that you will not bring them if [relatives] can't behave themselves. Tell them what the rules are, and tell them you don't expect them to give the boys special treatment, but you also don't expect them to instigate the boys." Once I put my foot down, things changed, but it took me a while to get to that point. We still have moments where my sister-in-law will say, "Well, I didn't do that with my kid," and I'm like, "Okay, well you didn't do it with your kid but these are mine."

## ESTABLISHING SUPPORT AMONG FAMILY MEMBERS

The landscape of the extended family has changed over time. Years ago, extended families often settled near one another, and children were raised communally by parents, grandparents, aunts, and uncles. For parents, these extended family members were a source of support and friendship as they raised their children. This family dynamic has changed considerably over time. Now families are spread across the country and often across continents. It is not uncommon for a person who lives in Virginia to have a brother in Oregon, a sister in Spain, and parents living in New England. Thus, the family support that was once ever present is now left to phone calls, video conferencing, and visits.

For families who live long distance, the primary form of support that they may offer is emotional; they can offer a listening ear to the parents so that they may share their daily struggles parenting a child with ASD, and also share their joy at the accomplishments the child has made. A mother shared the emotional support her parents provide: "They're constantly, when they can, saying, 'Wow, I can't believe how she's doing X now, that's so great. I can't believe how wonderfully she's doing.' So they will be supportive—they're all supportive."

The impact of extended family's emotional support can vary depending on whether they can demonstrate understanding of the parents' experiences. As indicated above, some family members may be out of touch with the impact of ASD on the family. Yet others can be incredibly empathic and offer support and information to the parents as they navigate new waters with their child. A mother recalled the support her mother gave her after her twin sons were diagnosed with ASD:

> My mom went out and she grabbed every book she could on anything that had to do with ASD. She read it and at first she was like, "You have to read this, you have to read this." I'm like, "Mom, I don't have time." [She'd say,] "I'll read it and I'll tell you all about it."

Grandparents and other family members who work to understand ASD can provide significant support to parents as they learn to cope with their child's diagnosis and their own response to the diagnosis.

In addition to emotional support, family members can also provide practical support (Hastings, 1997). For example, a family who lives long distance may be able to provide financial assistance to the parents of a child with ASD, which can be immensely helpful in alleviating the stresses associated with the climbing costs of caring for a child with ASD. Family members who live close by can provide additional practical support on a regular basis, like that shared within families that do not have a child with ASD. Running errands for the family, helping with housekeeping responsibilities, and childcare may be forms of support that grandparents and other relatives will take on when young children come into the family. In my own life, I am incredibly fortunate to have my in-laws live nearby; they will pick up milk for us when we run out, clean dishes when we fall horribly behind, and babysit our children when we do not have childcare. In a busy household, these additional sets of hands are immensely helpful and appreciated.

When a family has a child with ASD, this additional support can be especially meaningful. For parents who have additional childcare responsibilities, different from those experienced by other families, falling behind in housekeeping and other responsibilities may happen frequently. Extra help from family members can have an incredible impact on the stress experienced by these parents.

Local family members can also take a significant role in the care of the child with ASD. Because of the scope of symptoms exhibited by individuals with ASD, finding caretakers for them can prove to be especially challenging. Even if a parent is able to find caregivers willing to care for their child, *trusting* the caregiver is another matter altogether. For some parents, family members are ideal babysitters. A mother recalled, "My husband is actually the oldest of four, and his youngest sibling is 14 years younger so she was our best babysitter, and continues to be." Family members can provide considerable respite to overtaxed parents of a child with ASD, significantly reducing parent stress, as described by one mother:

At the time, my mom was still alive and so she would come over and help watch one kid while I was working with the other kid. I really needed assistance. I was completely exhausted. I was getting absolutely no sleep. I had this high-energy kid all day. So having a little bit of respite with having a relative come by and let me sleep for half an hour, or take one kid while I did something with the other kid was really helpful.

In some cases, family members may even be able to provide lengthy periods of childcare to give parents a significant break from their parenting responsibilities. A mother shared,

> [My niece] came and watched our boys, and we went [away] for my birthday. My husband splurged and took me on a cruise, and I had never been on a cruise in my life. He hired his niece to come and watch the boys so that we could do this. She came and was like, . . . "Oh, they are so wonderful, I would watch them anytime." I am blessed, then.

For some families, however, the ability of family members to help care for their children is limited at best. Especially for aging grandparents, the prospect of caring for children on the autism spectrum, especially those with challenging behavior, can prove to be difficult. Parents sometimes report significant involvement by grandparents when their child was younger, which diminishes over time as they feel less capable of care. "We both had both of our parents living at the time," a mother recalled. "They were accepting of her as she got older, and as they got older it got harder for them to take care of her." Another parent compared the support she received from her parents with what she sees provided to her peers:

> I think both sets of parents are a little fearful of taking [my daughter] on for any extended period of time because they're not quite sure what to expect, understandably. They've each probably had her for a night, maybe. I know many parents by this point, grandparents have had their kids for full weekends or a whole week or something special like that.

One additional point that should be added here, in terms of the impact that grandparents can have on parents' coping, is that significant challenges can arise when a parent is caring not only for the child with ASD but also for aging parents. As grandparents age, they will likely require an increasing level of care. Parents will take on additional responsibilities of managing their own parents' health care—home health aides, medication, finances—adding considerable burden to their already full plates. Even if parents do not live locally to their own parents, they may need to be involved by contacting agencies and health care organizations long distance, and they may feel additional stress because they are not able to visit their parents or contact caregivers easily. Practitioners should be aware if parents are caring not only for their own children but also for their aging family, as the additional burden may impact the parents' ability to work effectively with the practitioner and follow through on recommendations in the home.

## INCLUDING FAMILY MEMBERS IN TREATMENT

If a grandparent, aunt, or uncle does provide a significant caregiving role for the child with ASD, the practitioner must be sure to inquire about the arrangement to know how and when to incorporate that person into the child's treatment. Many grandparents eagerly jump into the role of treatment provider with their grandchild. As one mother remarked, "[My father] tried his best to understand. He'd say to me, 'I don't know what to do, but if you tell me what to do, I'll do it.'" Despite best intentions, however, I have worked with a number of families who consistently cite their family members' interactions with their child as a primary source of stress. No matter the parents' best efforts following through on treatment recommendations, they can be thwarted by well-intentioned grandparents who respond differently to the child with ASD.

As most professionals know, when working with individuals on the autism spectrum, experts in the field emphasize the importance of providing treatment consistently across settings to maximize appropriate responses and minimize problem behavior. For example, imagine you are treating a young boy with ASD who hits and kicks others when he is told he cannot have a favorite snack or toy. To reduce that behavior, a practitioner might recommend that caregivers at home and at school consistently minimize the extent to which he gets access to these items when he engages in problem behavior. Instead, the practitioner may help parents teach the child how to ask appropriately for them. Even if parents follow through consistently and work diligently with the child to increase his requests, a grandmother's visit may be the undoing when she hands over the favorite items as soon as the child hits her. The grandparent's behavior creates an inconsistent response to problem behavior in the home setting that could make the behavior more difficult to decrease in the future.

The reason behind the inconsistency across relatives is not difficult to understand. Grandparents especially are often viewed as doting relatives, and as such they may be less likely to implement what could be perceived as strict parental rules. Imagine those grandparents who let their grandchildren stay up late at night and bend the rules. These could be the same grandparents who have a difficult time imposing limits on their grandchild. One mother expressed how frustrating she found it when her parents challenged her implementation of an effective behavior plan when her daughter engaged in problem behavior: "When [I'm] running a behavior plan in the home, and I go see my parents, [they say] 'But it's okay.' [I say] 'No mom, it's not okay, these are the rules. We have rules. It's not okay.'"

Additionally, many relatives may feel unprepared or unable to deal with the consequences of the tantrum or other problem behavior that might ensue if they deny access to a preferred item. A grandparent who denies his grandchild a cookie following one instance of hitting may soon find the child in a full-blown tantrum. While the child's parents may be trained and physically able to manage this tantrum, a grandparent may be less capable and so more likely to give in to the behavior to reduce any further escalation.

If other family members are involved in the treatment of the child with ASD, professionals should take care that they are provided with specific training on how to provide treatment. Although some parents are capable of training other members of the family on the treatment to be provided, in some cases family members may be more likely to follow through on recommendations provided directly by the practitioner. I have invited extended family members into treatment sessions to share with them the rationale for the treatment, as well as the proposed recommendations. Providing the rationale can often be very important; although parents will likely become well versed in the treatment for their child with ASD, relatives are often a bit distanced and might not have a thorough understanding of ASD or the ways in which behavior—either adaptive or problematic—can be addressed. Providing the rationale firsthand and providing concrete real-life examples related to the child and to the relatives themselves can be helpful in getting buy-in from these family members.

Additionally, training on implementing procedures should be provided directly to the family members whenever possible. This is especially important when a practitioner is recommending a treatment approach that might not be feasible for an aging grandparent; the practitioner will quickly be able to recognize this limitation and adjust the treatment plan accordingly, especially if the grandparent is expected to provide considerable care for the child with ASD. Follow-up with specific family members will be immensely helpful; although a parent's report of how treatment is implemented by other family members can be helpful, observing firsthand implementation will provide the practitioner with the best information about what is going well and what needs to be improved.

## CONSIDERING EXTENDED FAMILY RAISING CHILDREN WITH ASD

Another consideration for professional is the family in which the child with ASD, and possibly his or her siblings, is being raised by grandparents, aunts, or uncles. When working in an outpatient clinic in an urban center, I learned to make no assumptions about the relation between the child and the caregiver when first meeting them. Though one might assume that the mother or father might bring the child to the appointments, often I found that I was interacting instead with the child's maternal grandmother or paternal aunt. For various reasons, extended family members may have to take on the caregiving role for the child with ASD. The challenges that arise in these situations are not dissimilar from those discussed above. For example, aging grandparents may have physical concerns that prevent them from being able to implement treatment in the way in which the professional would recommend, and treatments should be adapted with these concerns in mind. Additionally, grandparents may have significant emotional concerns not only about their child with ASD but also about the welfare of their grown child, who may have health or financial issues that make him or her unable to care for the child with ASD.

Additionally, I have discussed how parents may experience a feeling of loss for their plans for their own future as they watch their peers transition to a period of their lives when their children become more independent. Similarly, grandparents, aunts, and uncles may experience the same feeling of loss as they recognize their inability to pursue their own future plans, especially as they reach the age of retirement. Depending on the family situation, feelings of resentment toward the parents may emerge as the extended family member expends considerable effort caring for the child in the parents' absence. When working with family members who are caring directly for the child with ASD, practitioners should carefully assess their emotions about the role they have taken on in the child's life and their emotional and physical ability to work with the practitioner and implement treatment successfully. The recommendations provided within this book will benefit extended family caregivers as much as parents, and the practitioner should not hesitate to apply these recommendations to these unique family constellations.

## CLINICAL TAKE-AWAYS

Although parents note that extended family can pose significant challenges in the diagnosis and care of their child with ASD, they can be unbelievable sources of support when their views of the child are aligned with those of the parents. Practitioners can play a role in facilitating effective communication between family members and including extended family members in treatment to ensure coordinated efforts by parents, grandparents, aunts, and uncles. Recommendations for practitioners are as follows.

Practitioners should:

- Value extended family members as important sources of support for parents of individuals with ASD, and understand that in many cases extended family members will be vital members of the team of caregivers with whom the practitioner should work.

- Understand the impact of the child's diagnosis of ASD on extended family members, recognizing that responses to diagnosis will be similar to those experienced by parents. Recognize that unengaged extended family members may be struggling with accepting the child's diagnosis as well as the impact of ASD on the child's parents.

- Validate parents' concerns about their child at the time of diagnosis, especially when parents are experiencing opposition to the diagnosis from family members. Offer to meet with dissenting family members to explain the diagnosis, its importance, and its impact on the child.

- Facilitate communication between members, asking parents to advocate for themselves and their child in the face of family members who appear unsupportive or unaware of the impact of ASD on the various dimensions of the family's life.

- Provide referrals for sources of support for family members, such as Internet resources, support groups, and therapists.

- Conduct training on how to effectively work with the child with ASD for all family members who serve as the child's significant caregivers. Invite family members to treatment sessions to promote their understanding of and motivation to support treatment for the child.

- Recognize the burden of extended family members caring for the child with ASD, and use the strategies provided in this book with these caregivers, with attention to any potential limitations they may encounter based on age and physical ability.

# CHAPTER 6

# Understanding a Family's Culture

As the prevalence of ASD in the United States grows, so does the country's diversity. According to the census (Mather, Pollard, & Jacobsen, 2011), approximately one in three persons in the United States now self-identifies as a member of a minority group. The diverse makeup of our population means that any practitioner in the field of ASD treatment will interact with families of different backgrounds and cultures. When working with these families in a therapeutic setting, it is imperative that professionals consider how a family's culture—their beliefs, values, religion, rituals, and traditions—can impact their view of the child's diagnosis. A family's culture will also impact the family members who will participate in treatment and their opinions of the practitioner and of how treatment should be delivered. A therapist who does not attend to these beliefs and views can quickly come in conflict with the family's values, making little headway in treatment. This chapter illustrates how culture can impact diagnosis and treatment of ASD so that therapists will be informed and adjust their own practices to be sensitive to a family's cultural values.

## APPRECIATING THE IMPACT OF CULTURE ON DIAGNOSIS

Decades ago, prominent scholars in the field believed that ASD was found only among middle- to upper-class White individuals (Bettelheim, 1967; Kanner, 1949). Of course, this misconception has since been dispelled, and we now know that ASD does not discriminate: the prevalence of ASD is the same across cultural groups (e.g., Fombonne, 2003). However, just because the prevalence rate of ASD does not differ across groups does not mean that ASD is diagnosed at similar rates among them. In some cases, individuals within certain groups might be overdiagnosed or underdiagnosed with ASD.

Unfortunately, researchers have consistently found that children of color, including African American, Hispanic, and Asian children, are less likely to receive an early diagnosis than are White children (Mandell, Listerud, Levy, & Pinto-Martin, 2002; Mandell et al., 2009). For example, Mandell et al. (2002) found that Black children were diagnosed, on average, 1.5 years later than White children. Further, Black children were 2.5 times less likely to be diagnosed with ASD during their first mental health specialty visit than were White children and more likely to receive a diagnosis of attention-deficit/ hyperactivity disorder, adjustment disorder, and conduct disorder prior to the eventual diagnosis of ASD (Mandell, Ittenbach, Levy, & Pinto-Martin, 2007). While the prevalence rate of ASD diagnosis has increased across all groups over time, overall, Black, Hispanic/ Latino, Asian, and Native American individuals are more likely to be underdiagnosed with ASD, while White individuals are more commonly diagnosed at a level proportionate to the prevalence rate (Mandell et al., 2009; Tincani, Travers, & Boutot, 2009; Travers, Tincani, & Krezmien, 2011).

The impact of the delay in diagnosis for children of color cannot be overstated. Such a delay also delays early intervention services for the child, and we know that early intervention can be critically important in the acquisition of skills in young children. For older children, a delay in diagnosis means that they have missed out on years of specialized treatment for ASD that could help improve their communication and social skills and reduce problem behavior. These are also years that parents may have spent wondering what is wrong with their child and why the child is not behaving like other children the same age. As discussed in Chapter 1, for parents who have received multiple incorrect diagnoses before they receive a diagnosis of ASD for their child, the stress and confusion that they experience can be overwhelming. Practitioners working with families of color must recognize that their road to diagnosis may have been challenging and less straightforward than that of other families, which may increase their level of stress and the pressure they feel to have effective services in place quickly. Further, practitioners should recognize the barriers to diagnosis for families of color, which are detailed below, and work to overcome these barriers in their own practice to minimize delay of services for these vulnerable children.

Recognizing signs of ASD. The reasons behind delay to diagnosis and general underdiagnosis of children of color are many. First, some families may be unfamiliar with the signs and symptoms of ASD and may have few opportunities to compare their child's development with that of other children. For example, families in under-resourced areas may not have access to high-quality schools (Evans, 2004) where educational professionals can help assess their child through comparison with other children. As mentioned in Chapter 1, teachers can often be the first people to flag signs of ASD for a parent. Additionally, these families may have less access to social situations (e.g., playgrounds, play dates, children's events) because of the physical constraints of their neighborhood (Evans, 2004). As a result, the parents may have little basis for comparison, especially if their child is their first.

However, as noted in Chapter 1, some parents who do notice some symptoms of ASD may not identify them as problematic, based on cultural expectations of child development. For example, in Asian cultures, behaviors such as pointing with an index finger are not as important as in White families, and family members may see behaviors such as direct eye contact with adults as disrespectful (Zhang, Wheeler, & Richey, 2006). Some groups may believe that the symptoms they observe will be outgrown over time, or that they can be corrected with different parenting strategies. In a study by Burkett, Morris, Manning-Courtney, Anthony, and Shambley-Ebron, one parent noted, "The Black community does not believe that autism happens in Black families. And that the only problem with these children is a lack of being able to deal with their behaviors" (2015, p. 3249). This same parent continued on to refer to another concern among families: that the diagnosis of a disability carries significant stigma for many members of certain groups. "Black mothers do not want to face that their child may have autism; they hide from it and do not want to accept why it happens and what it is" (pp. 3249–3250).

As is expected of many health professionals, practitioners working in the area of child development should be prepared to provide all families with information on the signs of ASD, as well as referrals for diagnosis, should concerns arise, and be sensitive to the potential for culture-based resistance and misunderstandings. Further, stressing the importance of a diagnosis as a means to access appropriate services for the child may help some families overcome concerns about the stigma of the diagnosis. Resources for diagnostic information for families of diverse backgrounds are provided in the Resources section of this book.

Working with diagnostic professionals. Parents who cannot rely on their own knowledge or social comparison to identify symptoms will need to rely on the advice of medical professionals for a diagnosis of ASD. However, families of color experience clearly documented disparities in health services. For instance, research indicates that Hispanic/Latino, Black, and Asian families are less likely to access youth mental health services than are White families (Gudino, Lau, Yeh, McCabe, & Hough, 2009), and African American children see a primary care physician less frequently than do White children (Kass & Weinick, 1999, cited in Mandell & Novak, 2005). In some cases, this underutilization of medical services may be due to difficulties in access due to limited transportation and monetary resources. In other cases it can be related to reluctance to engage with the medical system. Even if parents are concerned about their child's diagnosis, they may be dissuaded by other members of the family, such as the spouse or grandparents. They may discourage parents from seeking a diagnosis because of distrust of the medical/health professions, because they do not believe that anything is wrong with the child, or a combination of the two. Without a regular check-in with health professionals, families who are unaware of the symptoms of ASD will not be alerted to them.

The prevalence of non-ASD diagnoses among children of color

suggests that practitioners may hold unconscious biases that result in less frequent ASD diagnoses for individuals of specific groups. Some families may not know enough about the symptoms of ASD to question their doctor's diagnosis. Still others, such as those in Hispanic/Latino and Asian cultures, may hesitate to question the diagnosis or the medical provider's choice not to screen the child for ASD because of cultural expectations for how doctors should be treated (e.g., Jegatheesan, 2009; Rogers-Adkinson, Ochoa, & Delgado, 2003). For example, an Asian mother in a study by Jegatheesan (2009) stated,

> Medical professionals are highly esteemed and we are not supposed to question. Also, we are trying to be respectful, so we may not even ask them questions because in the Asian culture when we ask questions, often it is considered that we are challenging them. . . . That Asians being silent does not mean we are agreeing with you. Often when we Asians are silent, we are really disagreeing with you, but we are too polite to say it. (p. 129)

Additionally, families of children whose primary language is not English may be told by their physician that any language delay is because the child is bilingual and that the child does not need to be assessed for ASD. Families also may be told this by relatives and friends and so might not seek a diagnosis at all. The same mother above shared,

> I was saying [to the doctors], you know, this child, she is not doing this and that. There are quite a few things I am concerned about. They said that she looks fine and healthy. Then they said that we are a bilingual family and that many children of bilingual families tend to be late talkers. That was pretty much the explanation they gave us. And another thing, this came from three different doctors. They said I am just a typical Asian mom who is overanxious, over involved with my child, who really wants to push my child. . . . They said they have seen so many Asian moms. They push their kids so much. So if you relax then your daughter will start

talking. . . . They are impatient, dismissive and pretty condescending. I often thought they dismissed me because I am a minority. . . . I felt horrible. Maybe I am doing a disservice to my child by being a minority. (Jegatheesan, 2009, p. 130)

Professionals may also hold biases based on socioeconomic status (SES). A diagnosis of ASD is more common among individuals of higher SES (Durkin et al., 2010), and one study found that doctors are more likely to provide a family with a diagnosis of ASD when the family has a higher SES (Cuccaro et al., 1996). In some cases, professionals may be suspicious of the family's motivation for seeking a diagnosis when they are of lower SES and may believe, for example, that the family is pursuing the diagnosis to gain additional monetary assistance for their family.

Even if a professional does screen for signs of ASD, the standardized tools that are used to definitively diagnose ASD may not be well fitted to the cultural background of the family. For example, the ADOS-2 has been subject to analysis of its validity and reliability with individuals from various backgrounds (e.g., Overton, Fielding, & de Alba, 2008). However, researchers point out that little guidance is provided for professionals on how to administer and interpret the ADOS-2, or other diagnostic tools, to account for differences in cultural and language background (Tincani et al., 2009).

Diagnostic professionals should recognize the underestimation of ASD among children of diverse cultural backgrounds and carefully consider their own diagnostic process and the role in which their own cultural biases may affect their conclusions. Without a doubt, children of families of diverse cultures should be screened and offered diagnostic evaluations with the same regularity of any other families, regardless of their cultural or language background. Professionals should be aware of their own possible inclination toward a diagnosis of conduct disorder, adjustment disorder, or attention-deficit/hyperactivity disorder for children of color and consider the symptoms (e.g., ritualistic behavior, undeveloped social skills) that may help differentially diagnose ASD.

## INCREASING ACCESS TO SERVICES

Once a child receives a diagnosis of ASD, many of the same cultural challenges can arise when parents are seeking treatment for
their child. Again, treatment may be difficult to access for families
from disadvantaged communities. First, the quality of programming
within their school system may be poor. I vividly remember working with individuals with ASD in inner-city public schools and being
completely dismayed and discouraged at the quality of the services
available for the children. One child I worked with was a highly
engaging 9-year-old girl with ASD. She had tremendous potential for
improvement in social and academic areas, but her mother reported
that her school was not addressing concerns. When I visited the
classroom, I was taken aback by the services provided. While she
had a one-to-one aide, that aide had no training in working with
children with ASD, let alone in providing effective services. Without
effective supports in class, the student, who was perfectly behaved
during her sessions in our clinic, wreaked havoc in the classroom:
climbing on tables, hitting and kicking the staff, and running out
of the classroom. She was strong, and the only way that the aide
could control her behavior was physically. Over time I continued to
work with this aide to provide training in how to effectively address
her needs, but progress was sidelined by the aide's frequent absence.
This case really opened my eyes to the limited services that students
with ASD might receive in underfunded schools.

Unfortunately, many families are not aware of the deficiencies in
their school system because they do not know what to look for in a
quality program for their child. Because these parents are not professionals in the area of ASD treatment, they do not know how to
measure the effectiveness of their child's program. Again, they may
defer to people of authority within the school system who assure
them that their child is receiving the best care possible. Compared
with the education and services that their child would receive in
their country of origin, many parents may believe that the services
that their child is getting are far superior. As one mother shared in

Jegatheesan's study, "U.S. is children's heaven. It would be hopeless if we were in Vietnam. We are lucky to be here. Children are priority in U.S." (2009, p. 130). However, in conversations with parents, professionals may find that the family does not even know what an Individualized Education Program (IEP) or Individualized Family Service Plan (IFSP) is (Jegatheesan, 2009) or how it applies to their child. Most important, these families may have no idea of their educational rights and may not know that they can request assessments and accommodations for their child that would improve the child's progress in the school setting.

Practitioners should be prepared, when working with families of diverse cultures, to help inform them of their rights within the educational system as it pertains to their child, and also to help facilitate meaningful, productive dialogue between the school and the family to improve the services the child receives in that setting. Information on how to provide parents with the sense of efficacy they need to effectively advocate for their child in the schools is included in Chapter 9.

Families may also have difficulty accessing additional services outside of their school system. Limited transportation may preclude some families from traveling to clinics that provide high-quality services. When recommending services to families, professionals should consider the transportation needs of the family and suggest local services that can be easily accessed by public transportation or for which transportation can be easily arranged. Some families may be eligible for transportation services provided by Medicaid. Families may also be hesitant to participate in services that occur in locations they are not familiar with or that they distrust, such as universities and hospitals. In these cases, providing services in comfortable locations, such as at a local church or school, may help set parents at ease (Harris, 1996).

Even with appropriate resources, some families may hesitate to contact professionals about services because of stigmas associated with receiving medical and mental health care. Some parents, or their spouse or extended family, may be discouraged from seeking care from professionals because culturally it is not a highly accepted approach. If a family does seek services from a professional, they may not be forthcoming about the details of their family or their concerns for their child. Different cultures have different ideas about sharing private family information with strangers, especially if they fear that the information shared in therapy will be passed on to other members of their community and bring shame to them (Jegatheesan, 2009). As a result, the treating professional may not receive all of the pertinent information needed to prescribe an effective treatment.

Other families may distrust medical and other health professionals, or have concerns about how their child will be treated based on their ethnicity or religious or cultural beliefs. For example, some families may be concerned that their child will be more likely to be abused by care staff. As one parent in Burkett et al.'s (2015) study shared,

> [In the White community] it's an automatic . . . assumption that "I will be received well no matter what." But that's not the case . . . for most people of color. . . . [People] see color first and therefore the treatment follows that color. (p. 3248)

Concern about the treatment of their child may prevent some parents from seeking services for their child outside of the home or their local school. Professionals should be aware of the concern that families may have about the treatment of the family and their child, and speak with the family explicitly about the services that they plan to provide.

Further, practices should recognize the perceptions families have of specific professionals and attempt to mitigate negative preconceptions. For example, some practices employ social workers who help coordinate Medicaid or other funding for families, but some families may harbor an inherent distrust for social workers based on their traditional roles within society (e.g., evaluating families, removing children from homes). Practitioners can improve the effectiveness of families' relationships with social workers, and many other professionals, by directly explaining the role social workers play within the context of the practice. Additionally, especially when the child is young, all practitioners should be highly transparent and invite families into sessions with the child so that they can observe the practitioner and become more familiar and trusting of the treatment approaches used.

Another important barrier to recognize in providing services to families of diverse cultural backgrounds is the possibility of a language barrier. In families in which the parents are not fluent in English, considerable difficulty can arise in communicating with professionals. This difficulty may arise early on, following diagnosis, when professionals recommend the services that the child should receive. Parents may not understand what the professional is recommending and may not be able to remember what the professional said later. As a mother shared in Jegatheesan's (2009) study,

> We are Asians. English is our second language. We couldn't remember everything the doctors told us. They gave too much information at once and overwhelmed us. We couldn't absorb everything that they provided us and we forgot some or all of it when we came home. For example, I forgot some medical terms right away after I was told. I couldn't look up in the dictionary because I forgot how they were pronounced. (p. 127)

Unfortunately, families in this situation may not convey to the professional that they do not understand, out of shame and embarrassment (Jegatheesan, 2009). A strategy that may be useful for families, even those who are English speaking, is to ask families to repeat back the most important recommendations so that practitioners have the opportunity to clarify any misunderstandings.

Even professionals who provide written information to parents about ASD and treatment may be doing the family a disservice: the family may not be able to read and digest the information any better than if the doctor had explained it in the office. Further, parents who do not speak English will likely be unable to follow up on treatment recommendations because contacting other services over the phone will be limited by the parents' ability to converse, and progress in treatment can be made difficult by the practitioner's inability to effectively communicate with the parent.

The use of interpreters can be an effective tool in treatment, if the interpreter is well trained. Common complaints of parents are that the interpreter either does not have the language skills to fluently facilitate conversation or does not understand ASD and treatment well enough to effectively communicate the professional's recommendations to the parent. The most effective interpreter with whom I have worked was the adult brother of a child with ASD, who translated for his mother. The use of a family member who understood the parents' concerns (and could share his own) made my understanding of the family's situation much clearer. Others have noted that finding other parents of individuals with ASD who understand parents' concerns, and are also well versed in the language that accompanies ASD treatment, to work as interpreters would be ideal. At the least, practitioners should strive to work with interpreters who have some knowledge of the family, ASD, and effective treatment.

Parents can also become frustrated by interpreters who summarize, too briefly, what practitioners have said. To minimize the frustration of parents working with interpreters, practitioners should take care to use clear language that does not contain jargon, to minimize the misinterpretation of recommendations. Additionally, practitioners should use the minimum language necessary to convey their meaning so that the practitioner's long phrases are not condensed to shortened and sometimes meaningless phrases. Similarly, asking specific questions of the parent, to limit the length of their responses, can be helpful in reducing the amount of information that has to be passed through the interpreter (Jegatheesan, 2009).

## UNDERSTANDING THE FAMILY'S PERCEPTION OF AUTISM

Once a family is receiving services from a practitioner, the practitioner should be aware of how the family views ASD and their role in caring for the child with ASD over time. Many practitioners may take a very Westernized view of ASD and treatment. This view may focus on the need to increase the child's independence and self-sufficiency over time. However, some parents may be confused by this clinical focus, because it clashes with their own view that children with disabilities should be continuously cared for, protected, and nurtured (Zhang & Bennett, 2003). For instance, I remember working with a Muslim child with ASD on increasing his independence in different self-help areas, including feeding himself with a fork and a spoon. I was discouraged when I observed his parents feeding him with a fork, although we had been working on that skill diligently at school. I remember feeling as though my hard work was being undermined by the parents. However, now I take a different view of this family. Stepping back, I can see that their view of their child and independence was much different from my own. They felt their role as family members was to care for their child well into adulthood, and they did not push for his independence as much as we did at school.

Another perception of disability shared by many diverse cultures is that a child with a disability has special religious significance. For example, in one sample of Latino families, over half considered a child with ASD to be a "sign from God," and most of these families believed that the child was sent to them to make them more compassionate (Skinner, Bailey, Correa, & Rodriguez, 1999). Similarly, Orthodox Jewish and Asian Indian Hindu families believe that individuals with disabilities have a high spiritual status within their community (Gabel, 2004; Shaked, 2005), and Muslim families believe that they were chosen by Allah to raise "his special child" (Jegatheesan, Miller, & Fowler, 2010). As a father in Jegatheesan et al.'s (2010) study shared,

> This is a kind of test for us. And I am sure we will get through this. But I must pass the test with total integrity because I believe in Allah and have nothing else besides Allah. I embrace what He gave me. This will make me a better man, strong and I will do all that it takes to be worthy of His child. (p. 102)

Practitioners should be aware of the religious views of ASD, because it also impacts the role that parents take in caring for their child. If they believe that their child was sent to them by a spiritual being, they may strongly believe that they hold a sacred obligation to be highly protective of their child and may seem resistant to working with the professional to increase their child's independence.

Religious views and other cultural beliefs may also impact how parents view their child's disability. Parents who believe that their child is sacred may hesitate to focus on the child's deficits and react poorly to professionals who approach their child from a negative viewpoint. They may be confused and turned off by professional reports that focus on what the child is not able to do rather than the child's strengths (Jegatheesan et al., 2010). Again, this view may greatly impact the parents' understanding of what their child is capable of in the future and the goals they have for the child. The professional's view of the child's outcome may differ considerably from those of the parents, as illustrated by this Muslim father's statement in Jegatheesan et al.'s (2010) study:

> How you can say for sure he cannot do these things? Why do you say from the beginning that we have to change our expectations? . . . We think our son can be married and have a family like a normal person. We believe he can live a normal life, have children, be a father and a husband. (p. 103)

Likewise, the professional should be aware of cultural values that will cause parents to push for skills that may seem, to the professional, to be beyond the child's abilities. Many cultures value academic performance highly, and for some parents challenges in this arena may be more difficult to accept than challenges in social areas. Thus, they may continue to request that specific skills be taught to their child that seem currently unreachable to professionals. Practitioners must be aware of the impact of cultural values on the goals identified by parents and be sensitive to how parents develop these goals. Working with parents to understand goals and then to break the goals down into smaller, more achievable short-term goals may be helpful.

When working with any family, the practitioner should make efforts to understand the family's conception of disability broadly and ASD more specifically. Understanding how the family views the child, but also how they view their obligation toward caring for their child, will help mitigate potential stumbling blocks as the practitioner works with the family. Mandell and Novak present a rubric for asking parents questions about ASD and its impact on their child, which includes such questions as, "What did you call your child's problem before it was diagnosed?," "What do you think caused it?," "Will it have a short or long course?," and "What kind of treatment do you think your child should receive?" (2005, p. 113). Additionally, asking questions about the family's short- and long-term goals can help the practitioner better understand the family's values and identify common goals to work toward (Tincani et al., 2009).

Respecting cultural traditions and rituals. Therapists should be aware of and respect cultural traditions and rituals. Some families adhere to specific cultural or religious diets that will be important to uphold with their child. For others, the primary importance of their child's language development may be for the child to participate in daily prayers to ask for blessings and forgiveness. Some have specific holidays or customs that they celebrate and would like their child to take part. Some parents would like their child to be able to attend their place of worship. Working with parents to help develop manageable steps and modifications to achieve these goals is important to help the parents feel that their child is included in their culture and religion. For parents whose children are not integrated into their public school, participation in their faith may allow the child to be integrated into the parents' community. Many parents have to come to terms with the fact that their child will not accomplish many of the life goals they had for the child, such as living independently, getting married, or having children. For these parents, having the child achieve such momentous religious milestones such as First Communion, confirmation, or Bar/Bat Mitzvah may give the parents, siblings, and extended family an opportunity to celebrate and be proud of the child's development.

I once worked with a family for whom it was important that their child attend church with them. Although the church they attended was inclusive, some portions of the weekly service were difficult for him to attend. For instance, during periods of prayer, the period of silence was difficult for my student to tolerate and led him to not be able to attend this portion of the service. With the help of my colleagues, the parents developed a schedule of activities that the student could complete during this period. As the congregation kneeled, he pulled out his suitcase of activities and worked on coloring and worksheets on the pew while he waited for that portion of the service to be over. The family was thrilled to have him remain with them throughout the service. Years later, they happily shared pictures of him receiving his First Communion in their church. For both parents and professionals, many wonderful resources have been published about including children with ASD into faith communities. These publications, some of which are listed in the Resources section, can help guide professionals and parents in how to include children with ASD in religious customs and services in the best way possible.

Navigating family use of alternative treatments. A family's perception of the cause of ASD—be it medical, spiritual, or other—will greatly impact their choice of treatment for their child. Additionally, a family's views on whether ASD can or should be cured will impact how aggressively parents approach their child's treatment (Ennis-Cole, Durodoye, & Harris, 2013). For instance, Latino families are significantly more likely to use alternative treatments than are families of other ethnicities (Levy, Mandell, Merhar, Ittenbach, & Pinto-Martin, 2003). Many professionals may discount these treatments out of hand because of the lack of evidence supporting them. However, families who have different views of the etiology of ASD may be difficult to dissuade from using the treatments.

Asking about possible alternative treatments in a nonjudgmental way may provide the professional with valuable information about how the family views ASD and their approach to treatment. Mandell and Novak (2005, as adapted from Pachter, Cloutier, & Bernstein, 1995) suggested using the following question to ask parents about their use of alternative treatments: "Some of my patients have told me that there are ways of treating autism that are known in the community that physicians don't know about or use. Have you heard of any of these treatments?" If the parents tell the practitioner about a treatment, the practitioner could ask openly whether the parents are using the treatment with their child. Chapter 9 provides information about how to respond when parents reveal they are using an alternative treatment for their child, and how to guide them toward the use of evidence-based treatment while being sensitive to their cultural beliefs.

## CONTEXTUALIZING TREATMENT

One factor that is incredibly important to consider when working with parents is planning how the treatment will fit within the family context. Because of each family's beliefs, values, and daily rituals, simply providing parents with a written protocol to follow will likely not lead to successful implementation. Instead, the practitioner should tailor the intervention to match not only the individual but also the family members who will implement the treatment and the setting in which the treatment will be implemented (e.g., Moes & Frea, 2000). Chapter 9 gives in-depth information about training parents and the importance of contextualizing treatment for all families. This section addresses why contextualizing is especially necessary when working with families of diverse backgrounds, particularly if the background differs from that of the practitioner.

In general, when addressing a behavior of concern in the home environment, the important components for a practitioner to remember are the impact the behavior has on the quality of life of the individual with ASD and the family, the abilities of different family members to implement the intervention, and the impact that intervention will have on the daily routines of the family. Working with the family to identify routines and events within their day that will be most impacted by intervention will help identify the best routine in which to first implement the intervention (Moes & Frea, 2002). The practitioner can then work with the family to apply the intervention specifically in the context of that family routine. Identifying the family members who are available to support implementation of the intervention is vitally important, as is discussing how these family members would prefer to interact with one another (Moes & Frea, 2002). The family structure and the importance of specific members within the family differ across cultures (Harry, 1992), and extended family may play an important role in the daily care of the child. Practitioners must recognize that ascertaining input from these family members can be vitally important when working in the home.

As an example of contextualizing treatment, when training parents to teach their child to communicate effectively, practitioners should take into account who will be implementing the treatment, when they will be implementing it, and the family's typical daily schedule and interactions. It will be most effective to consider how the skill will be targeted within a family's day: Will they begin by teaching requesting at the dinner table? If so, who will be at the dinner table? How can they work together to ensure that the teaching procedures are put in place effectively? How will they respond should problems arise in this specific context?

Additionally, professionals should always take into account potential issues that may arise with language barriers. If a professional is introducing language instruction in a language unfamiliar to most of the family, the practitioner must consider the utility and effect it will have for the child, parents, and other family members. For instance, listeners who are non-native English speakers have difficulty understanding English language emitted by the voice output devices often used by nonvocal children with ASD (Alamsaputra, Kohnert, Munson, & Reichle, 2006). If a concern such as this arises, the practitioner should consider adaptations to the communication system or skills that need to be taught to the family members to overcome these barriers (Tincani et al., 2009). Research has demonstrated that treatments contextualized by taking into account the family's life, schedule, and structure will be more successful than those that are not (Moes & Frea, 2002).

If family members are unable or unwilling to implement components of the intervention in the home, the practitioner should talk about the barriers to implementation. Identifying cultural concerns and other impediments to successful implementation is crucial, because the practitioner can work with the family to identify alternative ways of implementing the treatment. For example, some families may have difficulty implementing treatments into their daily life because its instability prevents them from establishing a routine in which treatments can be consistently integrated. Working with families to identify supports that need to be in place to establish a routine will be crucial in overcoming this obstacle to effective treatment.

When some family members are unwilling or uncomfortable implementing an intervention, other family members may be willing to implement the treatment instead. For this reason, and to demonstrate respect for all members of the family, invitations to extended family to attend medical and therapy appointments may be beneficial. Family members who are unwilling to implement interventions should not be criticized or discredited, because their stance may be rooted in a cultural system. Recommending an intervention that does not match a family's cultural beliefs and values may doom the intervention at the outset. Practitioners incorporating the recommendations described above will increase the likelihood that the family will support the intervention and that it will be as successful as possible.

## CLINICAL TAKE-AWAYS

Working with families from various backgrounds will challenge practitioners to do some introspection and assess and analyze their own belief systems. Practitioners should consider their own beliefs with regard to family values, practices, personal goals, and concepts of disability. Recognizing these personal beliefs and values, and understanding those of the family, will better help the professional understand from where conflict with the family originates. A quick glance in the classrooms of any educational program reveals that most providers in early childhood education are female, white, and highly educated. The likelihood that the beliefs of these practitioners differ from those of families of diverse cultural backgrounds is high. Practitioners do not need to give up or change their own beliefs but, rather, learn to appreciate and respect the beliefs of others (Harry, Rueda, & Kalyanpur, 1999).

This chapter has broadly discussed the impact of culture and ethnicity on working with families of individuals with autism. I have also provided specific examples from research on beliefs that are frequently held by members of specific groups. Professionals should recognize that these research findings are group findings and do not necessarily reflect the values of individual families. When working with families, practitioners should not make assumptions about the family's beliefs and values and should instead ask directly about these important aspects of their culture. In doing so, practitioners will gain valuable insight into how they can best fit their work into the context of the family's particular culture.

On an organizational level, agencies offering services to individuals with disabilities and their families should strive to increase the diversity of their own staff to be better able to connect culturally with the families they serve. These staff could present culturally relevant workshops and training for families of individuals with ASD to speak to culturally specific values and understandings of the disorder. Another benefit of having diverse professionals on staff is that they may be able to more easily convey the content of training and interventions to parents who are non-native English speakers. Additional recommendations for practitioners follow.

Practitioners should:

- Understand that delays to diagnosis are common among families of color and may have serious impact not only on the progress of the child with ASD but also on the stress experienced by the parents.

- Provide easily understood information about the signs of ASD to all families.

- Carefully examine their own cultural biases and the ways in which these biases may affect their approach to diagnosing children of color, as well as the subsequent treatment they recommend.

• Inform families about their rights within the educational system, because parents may be unlikely to question the services provided by the schools or be unaware of the services to which their child is entitled.

• Offer recommendations for services that fit well with the family's access to transportation. For example, offer services that are easily accessed by public transportation, if that is available to the family, or by other transportation that may be available through auxiliary services.

• Consider providing services to families within spaces that are associated with a greater level of trust and comfort, such as churches or a local school.

• Be transparent about the services that will be provided to the child, and allow families to observe the work that is done with the child to help build trust with the family.

• Take the time to ensure that families who are not fluent in English comprehend the most important recommendations of any session, by having them verbally summarize these recommendations to the practitioner before they leave.

• Utilize interpreters who are familiar with the diagnosis of ASD and treatment, and ideally the family. Minimize jargon and ask direct questions when talking with a family using an interpreter, to minimize the risk of miscommunication.

• Directly ask families about their view of ASD, how it pertains to their child, and their role in caring for their child. Cultural and religious perspectives of ASD will highly influence the goals that are important to the family. Identifying these goals at the start of treatment will help reduce conflict between the family and the practitioner.

• Inquire about cultural and religious traditions and rituals that are significant to the family, because they may place considerable emphasis on their child's ability to participate in them.

- Inquire, nonjudgmentally, about the family's use of alternative treatments, to be aware of other treatments that may affect the delivery of the recommended treatment approach.

- Contextualize the treatment provided to the family by considering the family members who will implement the treatment and the routines in which the treatment will be implemented, and problem-solve barriers that may arise.

# CHAPTER 7

# Identifying Key Coping Strategies

$P$rior to any airplane flight, a short video reminds passengers of the safety features of the airplane. In all airplanes, in an emergency oxygen masks drop from the panel above each seat. In the safety video, parents are always given a special reminder to make sure that they put their own oxygen mask on first before they help their children put on an oxygen mask. The reason for this is simple: parents may have difficulty helping their children when they are unable to breathe themselves. I have heard this presented as an analogy to parents with children with ASD on more than one occasion. As one parent pointed out to me, "The biggest piece of advice I would have [for parents] is you need to take care of yourself to be able to take care of your child."

Yet, coping with a diagnosis of ASD can be exceedingly difficult, and caring for oneself in the midst of raising a child on the autism spectrum can be challenging. This chapter examines some of the coping strategies that are most effective in reducing stress for parents of children with ASD, to aid practitioners in identifying coping strategies that may be helpful to emphasize in their work with families.

## DEFINING PROBLEM-FOCUSED COPING

It is helpful to think about coping strategies as two different types: solving the problem at hand, and managing the emotions that result from the problem. The first type of strategy, problem-focused coping, involves actually changing the current situation so that stress is alleviated. The second strategy, emotion-focused coping, involves diffusing or avoiding the negative emotions that result from the current situation. I discuss emotion-focused coping strategies later in this chapter. First, we consider what problem-focused coping might look like for a parent of a child with ASD.

Problem-focused coping, also called engagement coping, typically involves working to solve a problem at hand through planning and taking action. Consider a parent's response to his child's diagnosis of ASD. The parent may learn of the ASD diagnosis and immediately launch into a full search of everything he can find about it. He may read books about ASD and treatment, scour the Internet for possible treatments, familiarize himself with the educational laws of his state, and begin to plan his child's transition to early intervention. While the parent is not changing the diagnosis, he is altering his ability to assess treatments, make decisions, and request services that his child needs.

One of the potential benefits of problem-focused coping is that it helps increase parents' sense of self-efficacy, or their belief in their own ability to conquer the problem at hand. Parents armed with information about their child's ASD diagnosis, the appropriate types of treatment, and the family's rights to education may feel confident in their ability to advocate for the child and to make sure the child has access to the most effective services possible. One mother shared her experience with advocating for her child:

> I remember one of the social workers said to me, "Oh, wow, you sure know a lot. How do you know all of this?" I said, "Well, I can read. And I read books that tell me what I need to do." I tried to just find everything that I could about what I needed to do so that [my son] could get what he needed, because I find if you don't speak up for your kid, no one else is going to.

This mother's approach to coping with her child's diagnosis was incredibly problem focused: she worked to build a strong knowledge base for herself so that she could effectively advocate for her son and bring change to his life.

Parents' sense of self-efficacy may also decrease the stress and mental health concerns, such as anxiety and depression, they experience (Hastings & Brown, 2002). Parents' sense that they have the skills necessary to tackle the challenge in front of them will greatly reduce the stress they experience when facing that challenge. That is why many parents find that arming themselves with information about ASD and ASD treatment is an effective method of coping. "Be knowledgeable and know what your rights are in the medical system so you can appeal when the insurance company denies autism claims," one parent noted. She continued, "In the school system, [prepare yourself] by knowing what your rights are, and what the district's responsibility [is]. . . . Because you must advocate, because otherwise people depend on you just going away." Many parents in the interviews spoke about how advocating for their child—whether for better school placement, better support within their placement, respite care at home, or communication devices and other materials—was an effective way of coping with the stress they experienced.

Parents' sense of self-efficacy can also be improved by learning about and implementing the treatments that will increase their child's adaptive behavior in the home. For that reason, professionals can play an important role in decreasing the stress experienced by these parents through training and supporting them as they work to implement treatments successfully. As discussed in depth in Chapter 9, professionals should be aware of the highly significant impact that training parents in managing their child's behavior can have on reducing parent stress through increasing parent self-efficacy.

Early research that compared problem-focused coping with emotion-focused coping suggested that parents who used problem-focused coping strategies fared better than did parents who used primarily emotion-focused coping strategies (e.g., Smith, Seltzer, Tager-Flusberg, Greenberg, & Carter, 2008). Especially in early stages of diagnosis and treatment, practitioners can play a significant role in helping parents engage in problem-focused coping skills with their child. By providing resources to parents, as well as effective training in the treatment of their child with ASD (see Chapter 9), practitioners can help strengthen parents' knowledge base, develop a plan for instruction and treatment, and help them become advocates for their child with ASD. These strategies may be highly useful in reducing parent stress when raising a child on the autism spectrum.

However, more recently researchers have considered the effectiveness of coping strategies specifically with parents of children with ASD. As discussed in Chapter 2, several aspects differentiate the experiences of parents of children with ASD from those of other parents and can cause greater stress among parents of children with ASD. For example, ASD impacts children across a number of different domains, including communication, socialization, and problem behavior. Further, the ASD diagnosis is unpredictable and unremitting. Thus, parents may find a problem-focused coping strategy ineffective at alleviating the stress of parenting a child with ASD, because they may not be able to solve some of the problems they face (Benson, 2014). For instance, they may not ever be able to change the fact that their child has an ASD diagnosis. Additionally, their child will likely be faced with considerable challenges throughout development, and parents may not be able to plan for and take action against all of those challenges. Some problem behaviors that emerge may be difficult to treat, and some children will never develop vocal language no matter the effort parents put forth. In these cases, parents may become frustrated with the amount of effort they expend to solve the problem, with little positive outcome.

Not surprisingly, then, research has indicated that problem-focused coping can actually increase the stress and negative affect experienced by some parents of children with ASD (Benson, 2014; Pottie & Ingram, 2008). For example, involving parents in treatment and working with them to identify ways to overcome the challenges their child faces may actually cause or exacerbate stress, and practitioners walk a fine line between involving parents in treatment and respecting their role as a parent first and foremost, rather than as an interventionist or case manager. Therefore, identifying additional means by which parents can cope with their child's diagnosis, including emotion-focused coping and social support, will be of paramount importance.

## ENCOURAGING EMOTION-FOCUSED COPING

Emotion-focused coping is recommended in situations where parents have little control over the current situation (Benson, 2014; Tunali & Power, 2002), as may often be the case when raising a child with ASD. Though early research indicated that emotion-focused coping was not as effective as problem-focused coping at improving parents' well-being, researchers have now identified that certain types of emotion-focused coping can be highly effective.

In general, one of the primary aims of emotion-focused coping should be psychological acceptance. This refers to parents being actively aware of their thoughts and emotions related to their situation—in this case, the child's diagnosis of ASD and related challenges—without attempting to change the content of or how frequently those thoughts and emotions occur (Hayes, Luoma, Bond, Masuda, & Lillis, 2006). Psychological treatment in acceptance focuses, in part, on teaching individuals to accept difficult thoughts and emotions and to clarify personal values and corresponding goals. Because psychological acceptance does not require the individual change the immediate situation, it can be especially well suited to parents of individuals with ASD who experience chronic stressors that are often immutable (Blackledge & Hayes, 2006). Acceptance has been found to be an important protective factor among parents of children with ASD. For example, parents who evidence high psychological acceptance experience fewer mental health problems such as anxiety and depression when faced with elevated levels of problem behavior in their child (Jones, Hastings, Totsika, Keane, & Rhule, 2014; Weiss, Cappadocia, MacMullin, Viecili, & Lunsky, 2012). With this benefit in mind, practitioners must recognize and teach parents how to use coping skills that are effective in achieving acceptance, while discouraging them from using strategies that can be ineffective.

Avoiding distraction and disengagement. A research study by Benson (2010) indicated that two ineffective coping methods sometimes used by parents raising a child with ASD are distraction and disengagement. Both of these coping methods involve avoidance and run counter to acceptance: they seek to avoid the problem and the emotions associated with it. Distraction coping strategies include trying to think about the problem less, or blaming oneself for the problem. Disengagement strategies include giving up, substance abuse, or denial of the problem.

In contrast to the problem-focused father I described above, imagine another scenario: upon learning of his son's diagnosis, the parent may begin to blame himself for his son's ASD, citing the frequently touted statistic that older fathers are more likely to have a child with ASD. He begins to withdraw from his family, avoiding time with them and not talking with his wife about their child's diagnosis. He begins to drink more heavily when he gets home from work in the evening. This father is employing distraction and disengagement to distance himself from the emotional reactions to his son's ASD diagnosis—if he does not talk about autism, it is not real. One father I interviewed shared his experience with emotion-focused coping by relaying a story in which a good friend, in a conversation with the father and his wife soon after their son had been diagnosed, shared that he had looked online for resources for friends of parents with children with ASD. The father shared with me that his wife was touched by his friend's gesture but that he had felt differently:

> I remember an image of leaping across the table and strangling him. That actually came into my head. Inside I was furious [at him] for bringing it up because it made [the autism diagnosis] real, and looking back on it, when someone mentioned it, it was a real thing.

This father recalled his early days following his child's ASD diagnosis as actively avoiding thinking or talking about the diagnosis—distraction and disengagement—to minimize his emotional reaction.

As this father's response clearly indicates, parents who engage in distraction and disengagement may be more likely to experience

anger, as well as symptoms of depression. The process of distancing oneself from the emotions and experience of raising a child with
ASD can have harmful effects on a parent's well-being (Benson,
2010, 2014). Fortunately, however, a number of other alternative,
effective emotion-focused coping strategies are available for parents
to help manage the stress of raising a child with ASD. Practitioners
should recognize when parents are using ineffective forms of coping such as distraction and disengagement and steer them toward
strategies that may be more effective, such as cognitive reframing
and mindfulness.

Recommending cognitive reframing. An effective way for
parents to deal with the negative emotions that they experience
in response to raising a child with ASD is to engage in cognitive
reframing. Using cognitive reframing, parents identify the negative way they perceive their child or the situation and then alter how
they think about it to change the way they feel about it. Research
indicates that parents of children with ASD who utilize cognitive
reframing report greater well-being than those who do not (Benson,
2014; Tunali & Power, 2002).

As an example of cognitive reframing, one mother described how
she struggled with her son's disability until she reframed her perception of it into a difference:

> I've started thinking of [ASD] as a discrepancy between how his
> brain works and how the world works, and seeing the therapy and
> education that we do with him not as a way of "fixing" or "curing"
> him but as a way of teaching him skills that he needs to get along
> in a world that is not set up for him.

When describing why this approach was helpful to her, she continued,

> It also helps when I encounter questions, even in my own mind,
> about why, when it seems like he is so advanced in some areas, are
> we pushing and focusing on the things that he struggles with? As
> in, he doesn't have to be advanced at everything, can't he be a
> math and writing genius and not a social one? Of course he can,

but my perspective is that he can learn those skills; he just needs a little extra help and support to learn them. If he was socially gifted but struggling to learn reading or math, I would get him a tutor because those skills are essential to being able to function in the world, and I look at this in the same way.

Similarly, another mother shared her process of changing her expectations of her daughter and reframing her cognitions about "success" after her daughter's diagnosis:

I was always kind of a perfectionist, and I believed in . . . survival of the fittest sort of thing, like you've got to get out there and try your best and do your best, and the cream will rise to the top. . . . But I just needed to realize that [my daughter is] not that kid and . . . as a result I started recognizing and paying much more attention to the people who weren't at the top. Where I had that a lot more in my life and in my career and my schooling, and even as I was raised by my parents, I now have a kid who is not in that strata. She is not going to be an independent, successful professional who has everything she wants and can do everything that she wants. She is going to be affected or inhibited or slowed down by her condition, and that's not to say that she's not an amazing kid and she's not going to do great things. . . . I don't look at her or at life the same way that I used to.

Many parents mentioned changing their expectations by "letting things go" as a way that they cope day to day. Prioritizing the obstacles that need to be tackled allows parents to minimize the amount of work that they face. "You can't get so down on every little thing," a mother shared.

You can't be like, "Oh no, he ripped a shirt," because he ripped a million shirts. Don't be like, "He's never going to go outside because he is always going to have a ripped shirt," that kind of thing. So I just calmed down a little bit. I accepted more of his things.

Additionally, letting go of unnecessary responsibilities, and the obligation that parents feel to meet these self-imposed expectations, may also help reduce their stress. "I always volunteered most of my life," one mother shared.

> I finally just stopped and said I'm going to garden, I'm going to quilt, I'm going to be there in my home and enjoy my home, and I don't take on things. I don't feel guilt anymore about not volunteering or about not going to church. I threw the guilt out the door. I like to get up every day and just enjoy that day.

Letting go of the expectations of others is also an important lesson that parents have to learn, though it is difficult. Parents may learn to focus less on other sources of approval to help adjust the emotions that emerge from their cognitions about their child but especially about themselves as a parent. Research indicates that parents of children with ASD focus less on the approval of others than do parents of typical children (Tunali & Power, 2002). One parent shared how she has shifted her concern about others' approval over time:

> It used to be really tough for me to have people staring at me and staring at [my son] or criticizing me. I would go to church, and some old woman would turn to me and say, "I have ten kids and they sit perfectly quiet all through mass. You need to be a better parent. That kid needs to be quiet." I would just be mortified. Now if somebody said that to me I'd say, "Oh, I'm sorry, he's autistic. Are any of your kids autistic?" And that would be the end of that discussion.

A second mother added,

> I would get so stressed with her in public, and especially because she is high functioning, it was like she was a major disruptive child and I was the bad parent, and we wouldn't even go to church. I just started telling people, . . . "This is what we're dealing with, and if you don't like it, I'm really sorry, and we will be out of here in a

half hour, but until then this pizza is going to be all over the place because she is not going to listen. But if you were here yesterday she was really good." That has helped me a little bit.

In addition to parents adjusting their own expectations and their sources of approval, cognitive reframing can also include looking for the positive in the current situation. We know that parents who think more optimistically about their child by focusing on the possible positive outcomes of the current situation experience less stress than parents who tend to think more negatively (Baker, Blacher, & Olsson, 2005). One father I spoke with repeatedly stressed the importance of looking at the positive aspects of his and his son's life when coping with the challenges of ASD. "We try and stay just focused on the positive," he said, "celebrating what [my son] can do and what we want him to do, as opposed to thinking about autism." He noted that one of the strategies that helps him and his wife focus on the positive is to "send out a holiday video with positive pictures from the year. I think that reliving the good moments as much as you can helps."

Focusing on the positive moments of their time with their child can be beneficial for parents, as this mother describes:

> [My son] doesn't really like to be touched too much. . . . We read books together; we read the Harry Potter series. When we read the book side by side, I read the left-hand page and he reads the right-hand page. We've gotten through the whole series that way. From time to time he's at ease and [he will] just lean over, lean his head on me, or he'll put his arm around me. There's a warmth, there's a feeling that goes through my entire body. It's so special, because it's genuine. . . . It's like an extra special treat because it doesn't happen all the time.

The impact of focusing on the positive aspects of parenting a child can have a significant impact on parents' overall mood. For example, research has shown that when parents are asked to log their cognitions for the day, those who log more positive perceptions of their child experience more positive affect than those who note more negative perceptions (Lickenbrock, Ekas, & Whitman, 2011).

Parents may also focus on the positive impact that raising a child with ASD has had on them. Research indicates that such positive impacts can include personal transformations, such a becoming more compassionate or becoming a better advocate for their child; relational transformations, such as a stronger marriage or better relationship with other children in the family; and altered perspectives on life in terms of what matters to them (Scorgie & Sobsey, 2000). One mother noted,

> I think that I am a much better person now than I was preautism. I think I am more passionate. I think that I am more patient. I think that I am more generous. I think I am a lot more accepting. . . . I think it just put my priorities in place really fast. . . . I don't get upset over little things because there are so many things, and it's sort of a relief.

Focusing on positive outcomes of an ASD diagnosis may help improve parents' positive affect. In turn, positive affect can serve as a buffer against the negative experiences parents may face raising their child and help reduce their stress (Ekas & Whitman, 2011).

Cognitive reframing is not the type of skill that develops overnight, unfortunately. Many parents have worked for years to be able to think differently or more positively about their child's ASD diagnosis and related symptoms. Practitioners who encounter parents who are not coping well with their child's diagnosis should refer them to professionals who can help parents learn effective strategies for cognitive reframing. Cognitive-behavioral therapists, in particular, may be well suited to helping parents develop effective skills in adjusting cognitions to improve mental health and well-being.

Promoting mindfulness. Another method of cognitive restructuring is mindfulness. For many parents, raising a child with ASD means always looking ahead toward what is coming and behind at what has not been achieved. It is common for parents to be reminded of what their child still needs to accomplish, which can bring stress and sadness to a parent. An area of parent support that has garnered considerable focus is that of mindfulness, which requires parents to focus on their child in the current moment, without judgment. When one mother described how she copes with her daughter's diagnosis, she stated, "I guess we've always not looked too far ahead on the little things."

Placing emphasis on staying in the moment can have considerable impact. Researchers have found that teaching parents to practice mindfulness reduces their stress. Mindfulness-based parent training teaches parents to be in the moment by attending to the immediately present environment (rather than past or future events), and to experience negative feelings and sensations without judgment. For instance, one exercise in mindfulness-based parent training may ask parents to play with their child mindfully by focusing their attention on the details of the current environment: what the child is playing with, how she looks, what she is saying. Studies have found this specific type of parent training improves parent mental health (Blackledge & Hayes, 2006) and child behavior and parent-child interactions (Singh et al., 2006) and has benefits over more typical skills-based parent training or training that teaches parents the skills to effectively improve the child's behavior (Ferraioli & Harris, 2013). Mindfulness-based parent training may help parents learn to focus on the here-and-now, rather than on the future, which could have considerable benefit for parents. One father recommended that other parents "don't look too much in the future. Narrow your focus as much as you can, if it's the day, or if it's the next hour or the last minute."

The use of mindfulness can also help parents focus more closely on their child and where he or she is, right now, developmentally, rather than continually focusing on what will come next. A mother shared,

> What I think sort of happened was a wave of epiphanies. I remember two or three times very clearly where I just felt like this is who he is, and this is what he has, and there is a limit to what I can do

to change it. I have to just love and accept him for who he is and enjoy him for who he is. I think that helped a lot. It really pulled me out of this mode of constantly trying to intervene and make things better—just kind of get myself more in the moment and enjoy him.

This parent found yoga to be a tremendously helpful form of exercise that also helped her develop a mindful approach to her son:

Yoga saved my emotional life. I really do think it did. I'm very physically active, and I need that to decompress, and I ran and I did yoga, and I think a combination of those things was hugely a big part of what helped me cope. I think the yoga piece helped me get into a mind frame of acceptance. There are things that I don't have control over, and I have to accept it. If I don't learn to accept it I'm not mindful, and I think my yoga practice was honestly one of the most important parts of what I did to help me get to that place. It would kind of calm my body and calm my brain and help me be focused.

Again, parents who are having difficulty coping can be referred to practitioners who specialize in mindfulness-based therapy. Professionals who would like to learn more about mindfulness can reference Steven Hayes's books on acceptance and commitment therapy (e.g., Hayes, Strosahl, & Wilson, 1999), which includes modules on mindfulness; and the 8-week course in mindfulness-based cognitive therapy by Segal, Williams, and Teasdale (2002), which can be modified for work with parents of children with ASD (e.g., Ferraioli & Harris, 2013).

## PROPOSING TIME ALONE

Many parents emphasize the need to take time for themselves among all of their efforts for their child. "I have to have time to myself," one mother shared.

> At night sometimes I can't even talk to my boyfriend. I have to
> have it to myself. Even if [my son] stays up really late, I stay up
> later. I have to be by myself for a half hour. That helps me out.

Parents may make use of that time differently, some using it to watch
television or cook, others to exercise. "I'm a runner. And that has
helped me tremendously. . . . I mean, that's the time that I carve out
for myself, and it helps me balance everything else." Time alone provides parents with opportunities to process their experiences and
think through some of the challenges that they face. Alternatively,
time alone allows parents to exercise and participate in other activities that may help them be more mindful in their lives.

However, as discussed in Chapter 2, finding time alone can be a
difficult feat for many parents. The substantial amount of childcare
required of them, in addition to other responsibilities, can make
carving out time difficult for any parent, let alone a parent of a child
with ASD. Some parents get creative in terms of finding time alone,
as one father described:

> I like walking. Up until a couple of years ago we had a German
> shepherd, and he and I would go out and walk. My regular route
> would be 8 to 10 miles, and I could go as far as 16. Typically, I
> would be outside anywhere between 10:00 P.M. and 3:00 in the
> morning. I know where all the foxes are. There's a small pack of
> Eastern coyote up the hill from us.

This parent found a quiet time after his children were in bed to slip
away and get time alone. However, for parents who cannot feasibly
stay up through the night, or do not have a spouse who can take
responsibility of the children at that time, making time like this can
be difficult. Practitioners can work with parents to identify times
during their day when they might be able to have some time alone,
perhaps before their children wake up in the morning, on a short
walk in the middle of their workday, or after their children are
asleep. Additionally, identifying sources of childcare that could help
give parents some time to focus on themselves regularly will be ben-

eficial, whether through family or respite care providers. While parents may struggle with feeling guilty that someone else is caring for their child while they are alone, they should be reassured that the time alone is important so that they can have the reserves to care for their child the rest of the time.

Practitioners may also talk with parents to help define what they consider "time to themselves," because their definition may differ from that of practitioners. For example, some parents may find that washing dishes while listening to music or a podcast on a set of headphones is a quick way to recharge. Others may find that sitting in their car for 5 minutes before walking into work may help them focus on themselves. I myself find that spending a few minutes in the shower, without child interruption, gives me a brief but sometimes needed break from parenting responsibilities. Just as practitioners may have to work with couples to define what might constitute an unorthodox "date night," working with parents on how they conceptualize "alone time" will help practitioners identify ways in which parents can find time for themselves in their busy lives.

## INCREASING SOCIAL SUPPORT

In my interviews with parents, one of the most often mentioned forms of coping was relying on social support. Some parents mentioned family as a source of support, such as conversations with their spouses or partners, or even their other children. Parents spoke of dear friends who offered help and respite during challenging times, really rising to the occasion. One parent shared,

> We have two close friends. One is a special ed teacher, and the wife is a teacher. They have been a tremendous form of support for us because they will take him, and they understand him, so I can leave him with them.

A distinction should be made between formal and informal forms of social support. Formal support refers to the support provided by professionals, such as through the child's school and clinicians, parents' own therapists, and structured social support groups. In contrast, informal social support refers to that provided by family, friends, and neighbors. Especially because families of diverse cultures may be more likely to rely on informal support than formal support (e.g., Aranda & Knight, 1997; Haley et al., 1996), practitioners should be mindful of the various types of support available and consider offering recommendations outside of the formal system of care when appropriate. Regardless of how social support is categorized, however, parents often report it to be an effective means of coping, and practitioners should be knowledgeable about how to strengthen parents' social support.

Notably, the impact that social support has on parent stress is related to parent perceptions of how much social support they receive. That is, parent stress is not related to the number of friends or family members who support the parent, or to the number of hours of social support they receive each week. Rather, it relates to their own sense of the amount and quality of support they receive from others. Parents who report a greater perception of social support also report better well-being and lower levels of depression (e.g., Benson, 2012). Parents who feel unsupported, even surrounded by friends and well-meaning professionals, will experienced increased stress.

Professionals working with children on the autism spectrum should consider the social support available for the parents. Even if the child is the primary focus of therapy, any therapist should be mindful of the support provided for parents and be ready to provide different avenues by which parents can connect with others. A simple survey that a parent completes (e.g., Social Support Questionnaire; Sarason, Levine, Basham, & Sarason, 1983) can provide information about how much social support they feel they receive and whether they are satisfied with it. Parents on the low end of the scale should be encouraged to seek out additional support, such as seeking out peers, support groups, and referrals to other professionals.

Seeking out peers. Chapter 3 discussed challenges with establishing a social support network when parents are raising a child with ASD. For example, many parents noted difficulty in turning to friends of children without ASD for support. It can be difficult to receive support from parents of neurotypical children because those parents truly may not understand what parents of children with ASD experience. They may not be able to, or may not want to, imagine what it would be like to have a child who faces the challenges of ASD. Additionally, these parents may not understand or be able to tolerate the behavior of the child with ASD. Parents who are unable to find childcare often find it difficult to attend group activities with their child with ASD.

Many parents note that other parents of children with ASD were the best forms of support they had found. One mother described her experiences with a group of parents of children on the spectrum:

> We could discuss stuff, and . . . I could say things like my kid is still wetting the bed and he's this many years old. And somebody would say, "Oh, I tried this, I tried that, have you tried this?" . . . [They were] a group of peers who I didn't have to be embarrassed about any of the crazy stuff that he was doing, and [knowing] that they actually had been there before. . . . We'd all share our experiences of what worked for us and what didn't work for us. So that was really helpful.

Another benefit of spending time with other parents of children with ASD, some parents mentioned, is putting their own lives in perspective, which interfaces with cognitive reframing described above. As one parent described,

> I realized through this group [of parents] that . . . there's just always someone with a bigger burden than you; that's what helps me get through. I will look at someone and say, well, she can do it so what am I complaining about? That's a huge coping mechanism.

Parents may find comfort in recognizing that other parents have the same experiences and, in some ways, may face more challenges than they do, which helps them find a source of strength in their own lives.

Finding places where other parents of children with ASD gather can provide parents with a level of support they do not experience in other settings, as one mother described:

> If your kid randomly has a meltdown over some random thing, or your kid goes up and says hi to someone and they don't say hi back, you know that the other parents get it, and they're not, like, "What is wrong with this kid?"

Many families cited Special Olympics as a great outlet for the entire family; it allows their child to be integrated into a community without judgment and provides the family with understanding and support from other families.

Practitioners should encourage parents to reach out to other parents of children on the autism spectrum by joining group activities that they attend, such as Special Olympics or other specialized classes for individuals with ASD. Additionally, some organizations sponsor community events that bring ASD families together and allow them to meet one another in safe environments. For example, locally I have seen organizations partner with restaurants for ASD-friendly family nights, where family members can eat out at a restaurant filled with other families who understand them and their child. Local theaters also offer special viewings of theatrical productions for individuals with ASD, which may include keeping the house lights on throughout the production, lowering the sound of the music, and providing areas where individuals can take a break from the performance. Being aware of these events and sharing them with parents is one way to improve their connection to others and to help them feel supported.

Accessing support groups. Some parents meet parents of children with ASD informally through social arrangements and connect with them over dinner or the telephone. However, many organizations offer formal meetings of parent support groups where parents can come together and discuss daily life raising a child with ASD.

"To be able to go and see and meet with other families who were parents," one parent shared,

> without my kids, and sit on a mat cross-legged and chat about and listen to other people chat about the tough stuff they were going through. It makes me feel like I'm not alone. Because autism is very, very isolating. Exceedingly so.

An important referral for practitioners to make is to local support groups. Parents who attend support groups are more likely to have been referred there by a clinician than parents who do not attend but, amazingly, even among parents attending support groups, fewer than one in four parents was referred (Mandell & Salzer, 2007). The importance of referring parents to local groups that could strengthen their support network cannot be overstated.

In addition to providing parents with a list of parent support groups in the area, helping parents overcome barriers to attending support groups or accessing other forms of support may also be help-ful. The logistics of attending a support group can be challenging, due to the location of the group, transportation, finding childcare, and the time required for attendance (Clifford & Minnes, 2012). Pro-fessionals working with families, at the time of diagnosis or later in treatment, should be prepared to help problem solve challenges parents face, such as finding ways to arrange childcare so they can attend. For example, some parents take turns attending a support group so one is always home to care for the child with ASD, or fam-ily members or respite care providers can be asked to care for their child for a few hours.

Additionally, practitioners should be knowledgeable about social support alternatives that do not require travel, such as online sup-port groups, and the Parent to Parent support program, in which parents of children with ASD are assigned as mentors to other par-ents whose children are newly diagnosed and can speak with them remotely (e.g., Singer et al., 1999). Seeking out parents who are willing to be in touch as a form of support, whether by e-mail or by phone, can also generate informal lines of support. Contact information for groups such as these is provided in the Resources section of this book.

Referring parents to other professionals. Some parents may decide that they need additional help or support beyond a group of friends. Formal social support that comes from professionals can be a significant form of support. Some parents find the support of a therapist to be especially helpful, as this mother describes:

> This point of my life when things went from busy and difficult but manageable to, "I am completely overwhelmed and drowning here." . . . It was right around the time when [my son] was diagnosed and [his younger brother] turned a year old and became mobile. The combination of those two things together—for a while I was drowning. I was just seriously not in a good place, just trying to manage things. It took me a while to realize that maybe this was something more serious going on and I need help with it, and so I think about a year ago I finally found a therapist.

Professional therapists can be key in offering parents specific skills they can use to minimize stress as they manage their household, jobs, and children. Cognitive behavioral therapists, in particular, will specialize in some of the techniques mentioned above, such as cognitive restructuring and mindfulness, and can teach parents how to effectively use these skills. For instance, the same mother above recalled one of the important cognitive reframing skills her therapist has helped her with:

> She is helping me be okay with just letting some things go. I can be really hard on myself with respect to the kids, if I let them watch too much TV, or if I get angry, or if I feel like I'm not doing enough for [my son]—I'm not doing enough research, I'm not finding all the services that he needs, I could be doing more of this or more of that. . . . Which doesn't actually help because I feel like I'm doing as much as I logistically really can be doing, given the time and energy that I have. She sort of helped me accept that and that if we're having a hard day and we watch too much TV, that's okay, they're going to be fine.

Practitioners, however, should be aware that the primary focus of professional therapists, in working with parents of a child with ASD, may be broader than simply helping the parents process emotions regarding their child. Therapists may help parents identify effective ways of coping across all areas of their life, including home, work, and peers and family, and how to balance everything in a healthy way.

## CARING FOR FAMILIES IN CRISIS

Despite professionals' best efforts to help parents develop coping strategies and seek out social support to reduce the strain of raising a child with ASD, they may encounter families in crisis. These families may find the challenge of raising a child with ASD unsurmountable, or struggle with the physical and emotional effort that is required to control their child's behavior. In these situations, professionals may be concerned about the potential for child abuse, or even concerned about the safety of the parents. Although it is an unpleasant topic, professionals should be aware of parental susceptibility to crisis. In 2013 I participated in a webcast panel of parents and professionals discussing the experiences of families of individuals with ASD. Viewers were able to send in questions for the panelists during the conversation, and the moderator was surprised by the number of questions from professionals about how to respond when they suspected that an individual with ASD was being abused by caregivers.

However, when one considers how physically, emotionally, and mentally taxing raising a child with ASD can be, and how difficult finding supportive resources can be in certain social contexts, the number of questions seems less surprising. I spoke with one father during my interviews who honestly and openly shared some of the thoughts that crossed his mind while he struggled to physically manage his daughter with ASD, who was very aggressive as a young child and continues to be so as an adult. "[She would] go into such a rage," he shared,

> and then I'm forced to really apply a lot of pressure [to control her behavior]. Not hit her, but hold her. You're getting nowhere, and

you're so frustrated, so angry, so distraught about the whole situation. It's hard to cope in those instances. You quickly regain your composure and say, "Maybe I hit her too hard. Maybe I grabbed her too hard."

Parents working to control the behavior of their child with ASD may inadvertently resort to an excessive level of physical control. In research, the numbers of children with ASD reported to be physically or sexually abused are inconsistent (e.g., Mandell, Walrath, Manteuffel, Sgro, & Pinto-Martin, 2005; Sullivan & Knutson, 2000), but researchers suggest that variables such as limited communication, long-term dependence on caregivers, and caregiver disappointment in the child's abilities may increase risk of abuse, though the relation between these variables and abuse remains understudied (Ammerman, Van Hasselt, & Hersen, 1988; Mandell et al., 2005).

Tragically, a few parents may reach such a state of desperation or hopelessness that the lives of their children and their own lives may be at risk. Parents may consider ways to eliminate the suffering in the family. In his interview, the father above continued,

At times, when she was going through those rages . . . I was thinking at times maybe she's better off dead. I never really verbalized that, but I know it was in my mind. Put her out of her misery. Put me out of my misery, and I won't have to deal with this anymore. When she was in a rage, do you really need to go through this, do I really need to? Maybe it's better. Because when someone is in that much pain, you're better off dead. . . . You see them suffering and you think, they'd be better off dead. And I had those feelings a few times with [my daughter].

This father's thoughts are not isolated to his situation; stories in the news about homicides and suicides in families of individuals with ASD tell us that other parents have these thoughts as well, and more. Professionals need to be aware of the possibility that the strain of raising an individual on the autism spectrum—care that often is required into the child's adulthood—may push parents to a point where they can no longer handle the challenges they face. All professionals should have on hand structured screening tools that help assess the severity of anxiety and depression symptoms and consider using the tools with all new families they encounter to identify potential concerns early in treatment. Further, practitioners should have a plan of action in the event that they are concerned about parents who are at risk, such as asking parents if they have readily available sources of mental health support. For families who do not have these supports in place, providing referrals could be beneficial.

If they are concerned about the potential for abuse in a family, professionals should make use of or refer parents to sources of support discussed in this chapter (e.g., respite care, parent support groups, and therapists). Additionally, practitioners should implement effective parent training to help them manage situations that may pose significant danger in the household, such as physically managing their child's behavior safely (see Chapter 9 for training strategies). When children pose significant physical risk to their parents or other family members, or family members feel unable to competently care for the child and maintain their own well-being, practitioners should discuss the possibility of and funding for short-term inpatient care or long-term residential care (as was the solution for the father above).

In addition, every professional should be aware of the signs of abuse, such as unexplained injuries on the child's body or less obvious signs such as a sudden change in behavior, avoidance of people or places, or withdrawal. They should also be aware of signs of neglect, such as inadequate supervision, food, or shelter. Professionals who suspect neglect or abuse are mandated to report the abuse to state child welfare authorities and should do so without fear of penalty. A professional need not have confirmed abuse before calling welfare authorities; it is the responsibility of the welfare authority to investigate and determine whether abuse has occurred. Family members in acute crisis, with risk of physical harm to themselves or others, should be referred immediately to medical or mental health services and professionals who can assess risk and create an action plan to reduce the possibility of harm to any of the family members. Contact information for agencies and hotlines that provide support for families in crisis are included in the Resources section of this book.

## CLINICAL TAKE-AWAYS

Parents experience considerable stress raising a child with ASD, and the level of stress some parents experience should be of significant concern for practitioners. However, over time we have identified effective means of helping parents cope with the stress that they experience, through constructive problem-solving approaches, reframing the way in which they think about their experiences with their child, and reaching out for support from others. In working with individuals with ASD, all practitioners should be attuned to symptoms of parent stress and related conditions such as anxiety and depression that could have a toll not only on the parent but also on the child with ASD. Helping parents identify ineffective means of coping and directing them toward more effective approaches, or other professionals who can help them learn these approaches, will be especially beneficial. Following are additional recommendations for practitioners.

Practitioners should:

- Help improve parent self-efficacy by providing parents with resources and training in how to effectively teach their child adaptive skills and manage problem behavior.

- Consider that, for some parents, problem-focused coping may increase stress as they struggle with challenges related to ASD that are not easily overcome. For these parents, emotion-focused coping may be better suited to their needs.

- Discourage the use of avoidant forms of coping, such as distraction and disengagement, and instead direct parents to therapists and other supports that can help them use effective emotion-focused coping strategies such as cognitive reframing and mindfulness.

- Help parents identify times of their day that they can spend alone, taking care to clarify what a parent defines as alone time.

- Share information with parents about local events or groups that will provide them with sources of formal and informal social support. For example, activities, events, and social support groups geared toward families of individuals with ASD may help introduce parents to others with similar experiences.

- Refer families to mental health professionals, when appropriate, to help build up the tools they need to cope with raising a child with ASD and the other concerns that may arise in their life.

- Identify parents at risk for crisis using structured assessments for anxiety and depression. Assess resources available to these families that may help provide support and reduce stress, but also be prepared to provide parents with referrals to community resources that may provide support (e.g., support groups, therapists), as well as those that can be used in emergencies (e.g., emergency respite, emergency hotlines).

- Be knowledgeable about signs of neglect or abuse among individuals with ASD, and as a mandated reporter, report all suspected cases of abuse to the proper authorities.

# CHAPTER 8

# Building a Strong
# Rapport With Parents

When interviewing parents for this book, one question I asked each of them was to describe an effective relationship that they had with a professional who worked with their child. What qualities did that professional—therapist, pediatrician, neurologist, or teacher—have, or what approaches did he or she use, that made the relationship so effective? In their responses, not one parent described a specific therapy or diagnostic technique that the professional used with their child. Nobody told me that they valued a professional for using ABA, or introducing them to a gluten-free diet, or implementing sensory integration therapy with their child. Instead, parents reported that the personal qualities of the professionals themselves, or the ways they went about working with the family, regardless of the type of therapy, was what made the experience so successful.

As parents talked with me, they often recalled one specific person with whom they had worked, and I could hear in their voices the admiration and gratitude they felt for having that person in their life. In fact, many parents said that the professionals they were speaking about were still in their life, even if their child was no longer receiving services from them. Oh, to be one of those professionals that parents hold in such high regard! What is the secret?

Fortunately, we can learn a lot from what parents say about such notable professionals. Listening to these parents, we hear a careful summary of the qualities and approaches of certain professionals that help develop effective rapport between professionals and families. Rapport is the quality of a working relationship between the practitioner and the patient—in this case, the parent or family member—and the degree to which the relationship is built on trust and cooperation. Understanding and empathy for the patient is at the heart of rapport (Norfolk, Birdi, & Walsh, 2007).

From research in psychological treatment, we know that building effective rapport with an individual can have an incredible impact on the outcome of treatment. For example, one research study found that stronger therapeutic alliance, or rapport, between the professional and a child with externalizing behavior (e.g., oppositional or aggressive behavior), as well as between the professional and the parent, predicted greater treatment success (Kazdin, Marciano, & Whitley, 2005). Though much of the research is based on rapport established between a psychological therapist and a patient, such as an individual with anxiety or depression, we can easily draw from this research to identify practitioner skills and qualities that can influence the development of rapport between professionals and parents of individuals with ASD.

Some factors that research indicates are related to treatment outcome include basic tenets from Carl Rogers's early work on how to encourage change in a patient in psychotherapy. Rogers is considered one of the founding fathers of psychotherapy research, and his work focused extensively on the conditions under which therapeutic change was most likely. Four of his six posited conditions were dependent on the therapist's behavior, rather than the patient's (Rogers, 1957). According to Rogers's person-centered approach, the therapist should build empathic understanding of the individual's perspective; communicate that understanding to the client; approach the client with "unconditional positive regard," or by clearly communicating nonjudgmental care and respect for the individual; and demonstrate congruence, that is, be nondefensive and genuine when working with the individual (Lambert & Barley, 2001). Over time, researchers have continued to add to the list of therapeutic skills that contribute to strong rapport (e.g., Lambert & Barley, 2001;

Leach, 2005; Norfolk et al., 2007), which largely overlap with these original thoughts put forth by Rogers.

Similarly, parents' ideas about what makes an effective professional map onto these therapy skills in building rapport. Take, for example, one mother's view on how professionals should interact with parents:

> Collaboration, mutual respect and communication, to listen to me, to take what I have to say seriously, to include me, to be respectful, to understand that even when I don't have a knowledge base, I have a knowledge base that they don't have.

This quote wonderfully summarizes the important components necessary to build rapport with parents. This chapter addresses these basic strategies for building rapport with a caregiver of an individual on the autism spectrum, discussing the ways in which to best develop understanding, communication, care, respect, and nondefensiveness with parents of individuals with ASD. Although the underlying principles of building rapport presented here are drawn from research in psychotherapy, the recommendations provided are not just for psychotherapists working directly with parents. Any professional working with the family, including diagnosticians, teachers, therapists, and medical professionals, should implement these strategies.

## EXPRESSING EMPATHY

As the title of this book suggests, one of the primary purposes of this text is to help practitioners develop greater empathy for and understanding of the experiences of families of individuals with ASD. Chapters 1 through 7 cover a wide range of considerations regarding the stresses and joys of raising a child with ASD, as well as how parents might cope with their experiences. I hope, however, that they also convey that the experiences of each family are different. As a result, practitioners should always strive to understand the individual experiences of each family rather than making assumptions about what they have gone through and how they cope. To better learn about and understand individual families' experiences, practitioners must first develop effective listening skills. To clearly convey their understanding of the family's experiences, practitioners must then also hone their skills in communicating with parents.

Listening to parents. In any relationship a professional has with a parent, listening to the parent should be one of their first steps in establishing rapport. Regardless of whether the professional is diagnosing a child, or providing the child with speech, occupational, behavioral, or any other kind of therapy, or providing medical treatment, or seeing a parent for counseling, listening will always be one of the first steps taken. If it is not, the professional should take a step back and reevaluate how to establish relationships and rapport with parents.

It may be the case, especially in schools, that a professional knows quite a bit about a student before meeting the parents. Perhaps a transition process was initiated between classrooms, and the teachers in the classrooms have spent time getting to know and learning about the student and the related programs before the transition. In these cases, the professionals working with the student may have an idea of where they feel the student should be headed educationally or vocationally before speaking with the parents. Even in these situations, however, the professionals should take the time to listen to the parents. Starting new parent-professional relationships with such questions as "Tell me about your child," "Tell me about your family," and "What are your goals in coming here?" will help the professional understand quickly where the parents are coming from. Their answers may run counter to the professional's own preconceived notions about where the student is headed.

In some settings, professionals may have the time to engage in joining sessions before initiating treatment, in which they get to know the family by asking the parents and child questions about the family structure and other topics, which offers the professional the opportunity to listen, validate, and support the family. In essence, the professional has a conversation with the family about the things that are important to them and the opportunity to convey interest and understanding. Particularly for families of diverse cultural backgrounds, joining can be particularly effective because it helps build trust and comfort with the professional prior to initiating treatment (Boyd-Franklin & Bry, 2000).

Joining typically takes place early in treatment, ideally in the first session, and can be quite prolonged depending on the amount of time available. The questions asked when joining with a family often include those that are commonly asked in background interviews, such as who lives at home with the child and what the parents do professionally. However, follow-up questions are much more personal in nature and take a friendly, conversational tone. For example, a colleague of mine uses this technique frequently in her work with families and shared questions that she might ask of the parents and children with whom she works. In addition to asking who lives at home with the child, she may follow up by asking about the ages, personality, and likes and dislikes of other siblings, as well as how they get along with the family. She asks about pets—breed, temperament, even asking to see pictures—and may ask parents to describe what they do for a living, or how they first met. These questions lead to natural interactions that provide the practitioner the opportunity to validate and express empathy for the parents' experiences and to help the family become comfortable with the practitioner.

If possible, drawing the child with ASD into the conversation also allows the practitioner the opportunity to see how the family interacts with one another. For example, asking the child if the family has talked about why they are visiting the practitioner may elicit responses about concerns that the family and child has; if the parent responds for the child, the practitioner can follow up to ensure that the child does indeed understand the purpose of the visit. Again, extensive joining may not be possible in quick appointments with a practitioner, but even 10 minutes of joining before diving into the purpose of the visit may help the practitioner build early effective rapport with the family.

During the remainder of the visit, in general, open-ended questions, or those that begin in *how, what, where,* and *when,* will allow the parent to introduce more novel information than if the practitioner asks yes-no questions that direct the flow of the conversation (Leach, 2005). One mother described an effective relationship she had with her son's neurologist: "He just listened to me. He didn't say, 'Oh no, I don't think this, I don't think that.' He just said, 'Tell me what your concerns are. What are you seeing?'" Through open-ended questioning, professionals will quickly identify areas where the parents might disagree with the professionals' own views and approaches and plan ahead for how those problem areas can be approached. Additionally, through these questions, practitioners will express their interest in the parents' experiences, which will begin to convey the practitioner's commitment to the well-being of the entire family and not just to that of the individual with ASD.

Practitioners can further express interest and warmth through the body language they use when listening to family members. When listening to parents, practitioners should imagine how the parents view them. For example, I have been to enough meetings to know that some professionals have very intimidating "listening" faces while in discussion with colleagues and families. My own listening face, I've been told, looks perpetually unhappy, and I have to be aware of this when I am meeting with parents and to make a concerted effort to provide encouragement to parents through smiles and eye contact. When listening, practitioners should remember to nod and smile, when appropriate, to affirm what parents are saying as they are speaking (Leach, 2005). Parents who are met with an expressionless practitioner may feel uncomfortable and wonder what the professional is thinking; this discomfort may make them less likely to self-disclose.

Awareness of the importance of eye contact and facial expression is especially important when clinics use a computer-based system to take notes when meeting with parents. The lack of eye contact between parents and professionals caused by the use of computers can make visits feel impersonal. Practitioners using computers should tell parents that they are using the computer to take careful notes and that, though they will not always look at the parents, they are listening to everything the parents say. Practitioners should recognize that computer use could detract from the warmth of their interaction with the family and should strive to mitigate these unintended negative effects.

Throughout conversation, practitioners should make a concerted effort to maintain natural eye contact with the parents and to sit in a way that conveys openness (Leach, 2005). Many practitioners get in the habit of crossing their arms across their body and slouching during interactions, which may make the practitioner seem stand-offish. A much more open posture—sitting upright with arms away from the chest—may seem less off-putting to parents. When possible, practitioners should evaluate their voice and posture in the moment to consider how a parent might view them during interactions. Practitioners should notice the nonverbal behavior of other professionals interacting with parents, and think about what they like and do not like about how those professionals interact with parents. If an interaction between a professional and a parent makes the practitioner uncomfortable, the practitioner should note what caused that discomfort and take care to avoid it in his or her own interactions. I remember observing one staff member who consistently, though probably unconsciously, rolled her eyes when she disagreed with a parent. The interactions between her and the parent made me so uncomfortable that I am always mindful to not unconsciously indicate my displeasure or disagreement to parents.

Asking open-ended questions and actively listening to the parent may also provide the practitioner with information about the family context. Asking who is at home with the child, who the brothers and sisters are, what other family members are involved, who is working outside the home, and if other stressors are present will provide the practitioner with valuable information about the family context so that plans for treatment can be created while keeping all of the players in mind and taking into account the many demands on the family. One father remembers how important it was that his son's home service coordinator took all of these aspects into account:

> She was seeing [my son] in the home, and she was seeing what was happening. Meeting with us as parents, she was getting the whole family picture, where other people aren't. At school, they're only

getting the school picture. . . . At his current school, while they do want to know what is going on at home, I don't think they would really want to know some of the gory details. I think [my son's home service coordinator] knew those, and so it helped us get him to a better place, and it helped us as a family get to a better place.

Professionals should be sure to write down key points for each family so that they can reference the information regularly and bring it back into context. Remembering the constellation of the family and their important goals and bringing them into conversation at a later time will demonstrate to the family that the practitioner remembers and values their goals and is invested in them as a unit. As one mother shared, "I think that would be my biggest piece of advice to any professional: Just make sure you know your patient. Know who you're talking to. Make sure you really get to know your patient. Even their name helps."

This parent's advice is sound. By listening to families, the practitioner will have a much better idea of who the individual is and the context within which they live. However, the last portion of this quote, "even their name helps," indicates how many professionals this parent has encountered who do not remember her or her son's name. Nothing makes an appointment with a professional seem more impersonal than when the practitioner is unable to recall such basic information about the family. With regard to remembering parents' names, practitioners should not try to dodge the responsibility by calling the parents "Mom" or "Dad," because it just further impersonalizes the experience and can distance parents, as one mother articulated:

The worst experience I have is the sort of feeling of being managed and placated [by professionals]. "Yes, yes, yes, Mom." I hate being called mom. I hate it. I have a freaking name. If you have to call me anything, you can call me [my son's] mom. I'm not *your* mom.

A quick look at a child's file before speaking with the family will remind the practitioner of the family members' names. Practitioners unsure of how to pronounce the name or what the parent would prefer to be called should simply ask, and make a note of it in the file. Parents would much prefer to give the information up front than to remain nameless throughout their interaction with the professional.

In my experience, I am always impressed when my children's medical professionals ask after other members of the family. For example, if I bring my daughter to visit our pediatrician, her doctor will almost always ask, "And how is that little brother of yours?" Such a simple question conveys an awareness of and investment in the overall welfare of the family. When discussing a behavior plan for home, for instance, a practitioner could ask such questions as, "How do you think this will work at home, with his brother and sister in the mix?" Parents value practitioners who take into account the whole family rather than just the individual with ASD.

Communicating understanding. Though listening to build an understanding of the family's experiences is important, rapport can only develop if the practitioner then communicates that understanding to the family. If the practitioner inwardly understands and appreciates the family's experiences and goals but then does not convey understanding with words to the family, rapport will be difficult to establish. Communication skills paired with listening will help practitioners effectively share their understanding with families. Additionally, if the practitioner does not actually understand what the parent has said, communicating this misunderstanding will help clarify things quickly.

When listening to families share their experiences and concerns, practitioners should remember to listen not to form a response composed of their own opinions and thoughts but to truly understand what the parents are saying. When the parents have finished speaking, practitioners can "reflect" back what the parents have just said by restating and summarizing it. Practitioners should not be afraid to also reflect back emotions that are observed while the parents speak, such as acknowledging that a parent must feel upset (e.g., he has tears in his eyes) or frustrated (e.g., her voice is raised). Reflecting the content of what the parents say will give them the opportunity to correct anything that may have been misunderstood and will also demonstrate that the professional has been listening and the parents have been heard. Prefacing reflections by saying, "Let me know if I get anything wrong" or following up reflections with "Am I hearing that right?" will provide families the opportunity to correct any misunderstandings the practitioner may have.

Professionals should be sure not to jump in too quickly to summarize what the parent has to say (or to share their own thoughts), because interruptions are detrimental to establishing effective rapport. Whenever possible, practitioners should wait for natural breaks in the parent's speech to reflect back what has been said. Practitioners may also ask parents to reflect back what the practitioner says at times to help facilitate open dialogue and trust between them and to ensure that the parent does not misunderstand the practitioner.

If a parent has shared information with which the practitioner does not agree, the practitioner should take steps to respond non-confrontationally. A dialogue approach developed by the Love Makes a Family organization, called LARA, can be an effective tool in responding to parents. LARA stands for *listen, affirm, respond*, and *add*, and it can guide practitioners through what might otherwise be confrontational discussions with parents. First, if the practitioner does not agree with the parents' view, the practitioner must listen to identify the underlying goals and values that are at the root of what the parents are suggesting. Identifying these values may help the practitioner respond from a place of common ground—shared values—and affirm what the parents are saying.

For example, if the parents state a desire to try an alternative treatment for the child with ASD and the practitioner does not approve of the treatment, the practitioner should first listen to the parents to understand what values are at the heart of what they are sharing, and then affirm, or reflect back, what the practitioner has heard by rooting it in a shared common goal. For instance, the practitioner might say,

From what you are saying, it sounds like you really want to place an emphasis on increasing your son's communication with others. I share your belief in the importance of building communication for him, since it will reduce some of the problem behavior that you are seeing at home and help you feel like you can address his needs. I would like to make that a primary goal as well.

This reflection will help the parents feel heard and understood and convey that the practitioner recognizes their goals and values.

Once the practitioner has shared this information and received affirmation from the parent that they are truly working from a place of commonality, the practitioner should then take the opportunity to respond by sharing concerns about the alternative treatment, and add some other methods that could be tried or ways in which the alternative treatment could be evaluated (see Chapter 9 for more information). After sharing ideas, the practitioner would then return to the listening stage to hear what the parents have to say about the practitioner's response (American Friends Service Committee, 1998).

## ESTABLISHING UNCONDITIONAL POSITIVE REGARD

In interactions with family, the practitioner should always strive to convey care and respect for all members of the family and to approach the family nonjudgmentally. Some of these skills can be difficult to develop with some families, especially if the practitioner and the family are not on the same page regarding goals for the individual with ASD. However, in these cases it is especially important to demonstrate that, regardless of differences in positions, the practitioner still cares for the child and the family, respects their values, and does not pass judgment.

Conveying care. Many parents I spoke with discussed the importance of feeling as though the professionals with whom they worked saw their child as an individual and cared for the child as an individual. Parents frequently recounted professionals who knew their child beyond just a name and diagnosis and could talk about, and sometimes laugh with the parent about, the unique characteristics of their child. One mother shared,

> We have been lucky with teachers that see him as [him] and not just as a diagnosis or a list of symptoms. They actually see *him*, and know that he is not necessarily going to fit their stereotypical [view of ASD]. They see him as an individual and go to him on that level, rather than trying to make him fit in with that. That is very helpful, to have them see him.

Parents value this approach of focusing on the individual in day-to-day conversations with professionals, and also in the reports written about their child:

> [I valued] the professionals that treated my son as an individual and got rid of that blanket IEP [where they had] just inserted the name. I can't tell you how many meetings we went to that somebody else's name was in there instead of my child's.

Part of recognizing the child with ASD as an individual is focusing on the whole child rather than just the symptoms that need treatment. Professionals often spend so much time focused on the goals that need to be addressed and the symptoms that need to be alleviated that they may forget to share with parents what they *enjoy* about the individual. By sharing these characteristics with parents and taking the time to enjoy these characteristics together, practitioners will convey to parents that they enjoy and care about the child. Conveying warmth and affection for the child will be a huge step toward building a strong relationship with the parents, as one father noted: "I think the first and most important thing is for it to be really clear that [the professionals] like him. They get him, and they like him, and they enjoy him. And really ultimately love him." Parents highly value professionals who clearly demonstrate affection for their child.

On a personal note, I brought my daughter to visit her old preschool classroom, and the way in which the teachers interacted with her by smiling, hugging, and talking with her made my heart ache in a good way: all parents want their children to be loved by those who care for them. A father shared this desire when talking about his definition of an effective professional:

It's the one who loved [my son]. The one who talked about the same kid that I see. . . . I remember there's a great description about Oliver Sacks. They said that . . . it was like your illness was a room and he had gotten in the room with you. Talk about the room. It was like those people [who cared for my son] were sort of in it with me. Also, I trust them because they love my kid—I can tell. I know when they love my kid that I have something incredible.

Another mother added her own take on this important quality in a professional: "Their being invested in [my daughter]. It is more than just their job."

By focusing on the positive qualities of the individual with ASD, professionals will convey that they see the whole child and not just the child's symptoms. This positivity can be very helpful to parents, as one father explained:

[My son] has a number of people that have worked with him for years and years, and the one thing is that they tend to overlook the things that some people see as issues, and they see all the positive things they can do with him. They have helped bring things to our attention, and it challenges them, and they want to work with him more to see what he can do. I think that has been a very positive thing. So those people who look more at these things, or even if they are small things, . . . they are just looking at the positives.

He continued to share advice for professionals:

Keep always on the positive rather than thinking about the negative so much. I can understand where it's hard, kids having tantrums—that's all you're thinking about. But it's narrow-minded in that thinking about the positive things I think helps.

Parents also respond well to professionals who demonstrate care and empathy for the parents and caregivers as well. Pausing to ask the parents how they are doing and referring to ways to help reduce parent stress through strategies discussed in Chapter 7 will help convey care and concern for parents. Though many professionals focus much of their work, appropriately, on the individual with ASD, they should also take time to focus on the needs of the parents by asking them about their experiences and helping them find resources that will best support them. One mother talked about a professional who had helped improve her situation:

> There wasn't just an appointment [where] you come in, you spend your time, and you leave. [I would say], "Okay, this is what I need," and then she would really beat the weeds to try and help find an answer for me. She has been really fabulous about finding resources or connecting me with people who could possibly help me.

Another mother shared an incredibly important quality in professionals: the ability to recognize the strengths of parents and to point out those strengths. In the field of ASD treatment, a good deal of emphasis is placed on providing individuals with ASD with positive feedback for the adaptive skills they learn. Similarly, praising parents for their hard work can have a positive impact and demonstrate appreciation for the effort they have put into caring for their child. This mother described her experiences with the son's developmental pediatrician:

> She said to me something to the effect of, "You're doing a really good job. He's doing well in part because of you." I nearly cried in her office because I so badly needed somebody to say that to me and to recognize that. I think that's something that parents probably don't hear enough of from anybody, because your kid is not going to turn around and tell you, "Mom, you're doing a really good job." I think all parents really need to hear that, but for parents dealing with something like [an ASD diagnosis], I think recognizing the parents for the work that they are putting in and for what they are doing well, from my experience, can be huge in terms of helping parents cope.

Demonstrating respect. Practitioner's respect for parents should focus on two primary areas. The first is respect for the parents' role in their child's life and the knowledge that they have because of that role. Many professionals have been working in the field of ASD treatment for decades and know a great deal about effective treatment for individuals with ASD. However, often professionals with the most experience can also be the worst at developing rapport with a parent of a child with ASD, depending on whether they acknowledge the unique contributions of the parent. Some parents find that they have to struggle to have their voice heard by a professional who single-mindedly develops how he or she plans to approach treatment without regard for the family. A mother of an adult with ASD shared,

> To this day, educators and now people in agencies, these are the people who are supposed to understand. But because I'm a parent, they don't take me seriously, so I had to do a lot of extra work to prove that I knew what I was talking about.

At all times, a practitioner should recognize that while the practitioner may have an expansive knowledge base about treating ASD, the parent will always have more experience with the specific individual with ASD. As one mother rightfully declared on behalf of parents,

> Nobody knows your kid better than you. . . . I don't care [what degrees a professional] has. I live and breathe autism 24–7. I know my child inside out. Swallow your pride and take my perspective into account for every little thing you do with my child.

A practitioner whose approach to treatment is close-minded and does not take into account the experiences or knowledge of the parent is not working effectively within the family system and not only will struggle to develop effective rapport with the family but also will miss opportunities to gain increased insight into the experiences of the child and family.

When working with families, as noted in Chapter 6, the practitioner must recognize that each individual with ASD, and each family, will be different from other individuals and other families. They will have different goals and values, as well as different abilities and resources to draw on. Parents' choice of ASD treatments will be lodged in the values they hold for their child, and understanding those values and goals will help. Assumptions about family values should not be made a priori, and practitioners should work to develop an understanding of the overall family system and how best to treat the individual within that system. Further, practitioners should strive to understand the family's perspective separate from the practitioner's understanding of the child's needs. A mother shared,

> It strikes me that [an effective relationship] is a cooperative relationship with the professional where they take time to pay attention to [the parent], too, even though the child is obviously the most important part. I have had so many good people [work with us], but the good ones were all based on having the give-and-take relationship with the therapist.

By presenting open-ended questions about parents' view of their child's disability and the goals that they have for the child, practitioners demonstrate respect for the family and the values that they hold. A mother illustrated this nicely:

> There's real individual differences for each child or adult. They're very different. Families will make different choices. Those are family values. No one else gets to say, "Oh, your family values are in the wrong place." I kind of feel like as a family we deserve that same respect. [My husband] and I make choices for what is most important to us for [our son], and it may not match what a teacher thinks, but we're making those decisions for a good reason. I've had the best working relationships with people who say, "Okay, what's important to you, and why, and how can we support that?" Or who say, "We're having trouble with this. What do you think we ought to do? Is there something you want to focus on? What do you do at home when this happens?" Those are things that I really, really appreciate.

Being nonjudgmental. A primary component of using unconditional positive regard is taking a nonjudgmental stance when
working with parents. This is one of the areas with which I see practitioners struggle, because ASD is such a hotbed of conflicting and
controversial information and treatments. Many practitioners stand
fiercely by their own treatment and leave no opening to consider
other treatments in their work; furthermore, they go so far as to
chastise parents for using other treatments. Even when practitioners
disagree with parents' position on a treatment or a goal that they
have for their child, practitioners should approach the disagreement
without expressing judgment of the parents (discussed further in
Chapter 9). Recognizing the underlying values and goals the parents
hold will help professionals better understand where the parents are
coming from and help them then effectively work with the parents to
determine how to approach the treatment goal collaboratively.

One parent shared how professionals judged her for considering
alternative causes for her child's problem behavior, aside from ASD:

> For me, [an effective professional] is about being open-minded,
> especially because kids can have comorbid conditions, in addition
> to having autism. If a child is banging his head, don't assume it's
> because he has autism; he could have another problem. I think for
> me those types of things were what we found extremely impor-
> tant, that people look beyond the diagnosis of autism and consid-
> ered these other things.

Another parent shared how detrimental it can be when professionals are not respectful of the treatment choices she has made for her
child:

> I feel like [professionals] need to be scientific, evidence based, *and*
> open-minded. I think that I've worked with practitioners who are
> very closed-minded about certain things. . . . I know people are
> like, "Oh, gluten-free diets are a fad and they're horrible," but I
> happen to have a kid that really needs to be on a gluten-free diet
> or he gets really sick. . . . I'm not jumping on a bandwagon because

I think it's cool or because I think it's going to cure [his] autism—
he needs it. It took me a really long time to figure out what he
needed.

This parent shared her frustration with practitioners who are not
open-minded but also with the fact that they are not respectful of
the efforts she has made as a parent to improve her son's health.

Again, a parent's words will reflect their view of ASD diagnosis
and treatment. Rather than passing immediate judgment on parents'
ideas, practitioners should listen and seek to understand the root
value that underlies what they are sharing with the practitioner. Professionals should always consider the ways in which parents' culture
can impact their choice of values and goals for the child, or the ways
in which emotions can influence the importance that they place
on the goals. For example, I have worked with many parents who
seem to hold what professionals consider "unrealistic" expectations
for their child. Some parents want to teach their son or daughter to
read when they have not yet learned prerequisite skills such as dis-
criminating between pictures or symbols. As discussed in Chapter
6, sometimes these expectations may be rooted in a cultural view of
ASD. Other times parents may be working through feelings of loss
with their child and may be seeking to capture some of the initial
expectations they had for their child. Passing judgment on these
goals may be confusing, disheartening, or in some cases devastating to a parent. Instead, the professional should identify the value
or goal at the heart of the parents' concerns or suggestions, such as
wanting their child to be as independent as possible.

Once they identify this value, professionals can express the ways
in which they agree with the parents (i.e., the values they both share)
before presenting their own ideas about treatment nonjudgmentally. Practitioners should take care to reflect the underlying values
that parents are expressing and then collaborate with the parents
to identify ways in which that goal can be approached, perhaps by
using smaller steps than the parents originally outlined. The goal of
reading, for example, need not be discarded; explaining to parents
the prerequisites that must be taught to help their child read may

help the parents feel that their ideas and hopes for their child are not being discounted.

I find practitioners can also be judgmental when evaluating parents' implementation of treatment strategies in the home (methods of training parents are discussed in Chapter 9). Professionals can take on judgmental attitudes when parents fail to collect data, practice a specific skill, or respond to their child in the specific way a practitioner has recommended. Parents' failure to follow through on treatment recommendations may be due to the number of responsibilities and emotions they are managing at any given time (see Chapter 2). Practitioners should be sensitive to how taxing it can be to care for a child with ASD, even without implementing interventions.

Practitioners should also recognize the extent to which putting an intervention in place can create conflict for parents, as this father explained:

> I think one big challenge that we struggle with a lot is the line between being the parent and being the implementer of the strategy. You have to still stay a parent, but sometimes the things that [professionals are] requesting make you not the parent. So I think that's a challenge. How you manage that I think is very tricky. Maybe in some situations, depending on what you're implementing, it's okay, like if you're trying to teach your kid how to go to the bathroom or something—well, all parents have to do that. You're just doing a stricter version of that, but that's okay. But when you're trying to do a [behavior reduction plan] or something like that sort of stuff, I think it becomes tricky. What we don't want is . . . [our son] to become unhappy with us or frustrated with us because we're implementing some kind of torture on him, whatever degree of torture we're talking about.

This father conveyed that implementing a procedure that will make his son unhappy is difficult for him; he does not want his son to associate his parents with that unhappiness. Parents struggle to connect with their child with ASD, and practitioners need to recognize emotional conflicts such as these and work with parents to identify how best to overcome them. The practitioner should not judge the parent for being unable to follow through on the protocol: the parent's feelings are valid and need to be respected. As another parent shared,

> It's really a little a bit about [the professional] putting [himself or herself] in somebody else's shoes. If families aren't following through with programs at home, help them figure out what's going on, or rewrite the program, or figure out what more support they need, or maybe give a little more positive reinforcement.

Self-disclosure can also be helpful in reducing the judgment that practitioners express. Self-disclosure, or sharing with parents experiences the practitioner has had that can be related to what the parents are going through, should be used thoughtfully. Used too frequently, sharing these experiences can make the boundaries between practitioners and parents fuzzy, or parents may get the sense that professionals just want to talk about themselves. But used sparingly and at the right moments, self-disclosure can head off making the parents feel as though the practitioner is being judgmental, as a parent shared:

> [With the professionals with whom I've worked effectively], I felt that I was talking with friends, but with a friend that got it—a friend that had the guidebook and [was] willing to share it with me. I could go into [sessions] and I could say anything, like my mother-in-law is acting like an a-hole, and [they] wouldn't look at me with this judgment look. [They'd respond], "Okay, this is what you do when mothers-in-law look like an a-hole." [They] could kind of relate to it even though [they] didn't have a child with a disability. [They] could relate it like . . . "When I was growing up my mom would do [this], and even though I didn't have a disability, this is what my mom would do." It was a relatable story as opposed to, "You have kids with special needs; do this special thing."

## STRIVING FOR CONGRUENCE

In their interactions with family members, professionals should strive to be nondefensive. I find this to be another particularly difficult skill for professionals, especially when they have put in a considerable amount of effort and care into teaching or treating an individual with ASD and parents seem unappreciative or displeased with progress. I have occasionally heard professionals say that working with children with ASD is not the hard part; it's working with their parents. Feeling unappreciated by parents is a primary concern for many professionals. Identifying how best to respond in these situations will be crucial to maintaining rapport with parents.

Truthfully, some parents do not share their concerns about their child's treatment with tact. When parents take on accusatory tones, practitioners can have difficulty not responding with defensive knee-jerk reactions. In these moments, however, the practitioner should make use of the strategies discussed earlier in this chapter and try to listen, not to respond to the criticism but, rather, to understand the family value or goal that underlies the parents' concern. By identifying common ground with the parents based on these values, and sharing it with the parents, the practitioner can respond without appearing defensive. Arriving at common ground will make the parents feel that they are not in an "us versus them" situation and may make them more open to hearing the professional's perspective on the child's treatment. The professional will also seem more willing to actively collaborate with the parent rather than steamroll over the parent.

Also in this process of listening, the practitioner may gain a better understanding of the family and of the individual with ASD. As one mother shared, "Professionals from the educational team should not consider parents' feedback as criticism. . . . Parent communication should be looked at as an opportunity to learn about that student. Don't you think?"

Another aspect of congruence is the extent to which the practitioner appears genuine and sincere to the parent. Practitioners should avoid body language or nonverbal mannerisms that indicate that they are not being truthful and honest in what they are sharing with the parent. For example, professionals who praise parents for their efforts with a treatment plan but do not make eye contact with the parents nor offer genuine indications of pleasure to the parents, such as a smile, may not appear sincere in what they are saying, and rapport will diminish.

Likewise, practitioners should be highly aware of the nonverbal communication they share with other professionals while the parents are present. One mother expressed her displeasure with a behavior often shared by professionals when they do not agree with something she has said in a meeting: "Looks around the table. I say something, and there are looks around the table. When you . . . walk out of there and you feel like everyone's talking about you. . . . It's so disrespectful." Shared glances or knowing smiles between professionals in a meeting with parents can be disconcerting to the parents and decrease their trust in the treatment team. A team that says one thing but then indicates another through body language could be described as phony, and the parents may have difficulty working effectively with them. Professionals should be aware of their nonverbal communication in these situations, again putting themselves in the parents' shoes and imagining how the parents must feel observing the interactions between professionals. If sideways glances would make the practitioner uncomfortable if placed in the parents' position, they should be avoided in interactions with the parents.

## CLINICAL TAKE-AWAYS

Throughout this text, I have emphasized the important source of support that professionals can be to families of individuals with ASD. However, the support provided by professionals—providing resources and effective therapy to the child and the family—will be limited if they are unable to build effective rapport with the family. A family that does not feel heard, or who perceives that beneath practitioners' efforts to help the family they are judgmental, disrespectful,

or disingenuous, will be less likely to be forthright or candid with practitioners. Using the strategies in this chapter, the practitioner can build effective rapport with the family to maximize collaboration as they work toward a common goal of improving the life of the child with ASD. A summary of recommendations for practitioners follows.
Practitioners should:

- Join with the family prior to the start of treatment by getting to know the parents, child with ASD, and other family members through questions about their family life. Joining will help families feel comfortable with the practitioner and establish rapport early in the relationship.

- Ask parents open-ended questions about their experiences and goals for their child to elicit novel information about the child, and to facilitate dialogue between the parents and the professional.

- Be aware of the effects of body language, such as eye contact, facial expressions, and posture—especially when using it to communicate with other professionals—when listening to a parent. Put parents at ease by conveying interest, openness, genuineness, and understanding through body language, increasing the likelihood that they will engage in conversation without reservation.

- Ask questions about the family constellation and goals for treatment for the child, and note parents' responses, for future reference in conversations with parents. Recalling information about family members and their values will demonstrate the practitioner's investment in the entire family.

- Reflect the information that parents share with the practitioner back to the parents to convey that the practitioner is listening, and to offer the parents the opportunity to clarify any misunderstandings.

- Employ LARA—listen, affirm, respond, and add—when the practitioner and parents are in disagreement. By responding to parents from a place of common ground and shared values, the practitioner can successfully maintain respectful interactions with the parents and minimize defensiveness.

- Convey care for the child with ASD by expressing to the family what the practitioner enjoys about the child; doing so will demonstrate affection for the child, which is highly valued by parents.

- Praise parents for the work that they have done with their child, to show appreciation for all their efforts to improve their child's life.

- Demonstrate respect for the parents' knowledge of their child. Even though the practitioner may have an in-depth knowledge of ASD treatment, parents will always know the child better than the practitioner. Taking the parents' input into account, as well as their values and goals for treatment, will help the practitioner develop effective rapport with the family.

- Work with families nonjudgmentally by respecting the values that underlie the decisions they make for their child, such as choosing to use alternative treatments or striving for what seems like an impossible goal for their child. Consider how families' values align with the practitioner's and work to collaborate with families from this common ground to maintain rapport.

# Guiding Parents in the Treatment of Autism

As I have shared previously, the purpose of this book was never to teach professionals the specific treatment skills they need to work effectively with individuals with ASD. First and foremost, the purpose is to engender a better professional understanding of the family's experiences so that the practitioner can work more effectively with the family. That said, in any treatment that we implement with the child with ASD we want to ensure that the treatment is as effective as possible to increase the child's adaptive skills and decrease parents' stress. Thus, I would be remiss not to highlight a number of general approaches that can be used within any program for individuals with ASD to ensure that parents implement treatments at home as they are intended and to evaluate the effectiveness of the treatment. These general approaches are important for the professional to keep in mind when working with families, regardless of the type of ASD treatment provided. A structured, systematic approach to parent training and treatment evaluation will ensure that the effects of treatments implemented in home settings are easily evaluated to determine whether they are improving the quality of life for the individual and, transitively, for the family.

To that end, this chapter first outlines the most effective methods for teaching parents how to successfully implement any treatment in the home and provides professionals with guidelines for how to help parents evaluate the effectiveness of the treatments they implement with their child with ASD. The chapter ends with a summary of the importance of teaching parents to advocate for their child—to ensure that effective treatments are also provided outside of the home.

## PROVIDING PARENT TRAINING

Many professionals know that implementing a treatment with high integrity, or according to the original treatment plan, is crucial to evaluate the true effectiveness of the treatment. Whether evaluating the effectiveness of a certain type of medication, therapy method, or alternative treatment, the treatment needs to be implemented as intended for any conclusion about effectiveness to be drawn. From a scientific perspective, if the treatment is not implemented with high integrity, two possible poor outcomes could result. First, if the symptoms of the individual with ASD do not improve, the family and professionals cannot be sure that the treatment is indeed ineffective, because it was not actually implemented as intended. Second, if the symptoms of the individual of ASD do improve, the family and the professional cannot be sure that the improvement was due to the treatment (or to components of the treatment), because they were not implemented with high integrity.

Based on this information alone, correct implementation of ASD treatment is imperative for accurate interpretation of results of treatment and decisions about whether to continue or discontinue the treatment. Identifying methods that are most effective in teaching parents and other family members to implement treatment—and those that are highly ineffective—will help professionals maximize the likelihood of accurate treatment implementation by family members and the best outcome for the individual with ASD.

Practitioners should also consider other potential benefits of effective parent training. Ensuring that the treatment is implemented as intended increases the likelihood of its effectiveness. As discussed in Chapter 7, parents' ability to implement an intervention that has a meaningful impact on the adaptive behavior of their child can improve their own feelings of self-efficacy—the feeling that they can capably tackle challenges that arise. This confidence leads to better management of child problem behavior and is associated with lower levels of parent anxiety and depression (Hastings & Brown, 2002). Once parents feel that they can effectively teach their child and manage problem behavior on their own, their perceptions of their life and of their child may alter dramatically. These tangential effects of parent training should provide professionals with extra motivation to ensure that they teach parents using the most effective methods available.

Avoiding pitfalls. Libraries and bookstores are full of books that provide parents and professionals with information on specific treatment approaches for working with individuals with ASD, including sensory integration, special diets, behavior therapy, and more. Parents can easily access these books at the recommendation of professionals, to gain an overview and foundational understanding of how specific treatments can be applied with a child with ASD, and a sense of support for their own experiences. However, using a book as the sole training method will be highly ineffective.

Even when we are training professionals who have had experience in the field of ASD treatment, we have learned that training methods such as giving them books to read about how to implement treatment, having them attend a workshop about the treatment method, or providing them verbal or written directions for how things should be done are highly ineffective (e.g., Moore et al., 2002). While these "trained" professionals may be able to clearly explain the steps of the treatment through spoken or written word, the translation of these directions into high-integrity practice is a different story. Often, implementation of treatment following only didactic (written or verbal) instruction is riddled with errors. Unfortunately, from research we have also learned that treatment implemented with low integrity may have variable benefit for the child with ASD (Carroll, Kodak, & Fisher, 2013), which highlights the importance of ensuring appropriate training methods are used with all caregivers, including professionals.

Though research has focused largely on the treatment integrity of therapy implemented by professionals, we can expect the impact of didactic instruction to be no better for parents. The field of ASD treatment is new, and digesting all of the information that is provided through didactic instruction will be very difficult, especially if a treatment plan is complex and includes several components. Parents also have many competing demands on their time, and their ability to find time to take in the information and fully understand it will be compromised. Fortunately, however, we have learned a number of teaching methods that are highly effective in coaching parents.

Utilizing successful teaching methods. When teaching parents a specific treatment method for use with their child, the practitioner should always provide a rationale for why the proposed treatment could be effective. Why should the parents spend the time and effort to implement this procedure in the home? What effects should they hope to see? For example, asking parents to teach their child to ask for desired items rather than having a tantrum, while simultaneously ignoring all tantrums, is a tall order. Parents who are asked to do this are likely to be daunted by having to deal with the tantrums that will result from no longer giving in to their child when the child pitches a fit. They may envision family visits where family members judge their parenting skills as their child throws a tantrum. They may think about how their lives will become more difficult when their child is allowed to engage in tantrums without giving the child the desired item. However, if the practitioner provides a rationale for the treatment, parents may be more likely to buy in to the treatment and be motivated to push through these potential challenges.

For instance, in the example provided above, the practitioner should highlight the parents' wish that the child communicate verbally more frequently, and then explain to parents that allowing the child to have tantrums to gain wanted items will decrease the child's motivation to ask appropriately using language. The practitioner may also inoculate parents to possible challenges that could arise with treatment, such as an initial increase in tantrums as the child persists in trying to get what is wanted. Inoculation will make the parents aware of the possibility of these challenges and decrease the possibility that they will discontinue the treatment early when they occur. By sharing with parents that their hard work up front may result in lower levels of problem behavior after they consistently implement the treatment, the practitioner provides parents with an informed perspective on the treatment that may motivate them to try it.

Once the rationale is explained, the practitioner can present a small amount of didactic instruction to introduce parents to the concepts they will be taught. What the treatment is, how it works, what the steps are, and what parents might do to respond in various situations will all be valuable information. Providing a written protocol will help parents better envision the treatment and answer questions they may have about how best to implement the treatment, especially as a reference when the practitioner is no longer present. A written protocol for the treatment may also increase the likelihood that multiple family members implement the treatment in the same way, though more in-depth training should be undertaken with all family members who will be key implementers of the treatment in the home.

However, practitioners must remember that didactic information alone is not sufficient for effective parent training. In fact, no type of teaching is a replacement for providing parents with the opportunity to practice the skills required for treatment implementation, first by role-playing and then with their child, while the practitioner is available to provide feedback on their implementation. As a first step, role-playing is a nice way for parents to practice skills without being in the heat of the moment with their child, and without the risk of mistakes impacting the child. The practitioner and the parent can take turns role-playing the treatment. The practitioner can act as the parent first, modeling for the parents how they should respond in specific situations; parents will be able to provide the practitioner with different examples of the child's behavior. Parents role-playing the child will allow them to act out all the "what if" situations they can think of to see how the practitioner would respond. Then, the roles can be reversed so that each parent has the opportunity to implement the treatment. This is a much more effective way of problem-solving possible challenges that may arise than having a conversation in which the parent repeatedly asks the practitioner, "What if . . . ?"

When parents take a turn responding to the child's behavior, the practitioner should vary the types of behavior and challenges that will arise so that parents must respond variably using the intervention. During this role-playing, the practitioner should provide the parents with plenty of feedback and praise for their implementation of the intervention. Steps that are incorrectly implemented should be practiced again in role-play to ensure that the parents know how to implement them.

Once the parents are proficient with the treatment in role-play, the practitioner may model the use of the treatment strategies directly with the child with ASD. Many parents are grateful for the opportunity to observe the practitioner work directly with their child and to see the approaches in action before they try them. The parents should then implement the treatment with their child.

Using the guidelines for contextualized treatment provided in Chapter 6, the practitioner should identify the periods of the day or the routines during which the parents will be most successful in implementing the treatment, and conduct the training in the context of those routines. The first time this happens, the practitioner should be present to provide feedback to the parents. This provides support for the parents so that they do not feel left alone, and it also provides additional learning opportunities. Without feedback, parents and professionals alike commonly begin to veer off the treatment course. Small errors can become patterns, and in no time the treatment could begin to look vastly different from what was intended. Providing feedback early on will help prevent some of those errors from emerging in the early stages.

Ahead of time, practitioners and parents should have a conversation about the ways in which the parents learn best, such as whether they prefer to learn the steps of an intervention by referencing a written protocol, plotting a decision tree, or hearing it explained, and whether they prefer to watch someone model the intervention first or learn best by doing it themselves. In this conversation, practitioners should ask whether it is best to provide feedback to the parents in the moment or after the parents have finished working with the child. The practitioner and the parents can weigh the pros and cons of each approach. Providing feedback in the moment allows parents to change their behavior immediately and may decrease the likelihood of the child's problem behavior escalating in response to treatment errors. However, providing constant feedback through-out parents' time with the child may unnerve parents and disrupt the flow of their work with the child. It may also decrease the likeli-hood that the parents will learn from their mistakes and correct the errors independently. Practitioner and parents can discuss the best approach, which may differ from parent to parent and from treat-ment to treatment.

The professional may also consider providing feedback by video recording the parents' time with the child. This approach can be especially effective because it allows the parents and the practitio-ner to watch the video of the parents' and child's behavior together and have a discussion without the child present about what was done well or what could have been done differently. Additionally, video feedback sessions could be used when the practitioner is not able to be present when the treatment is implemented but still wishes to provide feedback on the parents' behavior.

This type of in-person behavioral training with feedback is highly effective and has been incredibly helpful in teaching parents a number of skills, including how to teach their child adaptive skills and how to help reduce problem behavior (e.g., Bearss et al., 2015; Koegel, Symon, & Koegel, 2002; Tonge et al., 2006). For instance, a large-scale study by Bearss et al. (2015) demonstrated that behav-ioral parent training for problem behavior, including the use of direct instruction, role-playing, and coaching sessions, was more effective in reducing child problem behavior than simply providing parents with in-person training about the diagnosis of ASD and effective treatment and advocacy.

Numerous studies have also demonstrated significant impact of parent training on the well-being of parents of individuals with ASD (see the discussion in Chapter 7 on formal social support reducing parent stress). Overall, successful parent training can result in lower parent stress levels and a more positive outlook on the child (Bristol, Gallagher, & Holt, 1993; Koegel, Bimbela, & Schreibman, 1996; Tonge et al., 2006). For example, in a study by Tonge et al. (2006), parents were assigned to either a group in which they were taught about ASD and behavior management strategies to use with their child using the active skills training methods described above, or taught the same content but without any active skills training procedures. Parents who received active, hands-on training in how to manage their child's problem behavior experienced greater alleviation of mental health symptoms such as anxiety, insomnia, somatic symptoms, and family dysfunction following training.

How training is implemented may also have an effect on parents' well-being. Some research indicates that training with a more positive view of the children with ASD, such as focusing on what they can do and the skills that they do have, results in a more positive view of the children in the parents' eyes (Steiner, 2011). A more negative stance in the training—focusing on the child's deficits—results in the parents using more negative language about their child. As discussed in Chapter 7, a more positive parental view of their child will likely reduce parents' stress. This serves as another important reminder to professionals to be mindful of possible inadvertent emphasis on the child's weaknesses and challenges when talking with and teaching parents, and the importance of proactively focusing on capabilities rather than deficits.

Overcoming barriers. Despite their best efforts at providing effective parent training and contextualizing the treatment (see Chapter 6), professionals may find that treatment is not implemented the way it was intended in the home. When this happens, professionals must discuss with parents why this happened. Professionals should not make the assumption that parents were not listening to the professional, that they do not find the treatment valuable, or that they are lazy. Consider the numerous stresses and responsibilities that parents have (see Chapter 2). If the child is recently diagnosed with ASD, the family may still experience the heightened stress accompanying the diagnosis (see Chapter 1).

If parents are holding multiple jobs, or have multiple children, they may be pulled in so many different directions that they have been unable to implement the treatment. For example, imagine a practitioner talks with a parent and decides that teaching the child to request preferred food might be best implemented at the dinner table each night. However, after the practitioner teaches the parents how to prompt the child to request, the parents may find that further opportunities for teaching their child are completely sidelined by a busy family who is rushing through dinner to get to bedtime or other activities. Rather than becoming upset with the family for their failure to follow through with the treatment, the practitioner should ask the family what interfered with successful implementation and problem solve how to make treatment easier to implement for the family. Maybe another time of day would be better, or maybe the family might be able to divide up tasks more efficiently at dinnertime to leave time to focus on their child's requests.

What practitioners should not do is ignore that the treatment has not been implemented. Discussing lack of treatment implementation can be uncomfortable for many practitioners, especially if professionals prefer to avoid confrontation. I have seen some practitioners take a passive-aggressive stance when treatments are not implemented and become resentful over time with these parents. Instead, professionals should nonjudgmentally acknowledge that the treatment was not implemented (e.g., "What got in the way last week?") and restate the importance of the treatment to parents. Professionals should then have a clear discussion about the barriers that arise that prevent the parents from implementing the treatment successfully. By talking to parents about barriers, the professional fully acknowledges the numerous competing activities the family has in their life and how difficult it can be to add treatment for their child to their duties. The parents may welcome the chance to talk more about how to make the treatment easier or more integrated within their lives; if needed, the practitioner might need to take a step back and rethink the goal of the treatment and whether it could be achieved using another method.

In some cases, the professional may find that the barriers to implementation are not related to the home context, such as family schedules and multiple parent responsibilities. As discussed in Chapter 2, some parents face significant concerns with their own mental health, such as anxiety and depression, which can reduce their likelihood of implementing treatments in the home. If mental health concerns are standing in the way of parent implementation of treatment, professionals should first address those concerns before returning to training. Professionals may offer resources where parents may receive support from other parents or professionals to help reduce the symptoms they are experiencing and make them more open and available for training and successful implementation of treatment for their child.

## WEIGHING THE BENEFIT OF TREATMENT

Another role of the practitioner, from the earliest stages of the ASD diagnosis, is helping parents identify effective, evidenced-based treatments for their child. Type in "autism treatment" in your favorite Internet search engine, as many parents do, and see how many different treatments show up. The number of purported effective treatments for ASD is astounding, and for parents—novice or veteran—it can be completely overwhelming. Helping parents understand how to evaluate treatments will be critical to help increase the likelihood that the child receives effective treatment and to reduce the stress parents may experience in choosing treatments on their own. As a first step, parents must know how to evaluate the evidence for the treatments they consider by doing their own research. As a second step, they should understand how to evaluate the impact of a chosen treatment on their own child once it is implemented.

Examining the evidence. When parents are searching for initial treatments for their child, helping them understand the role of science in evaluating treatments is critical. This can be difficult, because science gets a bad rap with the general public—it conjures up images of clinicians in lab coats conducting medical trials that have nothing to do with the child in question. A parent may have difficulty digesting scientific information presented in studies but instead find considerable comfort in a website or blog post that supports a treatment that may not have been scientifically studied. So many parents are taken in by information online or shared in person by other parents reporting great effects of specific treatments on their own child. What parent does not want to hear that a specific treatment has unimaginable positive effects on an ASD diagnosis, and that a child experienced "breakthroughs" after exposure to the treatment?

Often, treatments that have not been scientifically studied are packaged on the Internet in such a way that parents are apt to believe the claims that are made about treatment success. Doctors may share their views on the success of these studies but without actual data to support their findings. Perhaps most influential, parent testimonials describe the success of the treatment with their own children. For parents of individuals with ASD, other parents of children on the autism spectrum are highly relatable and deemed trustworthy.

Some of the parents I talked with described how important they found hearing from other parents who shared the treatments that worked, in the hopes that some of these could be effective with their own child. One mother shared,

> We've met one or two other parents with kids with issues similar to [my son]. Not exactly the same, but it always feels like such a relief that I've found them. You can talk about, "Do you use this? Do you use that? What do you think of the school? What do you think of the IEP team? What do you about all of these different things?"

Another parent shared how she actively sought out the opinions of other parents when considering treatments for her young daughter:

> When my daughter was two and a half, and we were still working through early intervention, I got on the phone and started calling people in the community, people I didn't know, making cold calls and saying, "Hi, I heard you had a child on the spectrum in the

district. How have you addressed X, Y, and Z? Who have you gone
to? Who's helpful, who's not helpful?"

Parents place considerable value on the opinions and experiences of
other parents, and as a result the advice of other parents—whether
offered in person or online—can be one of the most influential
sources parents use to identify treatments for their child with ASD.

However, the opinions of other parents may be just that: opinions.
The conclusions that other parents draw about their child's response
to a specific treatment may not be based on data but may instead be
based on their subjective evaluation of effectiveness. Unfortunately,
parents who have invested a great deal of time and energy into a specific treatment (and want nothing more than their child to improve)
may consider it more successful than it was in actuality. Additionally,
many parents introduce several treatments at once and may attribute improvement in child behavior to one specific treatment when
another component caused the positive response.

While other parents can be an incredible source of information to
identify potential treatments for a child with ASD, the importance
of referencing the scientific evidence cannot be overstated. Unfortunately, the use of science may seem like an unnecessary step to
parents when other parents and professionals describe a specific
treatment that has been successful. Additionally, even though parents may recognize that a treatment is not evidence based, they may
be terrified that they will miss out on what could be the one break-
through treatment for their child, even if the chance of that break-
through is incredibly small.

In the face of persuasive parents and professionals who share
their opinions about effective treatments for individuals with ASD,
practitioners must be prepared to advocate for the important role
of science in evaluating any identified treatment. Therapists should
explain to parents that science is merely the method of evaluating
the effects of any treatment, be it medical or psychological, in a way
that is controlled and systematic. Professionals can also help parents
understand the different types of scientific evidence available for different treatments, based on different types of studies.

One type of research, known as a *group design study*, is used when a large number of participants are evaluated at once. For example, a medical researcher might evaluate the effects of a specific type of drug in reducing the repetitive, or self-stimulatory, behaviors of individuals with ASD. To do so, he might assign one group of individuals with ASD to the treatment group that receives the medication and also assign another group of individuals with ASD to the control group that instead receives a placebo, or sugar pill. The participants (and their parents) would not know whether they were receiving the medication or the placebo (a blinded study). Rather than relying on parent report of the child's behavior, in an ideal study raters would evaluate the impact of the drug on self-stimulatory behavior by recording each instance of the behavior during an observation period. These raters would also not know whether each child was receiving the medication or the placebo (a double-blind study). In this way, the researcher can evaluate whether the self-stimulatory behavior appears less in the medication group than in the control group without potential bias in parental or professional report, based on knowing whether the child is receiving the treatment or not.

While the group design is the most rigorous form of research, it does limit our ability to determine each individual's response to the treatment and whether that response was a meaningful change. Another type of research often used for children with ASD, called the *single-subject research design*, focuses on the effects of a treatment on individuals: an individual's behavior on the treatment is compared with behavior off the treatment or while receiving different treatments. Imagine, for example, that a psychologist wants to evaluate the impact of a sensory diet, or activities that provide an individual with desired sensory input such as swinging, spinning, or tactile sensations, on the self-stimulatory behavior of children with ASD. That psychologist would first clearly specify what that sensory diet would look like by describing the activities that would take place, the duration of the sensory sessions, and the frequency with which they are conducted. The psychologist would also clearly define what self-stimulatory behavior is so that it can be easily identified and measured by a trained observer. Then, the psychologist could use a few different methods to evaluate the impact of this treatment.

As one option, the psychologist could choose three students who all engaged in self-stimulatory behavior and observe their behavior when the sensory treatment is not in place (referred to as baseline). Then, the psychologist could start the treatment with the first student to observe the effects, while the second and third students remain in baseline. After the treatment has been initiated with the first student and effects observed, the psychologist could initiate treatment with the second student, and then with the third, to observe effects. If all students demonstrated a decrease in self-stimulatory behavior when *and only when* the treatment was put in place, we can be reasonably sure that the treatment was responsible for the change in behavior. This study design, called a *multiple-baseline design*, can also be implemented with only one child but staggered across three different settings or with three different but related skills or instances of problem behavior. Again, if effects are observed across all settings or behaviors only when the treatment is implemented, the effectiveness of the treatment is clearly demonstrated.

Alternatively, psychologists wanting to evaluate the treatment with only one student could implement the treatment on selected days while not implementing the treatment on the other days. The treatment days and the nontreatment days would alternate back and forth, with behavior data recorded to see whether self-stimulatory behavior was consistently lower on the days on which the student received treatment. In research terms, this type of research design is called an *alternating treatments design*.

Another way to evaluate this treatment at the individual level is to collect baseline data on the occurrence of self-stimulatory behavior for several days before the treatment is put in place. Then, the treatment could be introduced for another period of time (several days minimum) to evaluate the overall level of the behavior when treatment is in place. Once the practitioner determines that a change occurs when the treatment is implemented, treatment can be removed to see if the behavior again reverts to original baseline levels and that the changes in behavior are observed only when the treatment is in place. If the treatment seems effective, it can be reimplemented in a final phase. This *reversal design* can be a highly effective way to evaluate the effects of a treatment approach on a behavior that professionals feel will revert to baseline levels when the treatment is not in effect. It is not a good choice when professionals feel that the individual with ASD will maintain the skill or improvement in behavior once the treatment is implemented.

Regardless of whether group design or single-subject design is used, one of the most important components of scientific evaluation of treatments is that it is unbiased. Books, blogs, articles, and anecdotal stories that are based on parents' or professionals' perceptions of the effects of a treatment are very likely biased and are not scientific. Instead, behavior needs to be carefully measured with *and* *without* treatment in a way that controls for potential bias (e.g., blinding). That is the strength of scientific research, and why parents should rely on science to help them identify studies that are supported by research.

The problem, however, lies in the scientific community's inability to easily convey scientific results to parents and professionals. Often, scientific findings are buried in journal articles that can be difficult to understand. Also, the findings of just one journal article that supports a specific treatment is typically not enough evidence to conclude that the treatment is effective and evidence based. Instead, ideally a treatment is supported by several group design and/or single-subject design studies, all well designed with control and unbiased measurement, before considering it evidence based.

Fortunately for parents and professionals, many organizations have taken on the task of poring over the scientific studies for treatments of individuals with ASD to determine which are evidence based and which are not. This is exceedingly helpful for parents and professionals, because it takes the guesswork out of identifying effective treatments for a child with ASD. One mother described her reliance on some of these organizations for helping identify treatments that may be effective with her son:

I do try to rely on Asperger/Autism Network, or Autism Speaks, or those reputable organizations [to help identify effective treatments] because there's just too much. I mean, I think I'm decent at sifting through what's good and what's junk, but there's just too much of it.

Another parent shared high regard for a specific published resource:

The best publication was *Educating Children with Autism* from the National Academy Press because it looked at all of the interventions and what [clinical] research has proven effective. And I still stand by that—even though it is from 2001, I think it's the best thing out there.

With the growth of Internet resources, parents can easily access a wide range of publications and websites that provide information about the evidence base for specific treatments, and categorize those that are effective and evidence based, potentially effective but need more evidence, ineffective, and potentially harmful. Several of these are listed in the Resources section of this book. For example, the National Autism Center evaluates the evidence for available treatments for ASD according to stringent criteria and summarizes their findings in the National Standards Project, available online. Additionally, the website for the National Professional Development Center on Autism Spectrum Disorder not only lists treatments that are considered evidence based on their free website but also provides training materials for each of the different treatments, including written protocols, video tutorials, and data sheets.

Resources such as these will be helpful for both parents and professionals alike. For clinicians working in diagnosis, identifying some of these important organizations and sharing them with parents could go a long way in helping parents who are just starting to orient themselves in a maze of treatments. One mother expressed how overwhelmed she felt when tracking down early services for her son:

One specific thing I think would be super helpful for practitioners is to have a brief, not overwhelming list of resources they can hand to parents when they make a diagnosis so that the parents have someplace to start in learning about ASD and in locating services

for their kid and just generally figuring out what they are supposed to be doing. Would have helped a lot with that "lost" feeling I
had at first trying to work these things out and locate and evaluate
resources on my own.

A word of caution to practitioners, however: while the lists of
effective treatments can be a great starting point for families, we
still know little about which among these "effective treatments" will
be suitable for specific individuals with ASD. Not all of them will be
effective with every child, and some trial and error may be needed.
Preparing parents for this likelihood, and conveying that none of the
treatments should be considered a magic bullet, may help reduce
disappointment if their child does not make progress on a specific
treatment. Helping parents systematically evaluate the treatments
that will be a good fit for their child will be imperative.

Evaluating treatment. For many parents, there will come a
time when they would like to try a specific treatment with their
child. In the best of situations, the parents will have researched
the treatment and found a substantial evidence base for it but now
wonder whether it will be effective with their own child. In many
cases, however, parents may be unable to find evidence that supports the treatment but still wish to try it with their child. Perhaps
they read about it in a book a parent wrote about their child's gains
in the treatment, or they read about it on the Internet, or a friend
told them about it. Regardless of how they learned of it, the parents
are undeterred by the lack of evidence for the treatment, and the
practitioner must first understand why parents push for these treatments and also how to help them evaluate them (see also Chapter 8
on building rapport).

Parents are susceptible to non-evidence-based treatments for
many reasons. First, this treatment is for their child, and most parents will do anything to help their child have a better life. Second,
parents are bombarded with stories of children with ASD making
incredible gains, seemingly overnight, sometimes to the point where
they are indistinguishable from their peers and "lose" their diagnosis
of ASD. With stories like these comes the hope that there is a treat-

ment, somewhere, that will better help their child with ASD. Third, you may have heard Stephen Shore's oft-cited quote, "If you've met one person with autism, you've met one person with autism." Children with ASD differ from one another so significantly that sometimes it is easy for parents to refute research and tell themselves, "That treatment may have not been found to be effective with those children, but my child is different from those children." (And they are right! Their child is different from those children!)

Finally, many parents hear that a crucial period of time exists in early childhood when treatment will be most effective; after this point, children may be less likely to make gains from treatment. This warning to parents may cause them to frantically try different treatments in the hopes that one will work in that window of time. As one mother shared about the available treatments for ASD,

> We just try every single one. I tend to have a more holistic approach. . . . We were fortunate enough to have financially the ability to try a number of things. We did try the oxygen chamber because you hear such amazing things, you read these testimonials, and of course as any parents, you don't really know what to believe. But you hear enough, read enough, and say, "Alright, let's try it, it's just oxygen," stuff like that. So, we did that with supplements, and we did that with diets, and we saw changes, different things, different therapies. But at the same time, I'm really not going to say that anything was a magic pill.

One can see, then, why parents are likely to try treatments that are not necessarily backed by evidence. When this happens, a practitioner working with the parent has two jobs. First, the professional should be clear in describing to parents the body of evidence (or lack of evidence) that supports the treatment. If a treatment has been demonstrated as ineffective, or has been poorly studied, the professional should encourage the use—even if simultaneous—of effective treatment. For example, Mandell and Novak (2005) shared one way to nonconfrontationally share with parents concerns about potentially ineffective treatment:

I am not sure if this treatment is effective for treating autism, but I know that if used/taken as directed, it will not be harmful. If you believe it is effective, you can continue to use it. But I think that your child will show greater improvement if you use the treatments I have prescribed in addition to this other treatment. (p. 113)

Talking with parents about the evidence base for treatment is especially important if the evidence suggests that the use of the treatment could actually bring harm to the child with ASD, such as chelation, a medical procedure intended to draw heavy metals and minerals out of the body. In these cases, sharing these possible side effects (which in some cases can include death) is an ethical responsibility of any professional and should not be taken lightly.

However, unless the treatment proposed by parents has proven adverse risks for the child, the professional should not be so disparaging about alternative or non-evidence-based treatments that the parents then just stop telling the practitioner about their treatment choices. I have known parents who, in the face of critical professionals, continued to use alternative treatment choices but did not tell those professionals about it. Driving parents "underground" with their use of alternative treatments can be risky, because the use of those treatments, in secrecy, could have an effect on the child, positive or negative. Practitioners must be aware of all treatment use so that side effects and unintended effects of the treatment can be monitored.

Additionally, a large role that a practitioner can take is helping parents understand that because limited evidence exists for the use of the treatment, it is important that they, the parents and the practitioner, evaluate the effectiveness of the treatment. Ideally, we want to help parents develop the skills necessary to evaluate treatment for their child. One mother shared her own motivation to learn how best to do this:

I read, and read, and read, and I go and I talk to a lot of people. . . .
I'm always looking for someone who can provide me evidence of

[the effectiveness of the treatment] they do or how I can assess it
on my own child.

Evaluating a treatment with a child with ASD can be done using
any of the single-subject research designs described above in a systematic way. The mother above who said that she "tries everything"
shared how she tries them systematically to evaluate their impact on
her daughter's behavior:

> We tried a lot of different things, but we didn't try them just one
> after the next. We tried them based on what the research bore up
> to be the most popular or the most effective treatment. I would try
> them one at a time, and if I didn't see results I was done with that
> and moved on to the next thing. You can't try all of them at the
> same time.

She also expressed why trying one treatment at a time is important
to her: "They're your babies. . . . They can't make that decision for
themselves so it has to be systematic, it has to be scientific."

In addition to the use of a sound research design, the treatment
must be defined to describe exactly how it will be implemented each
day; a written protocol and effective training of parents and other
caregivers will help ensure that the treatment is implemented as
intended. Also, parents must identify the goal for the treatment in a
way that can be measured. For example, a parent's goal of "reducing
symptoms of autism" is not defined well enough to result in meaningful, measurable data. Instead, a parent may hope that the treatment
will increase how much the individual talks to others and the overall
level of eye contact made with others. Both communication and eye
contact can be clearly defined and then measured by the parents
or by an impartial observer, such as a teacher. Ideally, the behavior
may even be measured by someone who does not know whether the
individual has received treatment that day or not so that the data are
unbiased. The levels of behavior in baseline and treatment conditions can then be compared to identify whether the treatment was
effective. One mother shared her reliance on data when evaluating a

new treatment, compared with her husband's subjective evaluation: "My husband used to say, 'Oh, but I don't think this [treatment] is working,' and I'll say, 'You know what, I don't have enough data. I'm still doing it until my data show otherwise.'"

The use of data can also be incredibly important in building up trust with parents of individuals with ASD. Data will allow a professional to show a family in an observable way the impact of treatment on behavior. Without data, a parent may not trust a practitioner's subjective evaluation of what occurred following the implementation of treatment, especially if it runs counter to what the parent believes occurred. A mother shared one of the ways in which a practitioner developed an effective relationship with the family, which highlights the importance of data in evaluating treatment effects:

> She connected with us by building our trust, by working very, very hard, and by showing us her work. . . . We saw the work that was being done. We saw those data sheets, we saw those programs that were being run, we saw how much time was being put in, we saw the progress.

The use of single-subject research design is a hallmark of applied behavior analytic work with individuals with ASD. However, in my work with colleagues, I have used these methods to evaluate a wide variety of treatments that parents have wished to try. Many of the treatments are medications, but they also include special diets, such as gluten-free or casein-free diets, or sensory activities, hyperbaric oxygen chambers, or prism glasses. Through the use of scientific research design and careful measurement of behavior, we were able to share the results of these evaluations with parents to allow them (and professionals) to make informed decisions about whether the treatments were effective or not.

The point I am making here is that although single-subject research design is a hallmark of ABA, it can be applied to evaluate any type of treatment for individuals with ASD. A mother shared,

> I'm happy to try lots of different things, and some things work and some things fall flat on their face. One of the therapies [we

tried] was . . . this vision therapy, and that was . . . a total waste of time, and it did not help at all. But I'm willing to try anything and look at, is it making things better or is it making things worse? If it's making things better, go with it. If it's making things worse, see if it can be tweaked. If it can't be tweaked, give it up and go try something else. You bark up a lot of wrong trees, but you try everything. And the things that work, great. The things that don't work, let it go.

Providing parents with clear evidence that a treatment is ineffective, through the use of data, will be an incredible service to the family. While ineffective treatments will not always be dangerous to the individual with ASD, implementing them can take up considerable time that could be spent on another treatment that may be more effective.

The use of a valid scientific research design in evaluating a treatment is crucial. Sometimes in my work parents request evaluations of a treatment *after* their child has already started a medication. This approach is especially problematic, because my colleagues and I are not medical doctors and cannot recommend that the student take or not take medication on specific days (and many medications do not work like this; they need to be taken for a long period of time to be effective). Thus, we had little ability to evaluate the effects of the treatment. If the medication has already been started, and we have not been able to collect a period of baseline before it started, we are unable compare the medication period with a period when no medication was in place. Parents should be made aware that requests for these types of evaluations need to be made in advance of changes in medication. Also, whenever possible, the practitioner should be able to work with and contact the prescribing medical professional to determine how best to evaluate the impact of the medication.

## PROMOTING ADVOCACY

Another role a practitioner can play in guiding parents in the treatment of their child with ASD is helping them learn to advocate for their child. Having consulted for many school districts over the years, I sometimes found myself wondering whether parents knew about the services that could be most effective for their child and, if so, if they knew that they could ask that those services be provided. Many parents of children with ASD advocate for their child as if it were a job, but others do not know how or for what they should be advocating. Many parents may not even know that they have a right to advocate for changes to their child's services, as this mother articulated:

> When parents sit back and just let educators, or teachers, or principals, or heads of whatever it might be, steer the ship without them, I think they're doing their child a disservice. I think sometimes parents don't know that [they can advocate for their child]. They feel like they shouldn't—"That's not my place." You know what, it is your place. You're their parent and you had this child, and yes, it's a tough situation, but we've all got these things to do for our kids.

Introducing parents to the resources they need to advocate for their child is an important role that practitioners can fill, as the same mother continued: "That's how you start helping these kids, because the parent is the greatest advocate for that kid. No one's going to care more than the parent."

The first thing any parent needs in order to be a strong advocate for their child is knowledge about their child's rights within the educational system. As one parent pointed out, "Knowledge is power, and you've got to empower yourself. Because if you don't, no one else is going to do it for you." While professionals will be most effective if they themselves are knowledgeable about the ins and outs of parents' legal rights, if they are not confident in their knowledge of the educational system they should be able to direct parents to resources that will provide them with the information that they need. For example, states provide guidelines, often released by the state department of education, for students' rights in the special educational system under state regulations and the federal Individuals with Disabilities

Education Act. Many of these resources are available online. Additionally, local organizations may provide parents with workshops and training on how to understand their legal and educational rights. Professionals should be aware of these local offerings and share that information with parents. Additionally, professionals should be able to direct parents to professional advocates and lawyers knowledgeable about the rights of individuals with ASD in the educational system.

Professionals should also encourage parents to visit other programs that serve individuals on the autism spectrum, especially those that are largely regarded as highly effective, evidence-based programs for children with ASD. The purpose of these visits is not to determine whether the child would be well suited for that program (although that may be the purpose on occasion) but, rather, to observe the procedures that are implemented and consider whether they might be effective for their child. Attending parent-friendly conferences and workshops about treatment options will also introduce parents to treatments that may be useful for their child. One mother shared,

> I made it a point to go look at one program or go to one kind of conference a month on autism for something. Even the most updated apps for children with autism, I went to one of those [workshops]. There are certain schools I just love to go visit to learn.

Professionals should be knowledgeable about workshops and other resources that will teach parents how to advocate for their child, because advocacy is a skill that needs to be learned. Professionals should encourage parents to ask questions of their educators and other service providers so that they fully understand the services that their child is receiving. Teaching parents about common terms and acronyms they might hear when talking with other professionals could also be highly beneficial for the parent, because the information will help parents better understand their child's current services. One mother lauded the efforts of a professional who took that time to teach me . . . how to communicate with others about [my daughter]. So if ever I'm going to . . . have a conversation with her speech language pathologist, my head's not going to be spinning when she uses these words [I don't understand]. When there's a program that says X, Y, and Z, I'm going to know what it means versus be one of those parents who says [to the professional], "Okay, well, you know what you're doing."

Additionally, parents should be taught through advocacy training how to effectively communicate with professionals to avoid contentious debates.

Professionals should also encourage parents to be highly organized in keeping the numerous documents that will be generated about their child's progress and care. Practitioners should suggest that parents create a binder to file and transport diagnostic, cognitive, neuropsychological, and other reports, as well as past and current educational plans, progress reports, and behavior intervention plans. A strong organizational system will allow parents to easily access information relevant to their child's services and best advocate for their child based on previous assessments and reports detailing the needs of their child.

## CLINICAL TAKE-AWAYS

To many professionals, the types of training and evaluation discussed in this chapter may seem to fall solidly within the realm of ABA treatment for individuals with ASD, as they are largely supported by behavior analytic research and strongly recommended by behavior analysts. I may be highlighting my behavior analyst role in writing this chapter, but I argue that any professional working with families can use the methods described here to good effect. By carefully teaching parents to implement treatment in the home using the most effective methods of training, and by assessing the treatment using both a review of the evidence and systematic evaluation, practitioners can help family members identify the most critical components of their child's treatment. Further, evaluation can help families limit the number of ineffective treatments that take up valuable time that could be used for other, more effective treatments to help improve child functioning and reduce parent stress.

Further, the approaches described in this chapter are incredibly important to help practitioners build up parents' sense of confidence in their own ability to implement treatment and to choose effective treatments for their child. All parents would welcome the opportunity to feel as though they are doing the best they can for their child, and using the most effective methods of teaching and treatment will help them achieve that sense of accomplishment. To that end, all practitioners should look to broaden their therapeutic perspective by including these principles of evaluation in their work. The following list summarizes recommendations.

Practitioners should:

- Avoid substituting written protocols or verbal instruction for other, effective teaching methods when teaching parents to implement treatment with their child. Research has shown repeatedly that this type of didactic information is an ineffective method of caregiver training when used in isolation.

- Provide families with a rationale for the treatment that will be used with their child to increase their motivation for follow-through with the practitioner's proposed components.

- Inoculate parents to the potential challenges that will arise in treatment so that they will expect them and not give up on implementation when they occur.

- Utilize role-playing, as well as in-person practice with the child while the practitioner observes and gives feedback, to provide parents the opportunity to first implement the treatment with support from the practitioner.

- Deliver feedback to parents on implementation to ensure that errors are not repeated, because they can quickly become established patterns of errors. Discuss with parents ahead of time whether they would prefer feedback be provided while they are working with their child or afterward.

- Focus on a positive view of the children—what they can do or where they are improving—instead of focusing on a negative view, such as skill deficits. A positive view may help parents take on a more positive outlook on their child, which can help reduce parent stress.

- Address barriers that arise when families are not able to implement treatment successfully. Do not ignore parents' failure to implement treatment following a recommendation. Instead, nonjudgmentally inquire what got in the way of successful implementation, and problem solve ways in which to overcome the barriers.

- Be mindful of the possibility that mental health concerns may serve as a barrier to parents' successful implementation of treatment. In these cases, recommend support services such as those discussed in Chapter 7.

- Direct parents toward resources that summarize the evidence base for treatments, but caution parents that even evidence based treatments may not be effective for every child with ASD. Help parents develop ways to evaluate the effectiveness of a specific treatment with their own child.

- Strive to understand why parents may wish to try treatments unsupported by evidence, and be prepared to help parents evaluate the effectiveness of these treatments by using scientific design and clearly defining the procedures and the behavior the parents intend to change.

- Provide parents with resources they need to advocate effectively for their child, such as state regulations and national standards for special education. Encourage parents to visit other reputable programs in ASD treatment and direct them to workshops that teach parents how to effectively advocate for their child.

# Conclusion

Through the years, we have come to learn more and more about the most effective treatments for individuals with ASD. Medical professionals, psychologists, therapists, and other providers work tirelessly to identify the best course of treatment for each child with ASD, forever presented with new challenges that they must overcome. As each of us strives to perfect our science within our own area of treatment, however, we run the risk of becoming overly focused on the treatment and the child with ASD. As we carefully and devotedly work to ensure that our assessments are conducted with accuracy and treatments are implemented with the highest integrity, we may inadvertently begin to ignore the context within which individuals with ASD live, and with it the most important, influential people in their development: their family.

This book asks professionals to focus their attention on the entire family, including the extended family, when working with individuals on the autism spectrum. Using the recommendations in this book, I invite professionals to welcome parents into the treatment of their child not only by teaching them to implement treatment but also by considering the family's experiences and the ways in which those experiences will affect the family and impact the effectiveness of the intervention.

More than one hundred recommendations are provided in this book for how to understand and support parents, siblings, and other family members of the child with ASD. Even if practitioners choose to use only a few of these recommendations to help improve their relation with a child's family, inroads will be made in the care of individuals with ASD from the biopsychosocial approach that George Engel proposed decades ago. By approaching the family with empathy and understanding, the practitioner will spread positive effects beyond the treatment of the child to impact the family as well.

But how should practitioners begin to use the recommendations in this book? Where to start? At the very least, look beyond the child with ASD in treatment and get to know the family as a whole by asking questions about their experiences with their child, starting from diagnosis. Learn who they are as individuals, and recognize the numerous responsibilities they have in addition to raising their child with ASD. Work to better understand their perspective of ASD and the goals that they have for their child. Understand how their view of ASD is influenced by their culture, and respect these views when implementing treatment. Over time, practitioners should learn to let go of assumptions that they have about families' experiences and beliefs about their child's ASD, and get to know each family as a collection of individuals wholly different from any other family they have met. Most important, practitioners should convey to families that they see them as a group of individuals with unique needs and concerns.

Clinic and school programs for individuals with ASD should consider providing support specifically for parents and siblings. Designing workshops that address specific periods of development, offering support groups for parents, siblings, and extended family, and even providing group and individual therapy sessions that help teach parents effective coping strategies will help them overcome some of the largest stressors they face. Programs that cannot provide these resources should assemble a resource packet for families of local support services. For parents who are isolated and struggling to manage the challenges of raising a child with ASD, some of these services may be a lifeline. Training programs for teachers, therapists, and other professionals that provide treatment within the context of the family should offer instruction on how to integrate the family into treatment with understanding and empathy.

I have learned a great deal in writing this book, not only from the literature I have reviewed but also from the parents and siblings who shared their experiences with me. The amount I have learned, even after years of working in the field, illustrates how much more practitioners have to learn from families. Research should continue to focus on the experiences of parents and siblings and, most important, the ways in which practitioners can provide effective support to reduce the stress experienced by families of individuals with ASD. However, I hope that practitioners will also strive to learn directly from parents and siblings and become more effective, empathic professionals who provide support to the entire family.

Ultimately, practitioners should strive to be *that* professional: the professional that parents tell me about in interviews, the one who has had a meaningful impact not only on their child's life but also on their own (see Chapter 8). These are the professionals that parents tell me truly work to understand their experiences and to address their needs in addition to the needs of their child. Professionals should endeavor to be the doctor, psychologist, teacher, therapist, or support person that parents tell other parents to see, not only because of the effective treatment methods used but also because of the care and empathy expressed to the family. Please strive to be that professional, the one that parents hold in the highest regard and hold in their memory and hearts as one of the most positive experiences they have had in raising a child with ASD.

# RESOURCES

## GENERAL

### Online Resources

*Autism Speaks Resource Guide*
https://www.autismspeaks.org/family-services/resource-guide

A list of resources available to families of individuals with ASD by state, including diagnosticians; adult services; advocacy, financial, and legal resources; biomedical interventions; community and support networks; early intervention; school-age services; respite care; and health services.

*Autism Speaks Tool Kits*
https://www.autismspeaks.org/family-services/tool-kits

A collection of tool kits for professionals and families of individuals with ASD addressing such areas as toilet training, puberty, sleep, and challenging behavior.

*SEARCH Social Skills Resources for Children*
http://searchcenter.ucr.edu/social_skills_resources_for_children.pdf
http://searchcenter.ucr.edu/social_skills_resources_for_adolescents.pdf

Resources available to address the social skills needs of children and adolescents with ASD, distributed by SEARCH Family Autism Resource Center at the University of California, Riverside.

*SEARCH Resource Guide*
http://searchcenter.ucr.edu/images/pdf/resourceguide2014.pdf

An extensive national resource list for individuals with ASD and their families, distributed by SEARCH Family Autism Resource Center at the University of California, Riverside.

*Autism Internet Modules*
http://www.autisminternetmodules.org/

Free Internet modules for treatment for individuals with ASD. Modules include case studies, instructional videos, pre- and postassessments, and a glossary of terms.

*Autism Speaks Websites for Families*
https://www.autismspeaks.org/family-services/resource-library websites-families

A list of websites applicable to and useful for families of individuals with ASD.

*Asperger/Autism Network*
https://www.aane.org

An organization devoted to providing information, community, advocacy, and support for individuals on the autism spectrum.

*Autism Society*
http://www.autism-society.org/

A resource for parents about ASD, living with ASD, and identifying and navigating services.

*Autism Organizations*

http://www.researchautism.org/resources/links/Organizations.asp

A list of international, federal, and state organizations dedicated to providing support services to individuals with ASD and their families, compiled by the Organization for Autism Research.

*Guide for Military Families*

http://www.researchautism.org/resources/reading/documents/MilitaryGuide.pdf

A guide for military families raising a child with ASD, made available by the Organization for Autism Research.

## Books

Delmolino, L., & Harris, S. (2013). *Essential first steps for parents of children with autism: Helping the littlest learners*. Bethesda, MD: Woodbine House.

Koegel, L. K., & LaZebnick, C. (2005). *Overcoming autism: Finding the answers, strategies, and hope that can transform a child's life*. New York, NY: Penguin Books.

National Research Council (2001). *Educating children with autism. Committee on educational interventions for children with autism*. Catherine Lord and James P. McGee (eds.) Division of Behavioral and Social Sciences and Education. Washington, DC: National Academy Press.

Rosenblatt, A. I., & Carbone, P. S. (2012). *Autism spectrum disorders: What every parent needs to know*. Elk Grove Village, IL: American Academy of Pediatrics.

Volkmar, F. M., & Wiesner, L. A. (2009). *A practical guide to autism: What every parent, family member, and teacher needs to know*. Hoboken, NJ: Wiley.

## ASSESSMENT AND DIAGNOSIS

*Learn the Signs. Act Early.*
http://www.cdc.gov/ncbddd/actearly/

Downloadable materials on child development and screening resources, offered through the Centers for Disease Control and Prevention and available in several languages.

*Modified Checklist for Autism in Toddlers, Revised (M-CHAT-R)*
https://www.autismspeaks.org/what-autism/diagnosisscreen-your-child

A free online screening tool for ASD, made available by Autism Speaks.

*Early Intervention Offices by State*
https://www.autismspeaks.org/early-access-care/ei-state-info

A list of websites and phone numbers for early intervention offices within each state, compiled by Autism Speaks.

*Parents' Guide to Assessment*
http://www.researchautism.org/resources/reading/documentsAssessmentGuide.pdf

A guide for parents to the assessment process for their child, made available by the Organization for Autism Research.

*100 Day Kit*
https://www.autismspeaks.org/family-services/tool-kits

Free downloadable tool kit for families of children newly diagnosed with ASD, with separate versions for children under age 4 and school-age children, made available by Autism Speaks. Also available in Spanish.

*ASD Diagnosis: What Do We Tell the Kids?*
http://www.iancommunity.org/cs/articles/telling_a_child_about_his
_asd

Guidelines from the Interactive Autism Network on how parents can talk with their children about the diagnosis of ASD.

## SPECIAL EDUCATION RIGHTS AND SERVICES

*Navigating the Special Education System*
http://www.researchautism.org/resources/reading/documents/SPED
Guide.pdf

A guide to the rights of individuals with ASD under the Individuals with Disabilities Education Act, including tips for advocacy for parents, made available by the Organization for Autism Research.

*Your Child's Rights*
https://www.autismspeaks.org/what-autism/your-childs-rights

A summary of the educational rights of children with ASD under the Individuals with Disabilities Education Act, made available by Autism Speaks.

## SAFETY

*Guide to Safety*
http://www.researchautism.org/resources/reading/documents/Life
JourneyThroughAutism-AGuidetoSafety.pdf

Information for safety issues and strategies related to raising a child with ASD, made available by the Organization for Autism Research.

*Checkpoint Wristbands*
http://checkpointwristbands.com/pavblog/blog&id=23

Safety wristbands for individuals with ASD, equipped with QR technology, that provide important health and safety information for individuals in the event of an emergency.

*Big Red Safety Box*
http://nationalautismassociation.org/big-red-safety-box/

A free tool kit for families of individuals with ASD who are prone to eloping and wandering away from family, including a safety booklet, window/door alarms, and safety window clings and wristbands.

*Project Lifesaver*
http://www.projectlifesaver.org/

An organization promoting the use of tracking technology to aid in the search and rescue of individuals with cognitive disorders.

## TRANSITION TO ADULTHOOD

### Online Resources

*Guide for Transition to Adulthood*
http://www.researchautism.org/resources/reading/documents/Transition
sitionGuide.pdf

A guide to planning for transition to adulthood for an individual with ASD, including transitions to vocational placement and postsecondary education, made available by the Organization for Autism Research.

*AHEADD: Achieving in Higher Education*
http://www.aheadd.org/

A comprehensive college support program that provides coaching, mentoring, and self-advocacy skills for college-age students with ASD, as well as those with attention-deficit/hyperactivity disorder, dyslexia, and other learning difficulties.

*Programs for Students with Asperger Syndrome*
http://collegeautismspectrum.com/collegeprograms.html

A list of college programs (2-year, 4-year, and secondary support) by state for individuals with ASD.

*Postsecondary Education Resources*
https://www.autismspeaks.org/family-services/resource-library/post-secondary-education-resources

A list of postsecondary education resources for individuals with ASD, including scholarship opportunities, made available by Autism Speaks.

## Books

Palmer, A. (2006). *Realizing the college dream with autism or Asperger syndrome: A parent's guide to student success.* Philadelphia, PA: Jessica Kingsley.

## SIBLINGS

## Online Resources

*Autism, My Sibling, and Me*
http://www.researchautism.org/family/familysupport/documents/OAR_YoungSiblingsResource.pdf

A fun workbook created for siblings of individuals with ASD, 5–10 years of age, by the Organization for Autism Research.

*Life as an Autism Sibling: A Guide for Teens*
http://www.researchautism.org/family/familysupport/documents/OAR_TeenSiblingsResource.pdf

A guide that addresses the questions and concerns of teenage siblings of individuals with ASD, by the Organization for Autism Research.

*Brothers, Sisters, and Autism: A Parent's Guide to Supporting Siblings*
http://www.researchautism.org/family/familysupport/documents/
OAR_SiblingResource_Parents_2015.pdf

A parent's guide to effectively supporting siblings of individuals with ASD, made available by the Organization for Autism Research.

*A Sibling's Guide to Autism*
http://www.autismspeaks.org/sites/default/files/a_siblings_guide_
to_autism.pdf

An interactive guide for siblings ages 6–12 years to teach them about ASD, the way ASD will affect their life, and ways in which to interact with their sibling and parents, made available by Autism Speaks.

*Sibling Support Project*
https://www.siblingsupport.org/

A national program dedicated to supporting siblings of people with special health, developmental, and mental health concerns. This website contains links to books for siblings, online groups for teen and adult siblings, and local peer support groups for siblings of children with special needs.

*What Siblings Would Like Parents and Service Providers to Know*
https://www.siblingsupport.org/documents-for-site/WhatSiblings
WouldLikeParentsandServiceProviderstoKnow.pdf

A guide to sibling concerns for parents and service providers, based on online discussions with adult siblings of individuals with disabilities, made available by the Sibling Support Project.

*Sibling Blogs*
http://siblingleadership.org/services-and-supports/sibling-blogs/

A list of blogs written by siblings of individuals with disabilities, hosted by the Sibling Leadership Network.

## Books

Harris, S. L., & Glasberg, B. A. (2003). *Siblings of children with autism: A guide for families*. Bethesda, MD: Woodbine House.

## EXTENDED FAMILY

### Online Resources

*A Grandparent's Guide to Autism*
http://www.autismspeaks.org/sites/default/files/a_grandparents_
guide_to_autism.pdf

A resource to help grandparents understand the diagnosis of ASD, how to cope with the diagnosis, and how to interact with and support the child with ASD and the family, made available by Autism Speaks.

*Family, Friends and Your Child's Autism Spectrum Disorder*
http://raisingchildren.net.au/articles/autism_spectrum_disorder_
family_friends.html

Information for parents and grandparents of individuals with ASD on the grandparents' experiences, and how they can help support the family. Includes videos of how to talk with others about ASD and ask for support from extended family.

### Books

Melmed, R., & Wheeler, M. (2015). *Autism and the extended family: A guide to those outside the immediate family who know and love someone with autism*. Arlington, TX: Future Horizons.

Palmer, A. (2012). *A friend's and relative's guide to supporting the family with autism: How can I help?* Philadelphia, PA: Jessica Kingsley.

## CULTURE AND RELIGION

*Your Religious Community*
https://www.autismspeaks.org/family-services/your-religious-community

Links to resources on religion and ASD for parents, families, and religious leaders.

*Autism Speaks: Religious Resources*
https://www.autismspeaks.org/family-services/resource-library/religious-resources

A list of resources for information on integrating individuals with ASD into religious customs, including books, essays, online groups, and websites.

*Teaching Children with ASD to Attend Religious Services*
http://www.asatonline.org/research-treatment/clinical-corner/teaching-children-with-autism-to-attend-religious-services/

A guide to integrating individuals with ASD into religious services, made available by the Association for Science in Autism Treatment.

*Autism and Faith: A Journey Into Community*
http://www.djfiddlefoundation.org/userdocs/Autism_&_Faith_final-1.pdf

A free booklet on integrating individuals with ASD into faith communities, funded by the Daniel Jordan Fiddle Foundation.

*Considering Culture in Autism Screening*
http://www.maactearly.org/uploads/9/2/2/3/9223642/4_considering_culture_asd_screening.pdf

A guide for clinicians on how to consider and account for the effects of culture in ASD screenings, made available by Massachusetts Act Early.

*Pacer Center Translated Content*
http://www.pacer.org/translations/

Translated information on the special education rights of and ser-vices for children with developmental delays, produced by the Parent Advocacy Coalition for Educational Rights.

## PARENT COPING

### Online Resources

*A Parent's Guide to Understanding and Coping With an Autism Diagnosis*
http://www.kennedykrieger.org/sites/kki2.com/files/card-diagnosis_v8-final.pdf

A pamphlet that provides parents with recommendations for how to respond to their child's ASD diagnosis over time, made available by the Center for Autism and Related Disorders at the Kennedy Krieger Institute.

*A Parent's Guide to Autism*
http://www.autismspeaks.org/sites/default/files/a_parents_guide_to_autism.pdf

A guide to teach parents about ASD and help them identify strate-gies and support to reduce the impact of raising an individual with ASD on the family, made available by Autism Speaks.

*Autism and Your Family*
https://www.autismspeaks.org/what-autism/autism-your-family

Tips for parents, siblings, grandparents and other extended family on how to cope with the diagnosis of ASD, made available by Autism Speaks.

*Parenting for Service Members and Veterans*
http://www.veterantraining.va.gov/parenting/

Although primarily a resource for military families, Module 5 of this parenting course offers information on managing parenting stress and emotions that is applicable to parents of any child.

*The Five Main Tenets of Mindful Parenting*
http://www.huffingtonpost.com/lisa-kring/the-5-main-tenets-of -mindful-parenting_b_4086080.html

Tips for mindful parenting, authored by Lisa Kring and published by the Huffington Post.

*Find a CBT Therapist*
http://www.findcbt.org/xFAT/

Therapist search engine offered through the Association for Behavioral and Cognitive Therapies.

*Find a Therapist*
https://therapists.psychologytoday.com/rms/

Therapist search engine offered through Psychology Today.

## Books

Eichenstein, R. (2015). *Not what I expected: Help and hope for parents of atypical children*. New York, NY: Penguin Group.

Naseef, R. A. (2012). *Autism in the family*. Baltimore, MD: Brookes Publishing.

Rezek, C. (2015). *Mindfulness for carers: How to manage the demands of caregiving while finding a place for yourself*. Philadelphia, PA: Jessica Kingsley.

Senator, S. (2011). *Making peace with autism: One family's story of struggle, discovery, and unexpected gifts*. Boston, MA: Trumpeter Books.

Senator, S. (2011). *The autism mom's survival guide (for dads, too!): Creating a balanced and happy life while raising a child with autism.* Boston, MA: Trumpeter Books.

## PARENT SUPPORT NETWORKS

*Parent to Parent USA*
http://www.p2pusa.org/

A national program that provides emotional and informational support to families of children with special needs.

*Mom to Mom*
http://www.mom2mom.us.com/

A support and crisis hotline for parents of individuals with special needs, providing peer support, mental health screening, and referrals to mental health services.

*Autism on the Seas*
http://www.autismontheseas.com/

Cruises offered specifically for adults and families of individuals with ASD.

*Autism Moms Support Group*
https://www.facebook.com/AutismMomsSupportGroup/

An example of a Facebook community of parents of individuals with ASD.

*My Autism Team*
http://www.myautismteam.com/

An Internet-based social network for parents of children with ASD.

*Autism Meetup*
http://autism.meetup.com/

A list of Meetup groups specifically for families of individuals with ASD.

## FAMILY CRISIS

## Online Resources

*Recognizing and Preventing Abuse and Sexual Abuse*
https://www.autismspeaks.org/family-services/autism-safety-project/abuse
https://www.autismspeaks.org/family-services/autism-safety-project/sexual-abuse

Guides for professionals on how to recognize and prevent abuse and sexual abuse in individuals with ASD, offered by Autism Speaks.

*Keeping Our Children Safe*
http://www.uscucedd.org/component/jdownloadssend/6-training-materials/62-keeping-our-children-safe

A booklet for caregivers and providers of children with developmental disabilities to reduce the risk of abuse, authored by Angela Bissada, Leslie Scher Miller, Ann Marie Wiper, and Michele Oya (2000).

## Hotlines

*National Suicide Prevention Lifeline*
http://www.suicidepreventionlifeline.org/, (800) 273-8255

A 24-hour, toll-free, confidential suicide prevention hotline available to anyone in suicidal crisis or emotional distress. Warning signs of suicide for professionals are also available on this site.

*Crisis Text Line*
http://www.crisistextline.org/, text START to 741-741

A 24-hour, not-for-profit organization providing free crisis intervention via text message.

*Childhelp National Child Abuse Hotline*
https://www.childhelp.org/hotline/, (800) 422-4453

A 24-hour confidential hotline staffed with crisis counselors (and
interpreters) who can provide crisis intervention, information, literature, and referrals for emergency and support services.

*National Domestic Violence Hotline*
http://www.thehotline.org/, (800) 799-7233

A 24-hour confidential hotline for those experiencing domestic violence or seeking support or resources.


## PARENT-PROFESSIONAL COLLABORATION

### Online Resources

*Making Parent-Mediated Interventions Work for Families*
https://www.autismspeaks.org/science/research-initiatives/toddler
-treatment-network/making-parent-mediated-interventions-work
-fam

Tips for professionals integrating families into the treatment of individuals with ASD, made available by Autism Speaks.

*Collaborative to Improve Care for Children with ASD*
http://www.nichq.org/childrens-health/autism/collaborative-to
-improve-care-for-children-with-asd

A description of the efforts of the National Institute for Children's

Health Quality to improve care for children with ASD, including videos on working with parents to improve care.

*Parent, Family, and Community Engagement*
http://eclkc.ohs.acf.hhs.gov/hslc/tta-system/family

Resources for educational professionals and service coordinators on how to engage family members in the education and treatment of the child with ASD, made available by Head Start.

## Books

Sanders, R. Q. (2008). *How to talk to parents about autism.* New York, NY: Norton.

## EVALUATING EVIDENCE FOR TREATMENT

*Association for Science in Autism Treatment*
http://www.asatonline.org/

A resource for parents and professionals to help them navigate evidence-based treatment for individuals ASD. A newsletter is available.

*National Standards Project*
http://www.nationalautismcenter.org/national-standards-project/

A comprehensive report on interventions demonstrated to be effective in treating individuals with ASD, distributed by the National Autism Center.

*A Parent's Guide to Evidence-Based Practice and Autism*
http://www.nationalautismcenter.org/resources/for-families/

A guide to the importance of evidence-based treatment for individuals with ASD, describing effective treatments and using data to evaluate to guide decisions in treatment, made available by the National Autism Center.

*Educator's Manual to Evidence-Based Practice and Autism*
http://www.nationalautismcenter.org/resources/for-educators/

A guide to evidence-based treatment for individuals with ASD, evaluating treatment decisions, and taking into account the values and preferences of families in treatment, made available by the National Autism Center.

*A Parent's Guide to Research*
http://www.researchautism.org/resources/reading/documents/ParentsGuide.pdf

A guide for parents on how to search, read, and interpret research on treatment for individuals with ASD, made available by the Organization for Autism Research.

*Interventions for Autism Spectrum Disorders: State of the Evidence*
https://www1.maine.gov/dhhs/ocfs/cbhs/ebpac/asd-report2009.pdf

A report on evidence-based practice for the treatment of individuals with ASD, including descriptions of treatment approaches, authored by the Maine Department of Health and Human Services and the Maine Department of Education.

*National Professional Development Center on ASD*
http://autismpdc.fpg.unc.edu/evidence-based-practices

A resource offering training modules for evidence-based practices. Each module includes a general description of the treatment, the supportive literature base, step-by-step instructions for implementation, and an implementation checklist.

*Autism Speaks: Advocacy Tool Kit*
https://www.autismspeaks.org/family-services/tool-kits/advocacy

A tool kit to provide basic knowledge of advocacy and negotiation skills to parents.

# REFERENCES

Abbeduto, L., Seltzer, M. M., Shattuck, P., Krauss, M. W., Orsmond, G., & Murphy, M. M. (2004). Psychological well-being and coping in mothers of youths with autism, Down syndrome, or fragile X syndrome. *American Journal on Mental Retardation, 109*, 237–254.

Alamsaputra, D. M., Kohnert, K. J., Munson, B., & Reichle, J. (2006). Synthesized speech intelligibility among native speakers and nonnative speakers of English. *Augmentative and Alternative Communication, 22*, 258–268.

American Friends Service Committee. (1998). *Responding to comments or questions: The LARA method*. Ann Arbor, MI: Author.

American Psychiatric Association. (2000). *Diagnostic and statistical manual of mental disorders* (4th ed., text rev.). Washington, DC: Author.

American Psychiatric Association. (2013). *Diagnostic and statistical manual of mental disorders* (5th ed.). Washington, DC: Author.

Ammerman, R. T., Van Hasselt, V. B., & Hersen, M. (1988). Maltreatment of handicapped children: A critical review. *Journal of Family Violence, 3*, 53–72.

Aranda, M. P., & Knight, B. G. (1997). The influence of ethnicity and culture on the caregiver stress and coping process: A sociocultural review and analysis. *Gerontologist, 37*, 342–354.

Baker, B. L., Blacher, J., & Olsson, M. B. (2005). Preschool children with and without developmental delay: Behaviour problems, parents' optimism and well being. *Journal of Intellectual Disability Research, 49,* 575–590.

Baker, B. L., McIntyre, L. L., Blacher, J., Crnic, K., Edelbrock, C., & Low, C. (2003). Pre-school children with and without developmental delay: Behaviour problems and parenting stress over time. *Journal of Intellectual Disability Research, 47,* 217–230.

Bearss, K., Johnson, C., Smith, T., Lecavalier, L., Swiezy, N., Aman, M., . . . Scahill, L. (2015). Effect of parent training vs parent education on behavioral problems in children with autism spectrum disorder: A randomized clinical trial. *Journal of the American Medical Association, 313,* 1524–1533.

Bengtson, V. L. (2001). Beyond the nuclear family: The increasing importance of multigenerational bonds. *Journal of Marriage and the Family, 63,* 1–16.

Benson, P. R. (2010). Coping, distress, and well-being in mothers of children with autism. *Research in Autism Spectrum Disorders, 4,* 217–228.

Benson, P. R. (2012). Network characteristics, perceived social support, and psychological adjustment in mothers of children with autism spectrum disorder. *Journal of Autism and Developmental Disorders, 42,* 2597–2610.

Benson, P. R. (2014). Coping and psychological adjustment among mothers of children with ASD: An accelerated longitudinal study. *Journal of Autism and Developmental Disorders, 44,* 1793–1807.

Bettelheim, B. (1967). *The empty fortress: Infantile autism and the birth of the self.* New York, NY: Free Press.

Blackledge, J. T., & Hayes, S. C. (2006). Using acceptance and commitment training in the support of parents of children diagnosed with autism. *Child & Family Behavior Therapy, 28,* 1–18.

Bouma, R., & Schweitzer, R. (1990). The impact of chronic childhood illness on family stress: A comparison between autism and cystic fibrosis. *Journal of Clinical Psychology, 46,* 722–730.

Boyd-Franklin, N., & Bry, B. H. (2000). *Reaching out in family therapy: Home-based, school, and community interventions.* New York, NY: Guilford Press.

Bristol, M. M., Gallagher, J. J., & Holt, K. D. (1993). Maternal depressive symptoms in autism: Response to psychoeducational intervention. *Rehabilitation Psychology, 38*, 3–10.

Brobst, J. B., Clopton, J. R., & Hendrick, S. S. (2009). Parenting children with autism spectrum disorders: The couple's relationship. *Focus on Autism and Other Developmental Disabilities, 24*, 38–49.

Bromley, J., Hare, D., Davison, K., & Emerson, E. (2004). Mothers supporting children with autistic spectrum disorders: Social support, mental health status, and satisfaction with services. *Autism, 8*, 409–423.

Brown, R., & Kulik, J. (1977). Flashbulb memories. *Cognition, 5*, 73–99.

Buescher, A. V. S., Cidav, Z., Knapp, M., & Mandell, D. S. (2014). Costs of autism spectrum disorders in the United Kingdom and the United States. *JAMA Pediatrics, 168*, 721–728.

Burkett, K., Morris, E., Manning-Courtney, P., Anthony, J., & Shambley-Ebron, D. (2015). African American families on autism diagnosis and treatment: The influence of culture. *Journal of Autism and Developmental Disorders, 45*, 3244–3254.

Carroll, R. A., Kodak, T., & Fisher, W. W. (2013). An evaluation of programmed treatment-integrity errors during discrete trial instruction. *Journal of Applied Behavior Analysis, 46*, 379–394.

Casey, L. B., Zanksas, S., Meindl, J. N., Parra, G. R., Cogdal, P., & Powell, K. (2012). Parental symptoms of posttraumatic stress following a child's diagnosis of autism spectrum disorder: A pilot study. *Research in Autism Spectrum Disorders, 6*, 1186–1193.

Celiberti, D. R., & Harris, S. L. (1993). Behavioral intervention for siblings of children with autism: A focus on skills to enhance play. *Behavior Therapy, 24*, 573–599.

Cidav, Z., Marcus, S. C., & Mandell, D. S. (2012). Implications of childhood autism for parental employment and earnings. *Pediatrics, 129*, 617–623.

Cleary, B. (1955). *Beezus and Ramona*. New York, NY: HarperCollins.

Clifford, T., & Minnes, P. (2012). Who participates in support groups for parents of children with autism spectrum disorders? The role of beliefs and coping style. *Journal of Autism and Developmental Disorders, 43*, 179–187.

Cuccaro, M. L., Wright, H. H., Rownd, C. V., Abramson, R. K., Waller, J., & Fender, D. (1996). Professional perceptions of children with developmental difficulties: The influence of race and socioeconomic status. *Journal of Autism and Developmental Disorders, 26*, 461–469.

Dabrowska, A., & Pisula, E. (2010). Parenting stress and coping styles in mothers and fathers of pre-school children with autism and Down syndrome. *Journal of Intellectual Disability Research, 54*, 266–280.

Dawson, G., Rogers, S., Muson, J., Smith, M., Winter, J., Greenson, J., . . . Varley, J. (2010). Randomized, controlled trial of an intervention for toddlers with autism: The Early Start Denver Model. *Pediatrics, 125*, e17–e23.

DeStefano, F., Price, C. S., & Weintraub, E. S. (2013). Increasing exposure to antibody-stimulating proteins and polysaccharides in vaccines is not associated with risk of autism. *Journal of Pediatrics, 163*, 561–567.

Donovan, A. M. (1988). Family stress and ways of coping with adolescents who have handicaps: Maternal perceptions. *American Journal on Mental Retardation, 92*, 502–509.

Durkin, M. S., Maenner, M. J., Meaney, J., Levy, S. W., DiGuiseppi, C., Nicholas, J. S., Kirby, R. S., Pinto-Martin, J. A., & Shieve, L. A. (2010). Socioeconomic inequality in the prevalence of autism spectrum disorder: Evidence from a U.S. cross-sectional study. PLoS ONE 5(7): e11551.

Ekas, N. V., & Whitman, T. L. (2011). Adaptation to daily stress among mothers of children with an autism spectrum disorder: The role of daily positive affect. *Journal of Autism and Developmental Disorders, 41*, 1202–1213.

El-Ghoroury, N. H., & Romanczyk, R. G. (1999). Play interactions of family members towards children with autism. *Journal of Autism and Developmental Disorders, 29*, 249–258.

Elliott, G. R., & Eisdorfer, C. (1982). *Stress and human health*. New York, NY: Springer.

Engel, G. L. (1977). The need for a new medical model: A challenge for biomedicine. *Science, 196*, 129–136.

Ennis-Cole, D., Durodoye, B. A., & Harris, H. L. (2013). The impact of culture on autism diagnosis and treatment: Considerations for counselors and other professionals. *Family Journal: Counseling and Therapy for Couples and Families, 21*, 279–287.

Estes, A., Munson, J., Rogers, S. J., Greeson, J., Winter, J., & Dawson, G. (2015). Long-term outcomes of early intervention in 6-year-old children with autism spectrum disorder. *Journal of the American Academy of Child and Adolescent Psychiatry, 54*, 580–587.

Evans, G. W. (2004). The environment of childhood poverty. *American Psychologist, 59*, 77–92.

Ferraioli, S. J., & Harris, S. L. (2011). Teaching joint attention to children with autism through a sibling-mediated behavioral intervention. *Behavioral Interventions, 26*, 261–281.

Ferraioli, S. J., & Harris, S. L. (2013). Comparative effects of mindfulness and skills-based parent training programs for parents of children with autism: Feasibility and preliminary outcome data. *Mindfulness, 4*, 89–101.

Fiske, K. E. (2009). A cross-sectional study of patterns of renewed stress among parents of children with autism. *Dissertation Abstracts International: Section B, Sciences and Engineering, 70*(11-B), 7193.

Fombonne, E. (2003). Epidemiological studies of pervasive developmental disorders: An update. *Journal Developmental Disorders, 33*, 365–382.

Fombonne, E., & Chakrabarti, S. (2001). No evidence for a new variant of measles-mumps-rubella-induced autism. *Pediatrics, 108*, e58–e66.

Freedman, B. H., Kalb, L. G., Zablotsky, B., & Stuart, E. A. (2012). Relationship status among parents of children with autism spectrum disorders: A population-based study. *Journal of Autism and Developmental Disorders, 4*, 539–548.

Gabel, S. (2004). South Asian Indian cultural orientations toward mental retardation. *Mental Retardation, 42*, 12–25.

Glasberg, B. A., & Harris, S. L. (1997). Grandparents and parents assess the development of their child with autism. *Child & Family Behavior Therapy, 19*(2), 17–27.

Glasberg, B. A., Martins, M., & Harris, S. L. (2006). Stress and coping among family members of individuals with autism. In M. G. Baron, J. Groden, G. Groden, & L. P. Lipsitt (Eds.), *Stress and coping in autism* (pp. 277–301). New York, NY: Oxford University Press.

Gray, D. E. (2003). Gender and coping: The parents of children with high functioning autism. *Social Science & Medicine, 56*, 631–642.

Gudino, O., Lau, A., Yeh, M., McCabe, K., & Hough, R. (2009). Understanding racial/ethnic disparities in youth mental health services: Do disparities vary by problem type? *Journal of Emotional and Behavioral Disorders, 17*, 3–16.

Haley, W. E., Roth, D. L., Coleton, M. I., Ford, G. R., West, C. A. C., Collins, R. P., & Isobe, T. L. (1996). Appraisal, coping, and social support as mediators of well-being in Black and White family caregivers of patients with Alzheimer's disease. *Journal of Consulting and Clinical Psychology, 64*, 121–129.

Harris, S. L. (1996). Serving families of children with developmental disabilities: Reaching diverse populations. *Special Services in the Schools, 12*, 79–86.

Harris, S. L., & Glasberg, B. A. (2003). *Siblings of children with autism: A guide for families.* Bethesda, MD: Woodbine House.

Harris, S. L., Handleman, J. S., & Palmer, C. (1985). Parents and grandparents view the autistic child. *Journal of Autism and Developmental Disorders, 15*(2), 127–137.

Harry, B. (1992). Developing cultural self-awareness: The first step in values clarification for early interventionists. *Topics in Early Childhood Special Education, 12*, 333–350.

Harry, B., Rueda, R., & Kalyanpur, M. (1999). Cultural reciprocity in sociocultural perspective: Adapting the normalization principle for family collaboration. *Exceptional Children, 66*, 123–136.

Hartley, S. L., Seltzer, M. M., Head, L., & Abbeduto, L. (2012). Psychological well-being in fathers of adolescents and young adults with Down syndrome, fragile X syndrome, and autism. *Family Relations, 61*, 327–342.

Hartshorne, T. S. (2002). Mistaking courage for denial: Family resilience after the birth of a child with severe disabilities. *Journal of Individual Psychology, 58*(3), 263–278.

Hastings, R. P. (1997) Grandparents of children with disabilities: A review. *International Journal of Disability, Development and Education, 44,* 329–340.

Hastings, R. P., & Brown, T. (2002). Behavior problems of children with autism, parental self-efficacy, and mental health. *American Journal on Mental Retardation, 107,* 222–232.

Hayes, S. C., Luoma, J. B., Bond, F. W., Masuda, A., & Lillis, J. (2006). Acceptance and Commitment Therapy: Model, processes, and outcomes. *Behaviour Research and Therapy, 44,* 1-25.

Hayes, S. C., Strosahl, K., & Wilson, K. G. (1999). *Acceptance and commitment therapy: An experiential approach to behavior change.* New York, NY: Guilford Press.

Jegatheesan, B. (2009). Cross-cultural issues in parent-professional interactions: A qualitative study of perceptions of Asian American mothers of children with developmental disabilities. *Research and Practice for Persons with Severe Disabilities, 34,* 123–136.

Jegatheesan, B., Miller, P. J., & Fowler, S. A. (2010). Autism from a religious perspective: A study of parental beliefs in South Asian Muslim immigrant families. *Focus on Autism and Other Developmental Disabilities, 25,* 98–109.

Jones, L., Hastings, R. P., Totsika, V., Keane, L., & Rhule, N. (2014). Child behavior problems and parental well-being in families of children with autism: The mediating role of mindfulness and acceptance. *American Journal on Intellectual and Developmental Disabilities, 119,* 171–185.

Kaminsky, L., & Dewey, D. (2001). Siblings relationships of children with autism. *Journal of Autism and Developmental Disorders, 31,* 399–410.

Kanner, L. (1949). Problems of nosology and psychodynamics of early infantile autism. *American Journal of Orthopsychiatry, 19,* 416–426.

Katz-Wise, S. L., Priess, H. A., & Hyde, J. S. (2010). Gender-role attitudes and behavior across the transition to parenthood. *Developmental Psychology, 46,* 18–28.

Kazdin, A. E., Marciano, P. L., & Whitley, M. K. (2005). The therapeutic alliance in cognitive-behavioral treatment of children referred for oppositional, aggressive, and antisocial behavior. *Journal of Consulting and Clinical Psychology, 73*, 726–730.

Koegel, R. L., Bimbela, A., & Schreibman, L. (1996). Collateral effects of parent training on family interactions. *Journal of Autism and Developmental Disorders, 26*, 347–359.

Koegel, R. L., Symon, J. B., & Koegel, L. K. (2002). Parent education for families of children with autism living in geographically distant areas. *Journal of Positive Behavioral Interventions, 4*, 88–103.

Kurita, H. (1985). Infantile autism with speech loss before the age of thirty months. *Journal of the American Academy of Child Psychiatry, 24*, 191–196.

Lambert, M. J., & Barley, D. E. (2001). Research summary on the therapeutic relationship and psychotherapy outcome. *Psychotherapy, 38*, 357–361.

Lazarus, R. S., & Folkman, S. (1984). *Stress, appraisal, and coping.* New York, NY: Springer.

Leach, M. J. (2005). Rapport: A key to treatment success. *Complementary Therapies in Clinical Practice, 11*, 262–265.

Lee, L., Harrington, R. A., Louie, B. B., & Newschaffer, C. J. (2008). Children with autism: Quality of life and parental concerns. *Journal of Autism and Developmental Disorders, 38*, 1147–1160.

Levy, S. E., Mandell, D. S., Merhar, S., Ittenbach, R. F., & Pinto-Martin, J. A. (2003). Use of complementary and alternative medicine among children recently diagnosed with autistic spectrum disorder. *Journal of Developmental and Behavioral Pediatrics, 24*, 418–423.

Lickenbrock, D. M., Ekas, N. V., & Whitman, T. L. (2011). Feeling good, feeling bad: Influences of maternal perceptions of the child and marital adjustment on well-being in mothers of children with an autism spectrum disorder. *Journal of Autism and Developmental Disorders, 41*, 848–858.

Lingam, R., Simmons, A., Andrews, N., Miller, E., Stowe, J., & Taylor, B. (2003). Prevalence of autism and parentally reported triggers in a North East London population. *Archives of Diseases in Children, 88*, 666–670.

Lord, C. (1995). Follow up of 2-year-olds referred for possible autism. *Journal of Child Psychology and Psychiatry, 36*, 1365–1382.

Lord, C., Rutter, M., DiLavore, P. C., Risi, S., Gotham, K., & Bishop, S. L. (2012). *Autism Diagnostic Observation Schedule, second edition (ADOS-2) manual (part I): Modules 1–4*. Torrance, CA: Western Psychological Services.

Macks, R. J., & Reeve, R. E. (2007). The adjustment of non-disabled siblings of children with autism. *Journal of Autism and Developmental Disorders, 37*, 1060–1067.

Mandell, D. S., Ittenbach, R. F., Levy, S. E., & Pinto-Martin, J. A. (2007). Disparities in diagnoses received prior to a diagnosis of autism spectrum disorder. *Journal of Autism and Developmental Disorders, 37*, 1795–1802.

Mandell, D. S., Listerud, J., Levy, S. E., & Pinto-Martin J. A. (2002). Race differences in the age at diagnosis among Medicaid-eligible children with autism. *Journal of the American Academy of Child and Adolescent Psychiatry, 4*, 1447–1453.

Mandell, D. S., & Novak, M. (2005). The role of culture in families' treatment decisions for children with autism spectrum disorders. *Mental Retardation and Developmental Disabilities, 11*, 110–115.

Mandell, D. S., & Salzer, M. S. (2007). Who joins support groups among parents of children with autism? *Autism, 11*, 111–122.

Mandell, D. S., Walrath, C. M., Manteuffel, B., Sgro, G., & Pinto-Martin, J. A. (2005). The prevalence and correlates of abuse among children with autism served in comprehensive community-based mental health settings. *Child Abuse & Neglect, 29*, 1359–1372.

Mandell, D. S., Wiggins, L. D., Carpenter, L. A., Daniels, J., DiGuiseppi, C., Durkin, M. S., . . . Kirby, R. S. (2009). Racial/ethnic disparities in the identification of children with autism spectrum disorders. *American Journal of Public Health, 99*, 493–498.

Mather, M., Pollard, K., & Jacobsen, L. A. (2011). *First results from the 2010 census*. Washington, DC: Population Reference Bureau.

Moes, D. R., & Frea, W. D. (2000). Using family context to inform intervention planning for the treatment of a child with autism. *Journal of Positive Behavior Interventions, 2*, 40–46.

Moes, D. R., & Frea, W. D. (2002). Contextualized behavioral support in early intervention for children with autism and their families. *Journal of Autism and Developmental Disorders, 32*, 519–533.

Moes, D., Koegel, R. L., Schreibman, L., & Loos, L. M. (1992). Stress profiles for mothers and fathers of children with autism. *Psychological Reports, 71*, 1272–1274.

Montes, G., & Halterman, J. S. (2008). Association of childhood autism spectrum disorders and loss of family income. *Pediatrics, 121*, e821–e826.

Moore, J. W., Edwards, R. P., Sterling-Turner, H. E., Riley, J., Dubard, M., & McGeorge, A. (2002). Teacher acquisition of functional analysis methodology. *Journal of Applied Behavior Analysis, 35*, 73–77.

Möslä, P. K., & Ikonen-Möslä, S. A. (1985). The mentally handicapped child and family crisis. *Journal of Mental Deficiency Research, 29*, 309–314.

Norfolk, T., Birdi, K., & Walsh, D. (2007). The role of empathy in establishing rapport in the consultation: A new model. *Medical Education, 41*, 690–697.

Olsson, M. B., & Hwang, C. P. (2001). Depression in mothers and fathers of children with intellectual disability. *Journal of Intellectual Disability Research, 45*, 535–543.

Orsmond, G. I., Kuo, H. Y., & Seltzer, M. M. (2009). Siblings of individuals with an autism spectrum disorder: Sibling relationships and well-being in adolescence and adulthood. *Autism: The International Journal of Research and Practice, 13*, 59–80.

Osborne, L. A., McHugh, L., Saunders, J., & Reed, P. (2008). Parenting stress reduces the effectiveness of early teaching interventions for autistic spectrum disorders. *Journal of Autism and Developmental Disorders, 38*, 1092–1103.

Overton, T., Fielding, C., & de Alba, R. (2008). Brief report: Exploratory analysis of the ADOS revised algorithm: Specificity and predictive value with Hispanic children referred for autism spectrum disorders. *Journal of Autism and Developmental Disorders, 38*, 1166–1169.

Pelchat, D., LeFebvre, H., & Levert, M. (2007). Gender differences and similarities in the experience of parenting a child with a health problem: Current state of knowledge. *Journal of Child Health Care, 11*, 112–131.

Pottie, C. G., & Ingram, K. M. (2008). Daily stress, coping, and well-being in parents of children with autism: A multilevel modeling approach. *Journal of Family Psychology, 22*, 855–864.

Price, C. S., Thompson, W. W., Goodson, B., Weintraub, E. S., Croen, L. A., Hinrichson, V. L., . . . DeStefano, F. (2010). Prenatal and infant exposure to thimerosal from vaccines and immunoglobulins and risk of autism. *Pediatrics, 126*, 656–664.

Robins, D., Fein, D., & Barton, M. (2009). *Modified Checklist for Autism in Toddlers, revised with follow-up.* Publisher: Author.

Rogers, C. R. (1957). The necessary and sufficient conditions of therapeutic personality change. *Journal of Consulting Psychology, 21*, 95–103.

Rogers-Adkinson, D. L., Ochoa, T. A., & Delgado, B. (2003). Developing cross-cultural competence: Serving families of children with significant developmental needs. *Focus on Autism and Other Developmental Disabilities, 18*, 4–8.

Rutter, M., LeCouteur, A., & Lord, C. (2008). *Autism Diagnostic Interview—revised.* Los Angeles: Western Psychological Services.

Sarason, I. G., Levine, H. M., Basham, R. B., & Sarason, B. R. (1983). Assessing social support: The Social Support Questionnaire. *Journal of Personality and Social Psychology, 44*, 127–139.

Scherman, A., Gardner, J. E., Brown, P., & Schutter, M. (1995). Grandparents' adjustment to grandchildren with disabilities. *Educational Gerontology, 21*, 261–273.

Scorgie, K., & Sobsey, D. (2000). Transformational outcomes associated with parenting children who have disabilities. *Mental Retardation, 38*, 195–206.

Segal, Z. V., Williams, J. M. G., & Teasdale, J. D. (2002). *Mindfulness-based cognitive therapy for depression: A new approach to preventing relapse.* New York, NY: Guilford Press.

Seligman, M. (1991). Grandparents of disabled grandchildren: Hopes, fears, and adaptation. *Families in Society: The Journal of Contemporary Human Services, 72*, 147–152.

Seltzer, M. M., Greenberg, J. S., Floyd, F. J., Pettee, Y., & Hong, J. (2001). Life course impacts of parenting a child with a disability. *American Journal on Mental Retardation, 106*, 265–286.

Shaked, M. (2005). The social trajectory of illness: Autism in the ultraorthodox community in Israel. *Social Science and Medicine, 61*, 2190–2200.

Singer, G., Marquis, J., Powers, L., Bancard, L., Divenere, N., Santelli, B., . . . Sharp, M. (1999). A multi-site evaluation of Parent to Parent programs for children with disabilities. *Journal of Early Intervention, 22*, 217–229.

Singh, N .N., Lancioni, G. E., Winton, A. S. W., Singh, J., Curtis, W. J., Wahler, R. G., . . . Sabaawi, M. (2006). Mindful parenting decreases aggression and increases social behavior in children with developmental disabilities. *Behavior Modification, 31*, 749–771.

Skinner, D., Bailey, D., Correa, V., & Rodriguez, P. (1999). Narrating self and disability: Latino mothers' construction of identities vis-à-vis their child with special needs. *Exceptional Children, 65*, 481–495.

Smith, L. E., Seltzer, M. M., Tager-Flusberg, H., Greenberg, J. S., & Carter, A. S. (2008). A comparative analysis of well-being and coping among mothers of toddlers and mothers of adolescents with ASD. *Journal of Autism and Developmental Disorders, 38*, 876–889.

Steiner, A. M. (2011). A strength-based approach to parent education for children with autism. *Journal of Positive Behavior Interventions, 13*, 178–190.

Strauss, K., Vicari, S., Valeri, G., D'Elia, L., Arima, S., & Fava, L. (2012). Parent inclusion in early intensive behavioral intervention: The influence of parental stress, parent treatment fidelity and parent-mediated generalization of behavior targets on child outcomes. *Research in Developmental Disabilities, 33*, 688–703.

Sullivan, P., & Knutson, J. (2000). Maltreatment and disabilities: A population-based epidemiological study. *Child Abuse & Neglect, 24*(10), 1257–1273.

Thoits, P. A. (1995). Stress, coping, and social support processes: Where are we? What next? *Journal of Health and Social Behavior, extra issue*, 53–79.

Tincani, M., Travers, J., & Boutot, A. (2009). Race, culture, and autism spectrum disorder: Understanding the role of diversity in successful educational interventions. *Research and Practice for Persons with Severe Disabilities, 34*, 81–90.

Tonge, B., Brereton, A., Kiomall, M., MacKinnon, A., King, N., & Rinehart, N. (2006). Effects on parental mental health of an education and skills training program for parents of young children with autism: A randomized controlled trial. *Journal of the American Academy of Child and Adolescent Psychiatry, 45*, 561–569.

Travers, J. C., Tincani, M., & Krezmien, M. P. (2011). A multiyear national profile of racial disparity in autism identification. *Journal of Special Education, 47*, 41–49.

Tuchman, R. F., & Rapin, I. (1997). Regression in pervasive developmental disorders: Seizures and epileptiform electroencephalogram correlates. *Pediatrics, 99*, 560–566.

Tunali, B., & Power, T. G. (2002). Coping by redefinition: Cognitive appraisals in mothers of children with autism and children without autism. *Journal of Autism and Developmental Disorders, 32*, 25–34.

Vadasy, P. F., Fewell, R. R., & Meyer, D. J. (1986). Grandparents of children with special needs: Insights into their experiences and concerns. *Journal of Early Intervention, 10*, 36–44.

Verté, S., Roeyers, H., & Buysse, A. (2003). Behavioural problems, social competence, and self-concept in siblings of children with autism. *Child: Care, Health and Development, 29*, 193–205.

Weiss, J. A., Cappadocia, M. C., MacMullin, J. A., Viecili, M., & Lunsky, Y. (2012). The impact of child problem behaviors of children with ASD on parent mental health: The mediating role of acceptance and empowerment. *Autism, 16*, 261–274.

White, S. W., & Roberson-Nay, R. (2009). Anxiety, social deficits, and loneliness in youth with autism spectrum disorders. *Journal of Autism and Developmental Disorders, 39*, 1006–1013.

Yamada, A., Suzuki, M., Kato, M., Suzuki, M., Tanaka, S., Shindo, T., . . . Furukawa, T. A. (2007). Emotional distress and its correlates among parents of children with pervasive developmental disorders. *Psychiatry and Clinical Neuroscience, 61*, 651–657.

Zablotsky, B., Bradshaw, C. P., Anders, C. M., & Law, P. (2014). Risk factors for bullying among children with autism spectrum disorders. *Autism, 18*(4), 419–427.

Zhang, C., & Bennett, T. (2003). Facilitating the meaningful participation of culturally and linguistically diverse families in the IFSP and IEP process. *Focus on Autism and Other Developmental Disabilities, 18*, 51–59.

Zhang, J., Wheeler, J. J., & Richey, D. (2006). Cultural validity in assessment instruments for children with autism from a Chinese cultural perspective. *International Journal of Special Education, 21*, 109–114.

# INDEX